Living without oil

The new energy economy revealed

Adjiedj Bakas and Rob Creemers

We dedicate this book to our forever young-at-heart fathers Bertus Creemers (1917–2005) and Adjiedj Bakas sr, who made us both, each in our own way, the men we are today.

Copyright © Adjiedj Bakas and Rob Creemers, 2010

The right of Adjiedj Bakas and Rob Creemers to be identified as the authors of this book has been asserted in accordance with the Copyright, Designs and Patents Act 1988.

First published in 2010 by
Infinite Ideas Limited
36 St Giles
Oxford, OX1 3LD
United Kingdom
www.infideas.com

All rights reserved. Except for the quotation of small passages for the purposes of criticism or review, no part of this publication may be reproduced, stored in a retrieval system or transmitted in any form or by any means, electronic, mechanical, photocopying, recording, scanning or otherwise, except under the terms of the Copyright, Designs and Patents Act 1988 or under the terms of a licence issued by the Copyright Licensing Agency Ltd, 90 Tottenham Court Road, London W1T 4LP, UK, without the permission in writing of the publisher. Requests to the publisher should be addressed to the Permissions Department, Infinite Ideas Limited, 36 St Giles, Oxford, OX1 3LD, UK, or faxed to +44 (0)1865 514777.

A CIP catalogue record for this book is available from the British Library

ISBN 978-1-906821-06-7

Brand and product names are trademarks or registered trademarks of their respective owners.

Research by Trend Office Bakas
Cover by Baseline Arts Ltd, Oxford
Text designed and typeset by Wentelwereld Grafische Vormgeving, Westkapelle, The Netherlands
Printed and bound in Malta

Contents

Foreword	9
Preface	13
Part 1. The energy economy, past and present	19
1. Two crises that lead to the *new energy era*	21
2. Energy: what and how?	45
3. The future of our energy supplies	61
Part 2. The new energy economy: outlines and trends	79
Megatrend I. Towards new energy policies	81
Megatrend II. Towards the greening of industry	97
Megatrend III. Towards the greening of consumers	119
Megatrend IV. Towards new transport innovations	137
Megatrend V. Towards increasing pressure on the aviation sector	162
Megatrend VI. Towards innovations in energy supply	181
Megatrend VII. Towards new concepts of life and work	203
Part 3. Energy agenda for the future	215
Sources	223
Index	229

Columns:
- *Nilas* by Marc Cornelissen — 93
- *The alternative from FreshDirect* by Professor Dr. Marcel Creemers — 107
- *Taking the plane out of the emissions equation* by Cor Vrieswijk — 177
- *Solar energy as a wildcard* by Professor Wim de Ridder — 200
- *Moving towards green sea-going cargo?* by Hans de Vink — 212

foreword

I had to smile when I received a request as an 'oil man' to write the foreword to a book entitled *Living without oil*, which will, moreover, be presented at the international head office of Shell. What would life be without humour? When I read this serious yet also elegantly written book on the transition to a new energy economy, I recognised much of what the two trend watchers Adjiedj Bakas and Rob Creemers were writing about. One day the oil will run out, although we can manage for the moment. Yes, we need to start thinking about a different energy economy, certainly because of climate change. In recent years I have been privileged to reflect in various capacities along with creative people from varied backgrounds, who are driven by a desire for progress, on a new energy economy and the way the transition to that economy might take shape. I found and still find this very inspiring.

This optimistic book is written for the ordinary citizen, and therefore not in energy industry jargon. The authors describe seven megatrends in the fields of energy, climate and transport, which will radically change the way the world looks in the coming decades. Combining home and work will take on new forms, as well as the way we manage our time and how we organise the manufacturing of goods. The manner in which we deal with energy will become an important subject, with economic, but also moral, ethical and religious aspects, such as the current burning issue – whether it is acceptable to manipulate bacteria genetically to produce oil.

The authors have painted a broad palette of trends and possibilities, as trend watchers usually do. You don't always have to agree with them. I certainly don't agree with all the trends described in this book. It is also the case that at Shell we are not going to turn everything the authors describe into company policy, even if the company supports most of what the authors say. This book fits in well with the future scenarios developed by Shell itself.

In fact it doesn't really matter that I don't agree with everything in this book. I am a great supporter of diversity, creativity and free thinking, of 'ouside-the-box' approaches, and I believe it is important during this time of transition towards a different energy economy for creative minds to be given the space to unfold their talents in thinking of the necessary

changes. That is what the authors have done. They have upheld a motto which I find very appealing, something once said by Martin Luther, 'Even if I know that the world is going to end tomorrow, I am still going to plant a tree today.' The authors are not doom-mongers, something I greatly appreciate. There are after all enough people predicting the end of the world as a consequence of the way we treat our planet. But you don't get anywhere by preaching doom and gloom, and the authors understand this very well.

All in all, I find this inspiring, stimulating and superbly presented book about energy trends very worthwhile. I hope and believe that this book will inspire you.

Rein Willems

President of Shell The Netherlands (2003–2007) and currently Member of the Senate of the Dutch Parliament.

foreword

preface

Many people are feeling depressed about the future, and if you aren't now you probably will be soon because of all the doom and gloom prophesied for us by the media. However, hidden behind all the headlines there is a more optimistic picture – the birth of a new world order.

The Chinese word for 'crisis' consists of the two characters 'opportunity' and 'threat'. This gives us a useful way to view an uncertain future. We feel that the deep economic crisis in which the world now finds itself is the perfect time in which to make the turnaround towards a radical new energy economy. Sustaining a habitable world for ourselves and for future generations is more important than realising the astronomical value of the oil and gas (£3,000 trillion) that still lies underground – let's leave it there. The technology for producing alternatives to fossil fuels is developing so fast that we have no excuse for not making this historic changeover.

We are convinced that the twenty-first century can, and will, bring many benefits, as well as posing dangers of course. We are equally sure that it is no coincidence that the current economic crisis, the coming energy crisis, the climate crisis and the anticipated food crisis are happening at the same time. They are all part of the end of one era and the beginning of a radical new era. We believe that one of the main foundations of tomorrow's world will be the new energy economy that this book explores.

As far as the figures quoted in this book are concerned, we have limited ourselves to only the most authoritative sources, such as reports from the Intergovernmental Panel on Climate Change (IPCC) and the International Energy Agency (IEA). There's no doubt at all that you will be able to counter 'our' figures with others, because the publications that deal with this subject are full of contradictory information. Keep an open mind when you are bombarded with statistics about oil reserves running out and global warming resulting from the greenhouse effect. But do take these problems seriously.

This book previously appeared in a Dutch edition. This was provocatively presented to the press at Shell's head office. It became a best seller in the Netherlands. You are reading the 'global edition'. In this updated version we give a picture of the coming energy economy, which in these times of recession, will develop very quickly. The book offers hope, faith and optimism in dark times. It has been written in a journalistic style, to make it as

accessible as possible. Thus it differs from many other books written about this topic, which are usually highly specialized and full of technical jargon. The book's title is intended to be both provocative and inspirational: we realize that in reality, even when looking at the greenest scenarios the world cannot do entirely without oil during the next few decades.

The book consists of three parts. In part one we talk about the history of oil and its importance in our world. Part two describes the seven megatrends that will be the cornerstones of the new energy economy. Part three offers an agenda for the new energy future. We will explain what real steps we all can take to prepare ourselves for the coming of this new energy economy. This is a wonderful prospect, but creating it will pose enormous challenges. We do not necessarily believe or agree with all the trends we describe. A good futurologist describes what he or she thinks is happening in society and will only very occasionally offer value judgements.

We have been working on this book for two years. It is the result of an intense collaboration between two futurologists who have pooled their knowledge and experience, each working from their own point of view. Two people from different generations and cultural backgrounds, but who share one over-riding passion – the future of our world. We are proud of this book, and are thrilled that so many people have helped us to bring it to fruition.

We had a great deal of help in the creation of this book. Our literary agents, RaftPR and Big Apple Tuttle-Mori, advised us on how we could rewrite the original Dutch book for the world market. Our Dutch publisher Scriptum and our British publisher, Infinite Ideas, believed in and invested in the book. Minne Buwalda coordinated the research and took care of the editing. Many, many experts from universities, companies and professional organizations contributed their ideas and suggestions, and provided us with inspiring case studies: Ricardo Fakiera (Merrill Lynch), Rein Willems (Shell), professionals from Peakoil and other environmental organizations. Yet more people lent their expertise: Wim de Ridder, Marcel Creemers, Cor Vrieswijk (EasyJet), Liesbeth van Dijk, Hans Nieukerke, Adriaan Theeuwes, Albert van den Brink, Frits Bussemaker, Annette Nijs, Ben Verwaayen, Dirk Aleven, Jan van Weijen, the team at Trend Office Bakas, the teams at Speakers Academy and Assemblee, Second Sight (Andrea Wiegman and Jan Bletz), Allan Li Fo Sjoe, Steve Austen, Bram Buunk, Paul de Ruijter, Carine de Meyere, Wiet de Bruijn, Dennis Koot, Emile Ratelband, Frans Afman, Frits Bolkestein, Frits Huffnagel, Annet Bertram, Grace Robinson, Hamilcar Knops, Jeroen Wortman, Jochum Haakma, John Wories, Karel Hille, Marjolein Wenting, Lans Bovenberg, Maarten van Nispen, MAS Media, Marjet van Zuijlen, Reinier Evers, Rembrandt Koppelaar, Rolf Meter and Ruud Lubbers. We were given ideas by various universities, news groups, companies and authorities. Wentelwereld did the design of the book and Baseline did the cover design. Thank you all so very much. Reviewers of the first edition of this book wrote that the authors' enjoyment and optimism was evident throughout the book. We hope that you will gain as much enjoyment and inspiration from the book as we did while we were writing it.

Mijdrecht, Amsterdam, Jerusalem, Beijing

September 2009
Adjiedj Bakas & Rob Creemers

part 1

The energy economy, past and present

Chapter 1

Two crises that lead to the *new energy era*

In 2007, the world's leaders agreed that we had to reduce our greenhouse gas emissions and create a new energy economy, in order to prevent global warming from getting out of hand. The urgency of the climate crisis was recognised not only by the media, but also by governments and business. We were convinced that measures needed to be taken quickly and that the problems demanded the highest priority. It now looks like circumstances have altered the situation. The urgency of the climate problems has been overshadowed by an apparently bigger task: surviving the crisis and the resulting recession. In 2009, the recession is demanding the full attention of decision-makers, citizens, business-people and politicians.

The recession has actually been more successful than all the climate treaties and emissions deals were in reducing greenhouse gas emissions. It is expected that in 2009 emissions will decrease world wide by 3%, while in 2007, they rose by 3%. Thus in the short term, it looks like the economic crisis might be a godsend for the environment. However, there is a longer-term downside. Because of the crisis, there is less investment in the new energy economy. According to researchers New Carbon Finance, European green energy investments fell to $21.2 billion during the second half of 2008 – 13.7% lower than the same period in 2007. In North America, the toll is even worse: Over the same period, clean energy investment in the USA fell by nearly half, to $10.7 billion. When we emerge from the crisis in a few years and the economy recovers, we will find that we have fallen far behind in the development of renewable energy.

So, in 2009 we are actually faced with two crises, both extremely urgent, which must be solved in tandem. Solving the crises separately is not an option. Saving the economy without doing something about limiting CO_2 emissions would mean that we would eventually find ourselves with irreversible climate problems. We have to take action on the climate front now. If we only focus on sustainability and fail to do enough to rescue the

economy, then we will be unable to finance the new energy economy. Bo Ekman, founder of the Swedish Tällberg Foundation, draws the following analogy: 'The world suffers from "double pneumonia" – financial and environmental crises, both likely to become disasters for many more people. We cannot cure double pneumonia by treating one lung at a time.'

What's more, these crises must be solved at an international level. Separate nations cannot tackle them alone. But we are not very good at global cooperation – just look at the United Nations for example. We must learn to work with global institutions so that together we can set up and enforce regulations to enable us to confront these crises. If we don't, we will be stuck with a system geared towards national interests and egotistical players who only pursue economic growth in their own countries and expect other countries to enforce limits on themselves. Rajendra Pachauri from the UN institute for climate, the Intergovernmental Panel on Climate Change (IPCC) reminds us: 'What we do in the next two to three years will determine our future. This is the defining moment.' There's a lot hanging in the balance right now. At the same time, let's not forget that crises also present opportunities. The collapse of the old system will clear space for new solutions to develop. These two current crises mark the end of one era and the birth of a new one.

Kondratieff waves and the economic winter

It was the Russian economist Nikolai Kondratieff (1892–1938) who, at the beginning of the twentieth century, suggested that the world economy develops in fifty year cycles. Within each cycle, the economy goes through four seasons, just like the seasons of the year. We are now living through an economic winter. Although Kondratieff was the first internationally recognized economist to describe these long-term waves, it is interesting to note that Mayan culture and the Israelites of ancient times had already recognized the existence of fifty year boom-and-bust waves.

Kondratieff waves or long waves are the names given to a sine wave cycle in the modern capitalist world economy. Long waves span a period of fifty to sixty years and describe the swing between high sectorial growth and slower growth. This economic cycle can be seen more obviously in international production than in individual national economies and has more to do with productivity output than with prices. Kondratieff identifies four separate seasonal phases, with a centre point (deflation) between 'summer' and 'autumn'.

Transition era

Every so often, an economic winter will be worse than usual, this occurs when there is a transition from one technological era to another. Since 1800 we have had five technological revolutions with particularly striking similarities. We are now in the throes of the transition to the sixth technological revolution.

According to Carlota Perez from Sussex University, this kind of revolution advances in phases. First comes the *installation period* during which technological advances can be integrated into business processes at a relatively low cost. Later in this phase, you get unrealistically high expectations with respect to the new technology. This results in technological euphoria and financial speculation, which causes a *bubble* in the financial markets. Once this bubble has burst, you have a *recession* or *depression*, during which the financial markets slow down. That is the *turning point*. The turning point signals the beginning of *deployment*, the period in which society adapts itself to a new techno-economic paradigm. The potential of the technological revolution comes to fruition. This period comes to an end when the strength of the new technology wanes and the world begins to anticipate the next revolution.

Five technological waves in 200 years
The five waves of the last 200 years were interrupted during the transition periods by a deep crisis in the financial world:

- The industrial revolution
- The era of the steam engine and railway
- The era of electricity and heavy machinery
- The era of oil, the automobile and mass production
- The current information and telecommunications era, that is now coming to an end.

We are standing on the threshold of a major transition to a new era, which will have the following trends:

- Genetics, automation, bio- and nanotechnology are advancing and will drastically transform our lives.
- The world will become multi-polar: there will be several centres of power.
- We will make the transition from the oil economy to a new energy economy.
- We will set up a global waste management system for all refuse (including CO_2) produced by humans and develop a sustainable relationship with nature.

This era, which will last for twenty to thirty years, is being preceded by the current grave financial crisis.

But if we don't react to current climate changes immediately, the financial crisis will be directly followed by a climate crisis. As the UN Secretary General Ban Ki-moon has said: 'Though we can overcome the financial shocks of 2008, we will not overcome the climate change crisis unless we act fast.'

The importance of oil
'The Stone Age didn't end because the supply of stones ran out, it ended because smaller, then larger groups of people decided to use different

materials' said Sheik Ahmed Yamani, the former Saudi Oil Minister in the 1970s. He intended his words to serve as a warning to the oil producing countries that were still driving up oil prices. He meant that high prices would encourage the world's oil users to develop alternative forms of energy.

Oil – we don't really think about it very much, but without oil, we would hardly recognize our world. Oil allows us to live in great comfort, it provides both many of the raw materials and the energy for our cars, washing machines, televisions, ovens, lights, computers, elevators and all the other items we take for granted. One hundred and fifty years ago, even kings didn't have the luxury that we enjoy today. We also don't often stop to think about how much energy is generated by oil. If you were to climb on to your exercise bike and pedal for all you're worth, you would generate enough energy to power one lamp. Just one litre of petrol will power an average car for about eight miles, even if it's carrying five passengers and travelling uphill.

Over the last hundred years, the world economy has become highly dependent on oil. Oil forms the basis of industry as well as of transport

part 1. The energy economy, past and present

and logistics. The world population, which in 1927 stood at around 2 billion people, has grown to 6.7 billion in the year 2009. All of these people are fed, clothed and transported thanks to a ready supply of cheap oil. Starvation, as we used to know it, has to a large extent been eradicated from many parts of the world thanks to oil. Food production (and all other production processes) have been improved thanks to oil. In many ways, oil has been a blessing.

CO_2 emissions
However, our hunger for oil has massive drawbacks that are becoming ever more evident. The use of fossil fuels such as petroleum, coal and natural gas causes the emission of greenhouse gases, including CO_2. Emissions are rising every year, and in some regions such as Asia they are increasing alarmingly. At the same time, we are compromising the capacity of the earth to absorb CO_2 by cutting down the rainforests on a large scale. The increased concentrations of CO_2 in the atmosphere intensify the process of global warming and climate change.

Oil and politics
'Oil is ten percent economy and ninety percent politics,' writes Daniel Yergin, the director of Cambridge Energy Research Associates. Indeed it is. Oil prices fluctuate all the time. They rise during crises and then they fall again, as we saw after the war in the Lebanon in the summer of 2006. In the days to come, citizens, politicians and business-people all over the world are going to have to make decisions about energy management. We will have to face the issue of reducing our consumption of fossil fuels. Oil is going to run out, or will become impossibly expensive because of its scarcity. But when? And can we – should we – just sit and wait until this

happens before we transfer our dependence to new energy sources?

There is also the fact that terrorist organizations such as Al Qaeda and terror-exporting regimes such as the Iranian government are financed with oil revenues. Oil has also made the Wahabites, who until a century ago were an unknown Islamic tribe in the Saudi desert, one of the most powerful groups in the world. Russia is using its oil and gas supplies as a lever for power ever more frequently and is growing in influence, particularly in Europe. These factors have resulted in European countries finding themselves in a dependent position and they now have three energy problems: *environmental*, *security* and *economic*.

OPEC: there is still enough oil

The media sends both alarming and calming messages about the shrinking petroleum reserves. Organizations such as OPEC, the group of oil producing countries, and various oil companies tell us that there is sufficient oil left for the foreseeable future in undiscovered oil reserves, and that technological innovations will allow us to exploit previously inaccessible or unprofitable fields over the coming years. The discoveries of large new oil fields in Brazil and Mexico seem to confirm this. The British futurologist, James Martin, suggests that the oil that is as yet unexploited has an economic value of approximately €3,000 trillion. The economic interests surrounding this jackpot are tremendous. The high oil prices of 2008 also made it commercially viable to exploit the oil-bearing sands in Canada, the so-called tar sands. However, the price of oil fluctuates greatly and during an economic recession it is always low because of the fall in demand. In July 2008, just before the crisis hit, the price of oil was $147 per barrel. When demand fell as a result of the crisis, the price per barrel also fell very quickly to $40 in December 2008. Because the oil producing countries can't cooperate in reducing oil production and the

part 1. The energy economy, past and present

economic recession looks like it will last for some time yet, the price will stay low for the time being.

However, we know that when the world economy picks up again, the demand for oil will increase dramatically and that the price will rise quickly. Fulfilling that future demand requires investment in infrastructure and exploration now. But when oil prices are low, the oil companies, who have to answer to their shareholders, reduce investment. So when the demand for oil eventually picks up, the price of oil will rise even more dramatically because too little investment will have been made in oil infrastructure.

Peak oil: oil starts to run out
Environmental organizations are disputing the reports coming from the oil producing countries. The influential blog, 'Peakoil', suggests that in the near future the relative balance between supply and demand in the oil market will come to a dramatic end. The emerging economies such as those of India and China will soon cause a gigantic rise in the demand for oil. Just imagine over one billion Chinese and another billion people in India deciding that they want to drive cars. 'Peakoil' estimates that within ten years, the unbalanced growth between supply and demand in the oil market will have caused a new, worldwide economic crisis, wars for raw materials and even an end to civilization as we know it.

We must also look beyond the arguments about undiscovered oil reserves and the technical capacity for their extraction. This is not just an 'underground' problem – the dangers on the surface are even more worrying. Even if, during the next 50 to 150 years, we could technically satisfy the global demand for petroleum, there are still a great many factors that could threaten energy supplies. The political instability in oil exporting countries such as Nigeria, Venezuela and Iran; the dangers of terrorist attacks on major refineries and pipelines; the financing of terrorists with oil revenues; the way in which Russia and Venezuela use oil as a geopolitical tool. These all pose real risks. On the other hand, the mutual dependency between oil producing and oil consuming countries generally ensures that none of the parties involved do anything (too) stupid.

Climate change
It is vitally important that we stop ignoring the environmental problems and changes to the global climate caused by our consumption of fossil fuels. In the 1970s, the Club of Rome issued alarming reports about our destruction of the earth. The message was loud and clear, but during the 1970s and 80s, other opinions surfaced that cast doubts on the findings of the Club of Rome, and this resulted in people pushing the doom scenarios aside and cheerfully throwing themselves forward in the pursuit of economic growth. Some years ago, the Club of Rome was reincarnated as the previously mentioned UN institute Intergovernmental Panel on Climate Change (IPCC). In the spring of 2007 the IPCC offered several scenarios for the future, of which even the most positive was still alarming.

People are creative creatures. But they only really make the effort to do something when forced into it by the urgency of the situation or if it has an impact on their lives and their very being. According to quantum physics, everything is connected to everything else at a basic level; everything is dependent on everything else and has influences that we don't yet fully understand. That means that our interference with nature can set things in motion in ways that, as yet, we cannot foresee. These are called *tipping points*. According to the British scientist, James Lovelock, the biosphere – the global ecological system – is a perfect, self-regulating system that automatically ensures the ideal living conditions on our planet. He sees the earth as a kind of super organism that he calls *Gaia*, after the Greek goddess of the Earth. Lovelock was one of the first scientists to sound the alarm and draw our attention to global warming. He warned that our activities were upsetting the balance of the earth's bio-system. He postulated that reforestation could help to avoid disrupting the Earth's balance. And he proposed turning to nuclear energy. We will explore this in more detail later.

Geo-engineering

Over the past few years, we have been made shockingly aware of the warnings of Lovelock and others, and governments all over the world have tried to reduce CO_2 emissions. Meanwhile, global warming seems to be increasing exponentially. It's as if Gaia is out of kilter and the biosphere is creating its own dynamic. Slowly but surely we are coming to realize that simply reducing emissions will not be enough. More drastic measures will have to be taken to limit the warming effect. That's why at the moment the scientific world is working on a 'plan B'. If plan A (reducing the emissions) doesn't work we can move on to more drastic measures. Some of these far reaching measures have been called *geo-engineering*.

One example of geo-engineering is the idea of positioning large mirrors in space to reflect sunlight away from the earth. A kind of umbrella made of mirrors. The US National Academy of Sciences calculated that 55,000 mirrors circling the earth would deflect enough sunlight to halve the greenhouse effect. But each mirror would have to measure a hundred square metres. Solutions like these are obviously very expensive and could bring all kinds of unforeseen problems in their wake.

There is another example of geo-engineering that might be easier to realize and also cheaper: bombarding the atmosphere with sulphur particles. This idea was conceived in 1991 during the eruption of the Mt. Pinatubo volcano when it was observed that the sulphur plume reduced the amount of sunlight reaching the earth. The disadvantage here is that the effect can't be controlled or steered. Sulphur also damages the ozone layer, so it could be a case of out of the frying pan and into the fire.

The most realistic and feasible current 'plan B' would seem to be scattering metal particles in the oceans. This would cause the seas to absorb more CO_2 so that some of the excess carbon dioxide in the atmosphere would be 'eaten' by the oceans. At the moment research is being carried out to find out how much greenhouse gas could be stored in underground saltwater reservoirs – so-called sequestering; we will be looking at this technique in more detail later in the book.

We must emphasize that geo-engineering techniques carry enormous risks. What might the side effects be, can we safely and reliably predict how Mother Earth will react? If it goes wrong, we are putting all life on earth at risk. Really, this way of playing God is unethical. Also, the prospect of a 'magic bullet' solution to climate change could reduce the willingness of governments and ordinary people to embrace change and create a new energy economy. We should be very wary of such plans.

John Sterman's Bathtub Analogy

John Sterman, an MIT scientist specializing in risk perception, says that we are still not fully aware of what's at stake. In the *New York Times* he explains the effects of CO_2 emissions using a very effective analogy:

'Basically, the atmosphere is like a bathtub with a partially opened drain. Carbon dioxide from burning fuels and forests is flowing in twice as fast as it is being absorbed by plants and the ocean, and some of those "sinks" are in fact getting saturated, meaning that the "drain" is clogging up a bit. In a tub, this is a recipe for a flood.'

Sterman states that many people think that the stabilization of our CO_2 emissions will also stabilize the climatic effect of greenhouse gases, but nothing could be further from the truth. Once CO_2 has been emitted, it breaks down very slowly, and its warming effects can last for a hundred years or so. Sterman continues:

'The amount of carbon dioxide in the atmosphere is like the level of water in a bathtub. The level rises as long as you pour more water in through the faucet than what drains out. Right now, we pour about twice as much CO_2 into the atmospheric tub than what is removed by natural processes. Stabilising atmospheric concentrations requires emissions to fall to the net removal rate. The net removal of CO_2 from the atmosphere is likely to fall as the elements that absorb all that carbon, particularly the oceans, fill up.'

In short, we will have to deal with even more emissions and even less absorption of CO_2. Sterman goes on:

'Yes, a certain amount of climate change, due to past emission, is inevitable, and will not be reversible. But it would be tragic if people concluded that there is nothing we can do, that it is futile to reduce emissions, and that all efforts should shift to adaptation. On the contrary: if nothing is done to cut emissions, the climate our children and grandchildren will face will almost certainly be far less hospitable, and there will be no turning back. By the time we know how bad it will be, it will be too late to take any remedial action.'

So, the issue of the climate question is extremely urgent, and we should not let the current economic crisis distract us.

Mobility: now and in the future

The consumption of energy is directly related to our mobility. More than half of the oil we use is employed in transportation. If we want to do something about our energy consumption, it's clear that we need to look closely at alternative sources of energy to fuel our transportation needs. In the wealthy countries, experiments are in full swing to find permanent alternatives to petrol, such as bio-fuels, hybrid motors, plug-in hybrids, electric motors and hydrogen technology.

This might seem like a step backwards. One of the first automobiles, the Model T Ford, was capable of running on bio-fuels, and before this all-American car set the standard for the rest of the automobile industry, there were cars in existence that could run on batteries. Later on, the car and oil industries became so intertwined that cars and oil now seem to be naturally linked together. We are now going back to the origins of the car, albeit with better technology. But this turnaround will take time, separating the car and oil industry won't be easy. The British futurologist, James Martin, argues that the infant  Chinese car industry is not yet inextricably intertwined with the oil industry, and as a result, has been able to mobilize the world's best brains to design an ultra-economical electric car, with plans to export it from China. They are on the right track. We have now reached the *tipping point* when the consumer is willing to switch to electric cars and *crowd sourcing* will allow this to happen internationally (*crowd sourcing* is taking a task and outsourcing it to a group of people or a community).

Towards a new food paradigm

Tim Lang, professor of Food Policy at the City University in London, is a member of the Food Council, which was called into being by the British government. Lang argues: 'The level of growth in food production per capita is dropping off, and we have huge problems ahead with an explosion in human population.' In order to tackle this problem, Lang listed a series of 'new fundamentals,' which need to shape future food production. Here are some of the areas where new fundamentals are needed:

- *Oil and energy:* 'We have an entirely oil-based food economy, and yet oil is running out. The impact of that on agriculture is one of the drivers of the volatility in the world food commodity markets.'
- *Water scarcity:* 'One of the key things that governments have to do in the coming years is to start auditing food by water. Currently, 50% of

the UK's vegetables are imported, many from water-stressed nations.'
- *Biodiversity:* 'Biodiversity must not just be protected, it must be replaced and enhanced; but that is going to require a very different way of growing food and using the land.'
- *Urbanization:* 'Probably the most important thing within the social sphere. More people now live in towns than in the countryside. In which case, where do they get their food?' Can we afford the transportation of all that food to the cities?

According to Professor Lang, in order to feed a projected nine billion people by 2050, policy-makers and scientists face a fundamental challenge: how can food systems work with the planet and biodiversity, rather than raiding and pillaging it?

Increased demand for energy from developing countries

Over the next twenty-five years, two thirds of the demand for energy will come from developing countries. There are approximately 1 billion cars in the world at the moment. Every day, these cars guzzle 10 million barrels of oil. In 2007, because of fast economic growth in the emerging economic powers such as Brazil, Russia, India and China (the so-called BRIC countries) the car industry predicted a 27% growth in car sales during the next five years. They obviously hadn't taken into account the crisis which caused stagnation in the demand for cars in 2008. But as soon as the crisis is over, the sales figures will rise again. It is estimated that in thirty years there will be more than 190 million cars in China alone. So, however hard the wealthy countries are working to find alternative sources of energy, the problem of climate change caused by CO_2 emissions won't be solved overnight.

Cheap coal

With an eye on rising oil prices, many countries are taking another look at coal fired power stations. This would be a complete disaster for the environment. The CO_2 emissions from these types of power stations are enormous. Their supporters point out the possibilities of sequestering: capturing greenhouse gases and storing them underground, in salt mines for example.

But so far, the 'clean coal' campaign has been more PR than reality – currently there's no economical way to capture and sequester carbon emissions from coal, and many experts doubt there ever will be. The cheap price of coal depends on the fact that external costs – climate change, and the health impacts of air and water pollution from coal – remain external, paid for not by the utilities or coal companies but by society as a whole. We have to weigh these costs against the real damage caused by coal and charge the polluter.

Growth in aviation after the current dip

We can also expect a substantial increase in air traffic after this economic dip. Tourism and holiday traffic are increasing and globalization has meant an increase in business flights. Outsourcing and off-shoring, the removal of factories to other countries, has caused strong growth in cargo transport. In the near future this will cause an increase in the consumption of energy and in CO_2 emissions.

The International Air Transport Association, which is responsible for 230 airlines, wants its members to use 10% alternative fuels by 2017; there have already been tentative experiments with bio-fuels. New types of aircraft are far more economical than their predecessors and yet more energy-saving planes are being designed. In fifty years' time, the airlines plan, with

part 1. The energy economy, past and present

the help of technology like fuel cells, bio-fuel or solar energy, to be able to fly emission-free. This goal won't help much in the short term but better late than never is obviously the mantra of the IATA.

Tele-working in suburbia
People have always travelled, and we have used many means of transport in our history. In our *nomadic era* we travelled far and wide, but we used only our muscle power as a source of energy for our wanderlust. We then created permanent settlements and changed from hunter-gatherers to farmers. You could say that we then started using solar power. That other energy source, wind power, also made its appearance early in our history with the invention of the sailing boat. Agriculture and animal husbandry were gradually eclipsed as trade, work sharing, technology and urbanization increased. Our impact on the planet increased dramatically. In this *settler era,* peoples' mobility quickly became more limited. We made short trips on foot, or by donkey or horse but the wanderlust seemed to be slowly but surely draining out of our systems.

About four hundred years ago, around 1600, the average Londoner spent their whole life no further than six miles away from their birthplace. The seventeenth century saw the first rather tentative use of fossil fuels, beginning with coal. From the middle of the nineteenth century, our horizons expanded with the invention of the steam train, the steam ship and later, the car. At the start of the twentieth century, it wasn't just the favoured few who were able to travel, but the upcoming middle classes also began to venture out, and were followed somewhat later by the commuter.

The *era of globalization* had begun. We suddenly began to travel more, first closer to home, then to more far-flung places. A holiday in the Canary Islands has gradually become quite normal.

In the second half of the twentieth century, we began to outsource work to far-flung countries to save labour costs. Thus the components for a simple electric toothbrush might come from eight different countries, which in turn calls for the transportation of parts.

On top of this, due to the rise in car ownership we discovered commuting. We used to live in or close to our work places. Farmers tilled the land around their farmhouse and craftspeople usually had a workshop in or near their home. When *suburbia* appeared after the Second World War, work and home were separated, so that it became quite normal for people to travel for several hours to get from home to work.

Now the clear division between home and work is disappearing once again. We work in our free time, or relax during traditional working hours. For many people, working from home, using new communication technologies, allows some of us (mainly in the wealthy countries) to reduce our day-to-day travel. This offers an attractive alternative to traffic jams and results in a trend that is leading to a relative drop in mobility and therefore, fuel usage.

Too many people

If the world's population continues to grow at the current explosive rate, we will simply not be able to cope with the problems of nature, supplying our energy needs and climate change. Homo sapiens would be a sustainable species if we had a world population of 0.5–2 billion people (at the very most) rather than the enormous numbers that will be walking, driving and flying around the earth in the coming decades.

It is obvious that a large and ever increasing world population is not helping in the urgent need to reduce CO_2 and energy consumption. Reducing the population would therefore be a major environmental measure. According to the UN's demographic studies, this is going to happen in time, without any ecological disasters. There are now 6.7 billion people in the world, and this will increase up to the year 2050 when the world population will have risen to around 9.2 billion. Then the demographic model shows a drop, to around 6 billion world citizens by the year 2100. This means that the next forty to fifty years are going to be the crunch time, when the world population is going to rise by 2.5 billion people. The biggest increases will be in Africa and Asia. In our opinion, population control must be tackled fast and with stringent measures. We suggest that the Chinese one-child policy should be implemented internationally, because the real environmental problem is that there are too many people on the earth.

Future scenarios
According to the Dutch economist Lans Bovenberg: 'When you create future scenarios, you especially take into account uncertainties. You divide them in two dimensions in four quadrants. At the moment in a lot

of fields an important uncertainty is the extent of internationalization. How will globalization continue, and how will local entities like states and regions relate to globalization? Will nation-states erode? Will city states come back? Will there be a backlash because of states trying to regain the power they lost during globalization?' In this current economic crisis, we are seeing a rise in nationalism and protectionism. When you have some countries that do not want to get involved in climate agreements because they feel that their priorities lie with their own short-term national welfare, you can see the countries who do want to cooperate scratching their heads. Why should they make all the allowances and pay the bills for those who won't take part? International solidarity is key when it comes to tackling climate change. Thus we come to the second uncertainty indicated by Bovenberg that will play an important role in future scenarios in respect of the environment and the climate: the development of a community spirit and individualism. Global solidarity is a vital variable when it comes to lowering our CO_2 emissions.

We think that the following scenarios for the coming decades are quite plausible:

1. *The Easter Island scenario.* This is a doom scenario that predicts that this will be mankind's last century, as the British Royal Astronomer Martin Rees describes in his book *Our Last Century*. In this scenario, there is no solution to the climate changes resulting from our energy consumption: the earth will survive, but we will not be so lucky. The earth is perfectly capable of withstanding climate change, as it has demonstrated many times in the past, but large numbers of humans will die as a result of an ecological disaster. On a global scale we are doing just what the inhabitants of Easter Island did on a small scale. They brought about the end of their

civilization and their own lives by cutting down all the trees on the island. This scenario predicts that we will have only ourselves to blame for our ruin, because we are, and will remain, selfish, and because we are unable to work together to make the proposed solutions a reality.

2. *The Lutheran scenario.* 'Even if I knew that the world was going to end tomorrow, I would still plant a tree today,' said the Protestant leader Martin Luther. This also seems to be the adage of those who put forward this scenario that predicts that a new energy era will be born in the short or medium term. It anticipates that we will manage to switch over to more renewable forms of energy, even though much of the damage we have already done to our planet cannot be reversed, and we will have to go though serious climate changes that will cause great damage and even cost lives. Many people, particularly baby-boomers (those born between 1945 and 1964) and the young, are starting to accept the reality of this scenario, which will require a great deal of international solidarity to address the problem of climate change. This means that in the West, we have to reduce energy consumption even further and that energy consumption in new super powers such as China and India has to be reined in. In this scenario, other innovative ways of using new forms of energy will develop very quickly. This will happen as a result of the pressure of public opinion.

3. *The Ostrich scenario.* This scenario is mostly embraced by those who want to carry on serving their own short-term interests under the motto 'it won't affect me, so who cares?', and those who refuse to believe that people are responsible for the phenomenon of climate change. Although there were those in the 1990s who cast doubts on the climate change theory, the evidence has, meanwhile, become crystal clear not only to meteorologists but also to the general public. All this matters not a whit to the followers of the Ostrich scenario. They serve only themselves and not a greater good.

The followers of scenarios one and three are highly ideological and politically driven, and sometimes inspired by their religions. In public debates they would be diametrically opposed. The followers of the second scenario are rather more pragmatic. They are not doom merchants, and they are quite aware of the urgency of the energy problems and understand that everyone, to a greater or lesser degree, mother or grandfather, voter or business-person, politician or voluntary worker, has to take responsibility for creating a new style of energy management. Not everyone realizes that in this scenario, civilization as we know it will end. We will be faced with ecological refugees who are fleeing from floods and droughts. Starvation and conflicts over food and water are unavoidable, mass migrations could follow (including from Africa to Europe) and that will cause tension and armed conflict, winners and losers. In this scenario, a significant portion of humanity will survive by making a creative and innovative transition to another energy era, but it is quite possible that many won't make it.

Alternatives

In this book, we will first examine the trends that will come from various players such as governments, businesses and citizens. Then we will talk about trends in specific energy-intensive sectors: the car industry, the aviation sector, the energy companies and finally the housing and office sectors.

We feel that whatever happens, solutions must be put into operation, even if it turns out to be too late to prevent climate change. If civilization does go under, as in the Easter Island scenario, then at least we'll have given it our best shot. And if the Lutheran scenario comes to pass, then the creative solutions of the citizens, companies and politicians will have had some success.

All of the scenarios predict disasters in our future. The ice caps and glaciers are melting and this will result in a significant rise in sea levels. Incidentally, research has shown that towards the end of the Middle Ages, Europe was warmer than it is now, with wine growing in England and green fields in Greenland (hence its name), while now it is a white island. There is evidence that it was once possible to circumnavigate Greenland; in other words there was less ice even though sea levels were no higher than they are now. The consequences of global warming, irrespective of its causes, will become ever more obvious. Also, increasingly, people are going to want to become independent in their energy supplies from regimes such as those in Russia and Saudi Arabia. Whatever happens, we will have to learn to adapt to climate change. We simply have to save more energy *and* develop new sources of energy.

Urgency
At the moment, our attention is focused on the greenhouse effect. It is a vital issue and we have to do something about it now if we still want to have a habitable planet in fifty years' time. However, the danger of *peak oil* and the explosion in oil prices also needs attention. However much the experts might disagree we can soon expect a situation where the demand for oil will exceed the supply. In the summer of 2008, the International Energy Agency predicted a peak oil situation in 2012 – that is, in just three years' time.

Meanwhile most of us just go on our merry way even though the ship is heading for the rocks.

It will take a real sense of urgency and decisiveness from governments, business and the general public to bring about a new energy era. We would like this book to be an inspiration to all those who now or tomorrow, or the day after tomorrow if needs be, want to find a different way of living with energy.

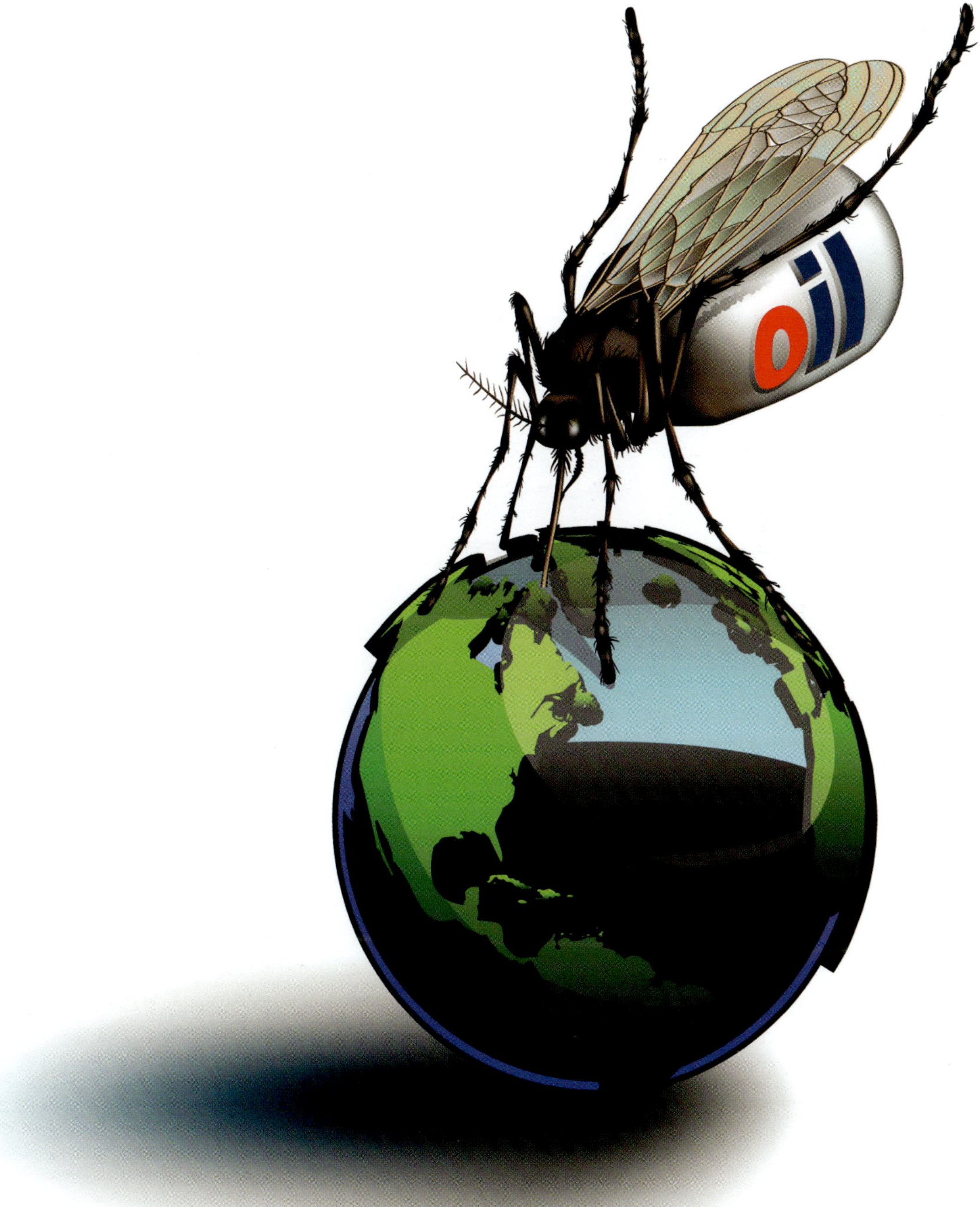
oil

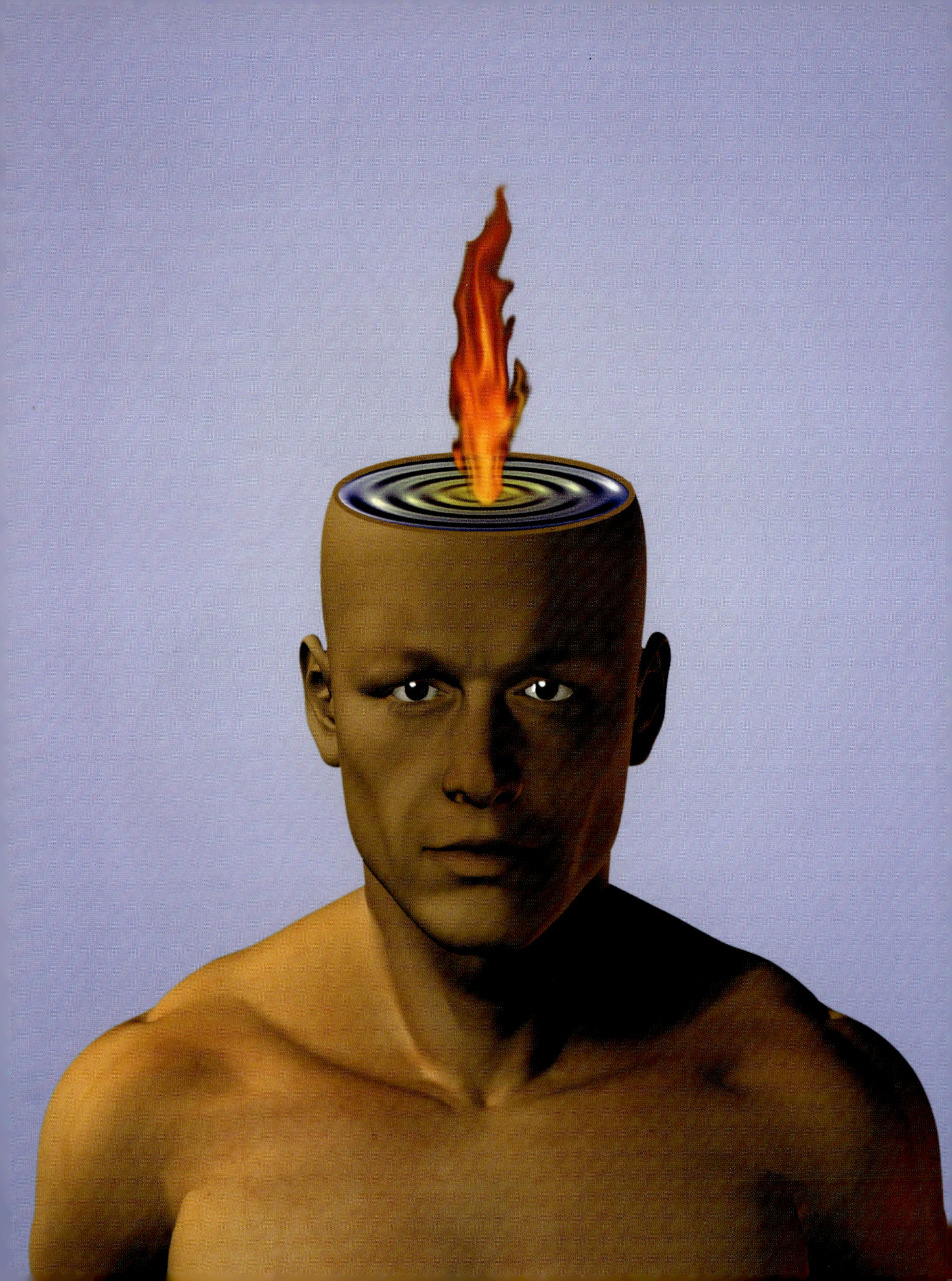

Chapter 2

Energy: what and how?

The future of energy
This is going to be one of the most important topics during the coming years. But what is energy? What are the most important sources of energy and how do the world's energy supplies actually work? What exactly are greenhouse gasses? How are they created and what effect do they have on climate change? How has energy use developed over the course of history? And how does this fit in with the way in which we live now? This chapter will look at these questions.

What is oil?
Oil supplies around 40% of our energy needs, which is a good reason in itself to take a closer look at this 'liquid gold'.

Oil and natural gas are formed from the residue of plankton and other marine organisms. When they die, they sink to the ocean floor where, because of the low-oxygen climate, they do not decompose completely and form a waxy substance called kerogen. Over the passage of time this layer of organic material is covered with new deposits. When the kerogen is covered by one to six kilometres of sediment and pressure causes the temperature to rise, the process of forming oil begins. Petroleum is formed in temperatures of between 60°C and 120°C. If the temperature rises higher than this, natural gas is formed. Oil and gas usually remain trapped underground by an impermeable layer of rock or salt, but some oil does naturally seep to the surface.

Since ancient times, people have used the oil that has surfaced naturally for various purposes. The ancient Chinese and Egyptians used it as lamp oil and in the United States, oil was being processed to make kerosene by the middle of the nineteenth century, so that Americans could light their homes, shops and saloons. Oil has been valued as a disinfectant, for vermin control, as hair oil, shoe polish and even as a remedy for kidney stones.

part 1. The energy economy, past and present

When the demand for kerosene increased because whale oil was becoming scarce, a group of American businessmen gave Edwin Drake the commission to drill for oil in Titusville, Pennsylvania. In 1859, after a great deal of hard work, Drake discovered a source of oil, and from then on, kerosene could be produced on a much larger scale. At first oil was processed very simply with the goal of producing kerosene, petrol was just one of the by-products. This began to change at the end of the nineteenth century with the invention of the petrol powered 'horseless carriage'. By 1920, there were approximately nine million cars in the US, more than half of which were Model T Fords, and a new petrol station was opening every day. A new business was born.

Oil interests

Slowly but surely, business and governments were discovering the importance of oil. Oil production began in Texas around 1930; in 1933 the Americans started drilling for oil in Saudi Arabia while the British were drilling in Persia, present-day Iran.

After the Second World War, it quickly became obvious that the world was going to need a great deal of petroleum. Prices rose and the oil producing countries, chiefly in the Middle East, wanted a share of the profits, which led to the founding of the OPEC cartel in the 1960s. OPEC stands for Organization of Petroleum Exporting Countries. OPEC has since become a power to be reckoned with in the world. The cartel can control oil prices by increasing or decreasing supplies.

In the 1970s it became clear just how powerful OPEC really was, and how political the question of oil had become. When the United States and some other Western countries, including the Netherlands, chose to side with Israel in the Yom Kippur War of 1973, all hell broke loose. On October 17, 1973, halfway through the war, a number of OPEC countries, including Saudi Arabia, Iraq and Kuwait, called for an oil embargo against the Western world. The first oil crisis was underway. The Arab countries increased the oil price by 70% and cut oil production by 5% each month so that the price per barrel went through the roof. Oil supplies were cut off altogether to countries that had supplied weapons to Israel or had acted as intermediaries, such as the United States, Portugal and the Netherlands. The Netherlands was faced with car-free Sundays and petrol was rationed. The United States chose a system whereby cars with even number plates could fill up with petrol on one day and those with odd numbers on the next. The measures put in place in the Netherlands and the US were actually an unnecessary panic reaction, because there never really was any question of a shortage. Western countries still received supplies via third parties, and the OPEC countries themselves couldn't afford to keep the boycott going for long because it would have depleted their treasuries too much, however on a global scale, the economic effects of the boycott were enormous. Many economies found themselves in a downward spiral. Because of the price agreements between the OPEC countries, the oil price never went back down to its 'pre-war' level after the crisis.

Of course, there were business-people who saw the oil crisis as an opportunity. The interest in alternative sources of energy was increasing and other less obvious companies also benefited. As a result of the higher prices demanded for (petroleum based) plastics, the German toy company Brandstätter introduced a range of smaller toys in 1974 that became immensely popular – the now classic Playmobil.

In 1979 the Shah of Persia's pro-Western regime was toppled. It was followed by that of the Ayatollah Khomeini and the country was re-christened the Islamic Republic of Iran causing panic to once again break out in the West. It was commonly thought that OPEC could make or break the Western economies. The cost of oil was $40 a barrel.

Oil as a raw material

Oil consists of hydrocarbons, molecules that are built up of only carbon and water. Crude oil can be made up of more than a thousand different hydrocarbons. The majority of these molecules have no more than thirty carbon atoms. In refineries, the various hydrocarbons can be 'sorted' according to size, then the larger molecules can be further reduced by 'cracking'. Molecules with six to ten carbon atoms are processed into petrol. Those with twelve to eighteen carbon atoms form diesel.

Oil distillation is based on the volatility (boiling point) of its various constituent materials. The following (combustible) fuels are listed from volatile to less volatile: LPG and butane (around 5%), petrol, kerosene, naphthalene, benzene and toluene (around 30%), diesel, domestic fuel oil, heating oil, lubricant and lastly asphalt (around 65%).

Naphthalene, benzene and toluene are used in the petrochemical industry as raw materials for chemical products, plastics, synthetic fibres and types of rubber. Chemicals extracted from naphtha can be used to produce base materials like ethylene oxide, phenol and isopropanol, from which products such as *antifreeze, medicines (including aspirin), cleaning materials, soap, solvents for cosmetics, paint and varnish, insecticides, pesticides, brake fluid and explosives* are made.

The list of products in which plastics, synthetic fibres and types of rubber are used is much longer, including (as a small sample): *rubbish bags, crates, toys, suitcases, PVC pipes, garden hoses, reusable plastic bottles, disposable beakers, CDs and CD covers, Styrofoam, Perspex, video tapes, tights, synthetic textiles such as nylon and Dralon, shoe soles, fishing lines, bullet-proof glass, golf balls, mattresses, fillings for chairs and settees, computers, glue, tennis rackets, boats, dashboards, car tyres, condoms, footballs and silicone implants.*

A glance through this list of day-to-day products that require petroleum demonstrates just how indispensable this raw material has become in our society.

These events made it clear that dependence on oil creates vulnerability, and measures to avoid this happening in the future began to be taken. One of the most important was to investigate more oil sources. Venezuela and Nigeria began to be exploited as oil suppliers on a larger scale. In the 1980s, new sources in Alaska and the North Sea secured a larger and more reliable oil supply. In addition the Western countries signed mutual cooperation pacts and agreements for less 'speculation susceptibility', and above all: the strategic oil reserves were increased, so that it was easier to absorb fluctuations in the market.

During the 1980s, a greater oil supply caused a drop in the price. OPEC was no longer holding all the reins and had to reduce production to prevent a further fall in the price. Even so, in 1986 the price per barrel fell from $29 to $10. In spite of a more stable oil market, the price per barrel still shot up at times, for example just after Iraq's attack on Kuwait, when the price per barrel returned to $40.

At the end of the 1990s, the energy question disappeared once again from political agendas. Oil prices had plummeted and with the tempestuous development of the 'the new economy' and the unsurpassed opportunities offered by the corresponding 'new media', an energy crisis seemed further away than ever. Everyone was focusing on companies like Yahoo! and Vodafone, and no one seemed to be interested in companies from the 'old economy', such as oil corporations.

When will oil production hit its peak?

For several years now, there has been an awareness of the importance of the demand for oil; there is particular concern about the expected peak in global oil production, usually referred to as *peak oil*. As mentioned in chapter one, experts can't agree as to when this global peak will take place. People in the oil industry and in the oil exporting countries estimate the global reserves to be higher than do people in environmental circles. It is almost impossible to determine which view is correct (and that isn't the aim of this book) but it is important to recognize that there are different perspectives on peak oil.

At the moment, oil production is still increasing world wide. The as yet unexploited oil supplies can be divided into three categories, proved, probable and possible reserves, also known as P90, P50 and P5. The figures after the P stand for 90%, 50% and 5% chance of recoverability of the relevant supply. The really large oil fields were discovered decades ago, mostly between 1959 and 1970. The fields that are now being found are small (50 million barrels) to medium sized (500 million barrels), which means that they could supply the world with oil for anything between one day and a week.

The total amount of petroleum still recoverable was, according to the oil company BP, around 1,200 billion barrels in 2006 which corresponds to forty times the current annual consumption. Of the total petroleum supplies 62% are in the Middle East, 12% in Europe and Eurasia, 10% in Africa, 9% in Latin America (excluding Mexico), 5% in North America, and 3% in the remaining parts of Asia. Saudi Arabia has the largest supply, followed by Iran, Iraq, Kuwait and the United Arab Emirates. Countries such as Russia, Venezuela and Nigeria also have notable petroleum supplies.

Due to the fact that in the long term the price of petroleum is sure to rise and because conventional petroleum will be harder to extract, the production of unconventional oil is going to play a much greater role. Unconventional oil can be produced from heavy oil or from oil shale, which contains a large amount (10%–50%) of fossilized organic material (kerogen), some heavy bitumens, or from tar sands. It is said that one benefit of unconventional oil is that it causes less pollution than ordinary petroleum, but this won't reduce our CO_2 emissions. It takes a lot of energy to extract petroleum from, for example, tar sand, as is being done in Canada at the moment. About twenty per cent of the extracted energy is already earmarked for the exploitation separation processes. At present, Canada is using gas for these processes but it won't be long before this will also become increasingly scarce. It is estimated that at least 1 trillion

(1,000 billion) barrels can still be produced from tar sands. However, extracting it will still be laborious because the tar sands contain only small amounts of kerogen, the actual raw material for petroleum. The most optimistic estimate for 2020 suggests a production level of 4 million barrels a day from the tar sands in Canada and 3 to 5 million from heavy oil in Venezuela (now 1.5 and 0.4 million barrels respectively).

It isn't just petroleum that is going to 'peak' either, other sources of energy look like they are heading the same way. Until recently it was predicted that the peak for coal would be reached in 2060, but when you consider that many of the coal reserves in China are of poor quality, we could be justified in thinking that the peak for coal will come much sooner. The German Energy Watch Group, founded by a group of scientists in 2006, now predicts that coal will peak around 2030 and uranium, the raw material for nuclear energy, around 2035.

The demand for oil
At the moment, petroleum fulfils about 40% of our energy needs, natural gas and coal about 25% each and all of the other forms of energy combined about 10%. The demand for oil is increasing. We have already discussed the two most important reasons for this: the explosive increase in the world's population and the ever-increasing affluence of the BRIC countries (Brazil, Russia, India, China). Energy consumption is linked to prosperity. The richer people are, the more energy they use. It is therefore the industrialized countries that are the greediest. According to information from the IEA, we can expect that the demand for oil will increase annually by 2% until 2025, to no less than 120 million barrels a day. This increase will be caused to a great extent by countries like India and China. In Western Europe the demand will barely increase between now and 2025, consumption in countries such as the US and Canada will continue to rise, and it looks like the Chinese demand will increase by about 80%. The demand for other fossil fuels such as coal and natural gas will also increase.

The crisis has caused a drop in the demand for petroleum. At first glance this looks like good news, but we can expect demand to increase dramatically when the economy eventually recovers. In addition, oil producers have abandoned any thought of new investments because oil prices have fallen so quickly and in the long term that is bad news for both the environment and the economy. The oil companies are investing less in alternative sources of energy and the search for new oil fields has been postponed, so that economic recovery will be quickly followed by an oil shortage. In other words, a low oil price has a negative effect on the environment – a guaranteed minimum price for oil would be a very good thing indeed for Earth's climate.

Energy as a means of exercising power
It isn't just the depletion of the earth's supplies of fossil fuels that should make us really start looking for alternative sources of energy in the next few years. There are plenty of other urgent reasons for reducing our oil dependency.

We have already mentioned how powerful the OPEC cartel is, but individual oil and gas producing countries such as Iran, Russia and Venezuela also use their oil wealth for political gain. Countries that are dependent on oil are vulnerable to pressure from these countries. Russia already punishes countries with which it is in conflict by cutting off energy supplies, as it did recently to Georgia and the Ukraine. Russia also has OPEC-style ambitions – in December 2008, under the inspired leadership of the Russian ex-president Vladimir Putin, the Gas Exporting Countries Forum (GECF) was set up, a cooperative of the twelve largest gas exporting countries, who want to regulate gas production and gas prices. Gas importing countries are not happy about this development, because they fear the abuse of power by countries like Russia and Iran.

Iran is a potential oil aggressor in other ways as well. After Saudi Arabia, this country has the largest oil supplies in the world, and after Russia, the largest gas supplies. If Iran wanted to strike out at the West it could easily blockade the 50km wide Strait of Hormuz, which divides the Persian Gulf from the Indian Ocean. At least two-fifths of the world's oil production is transported through this strait, making it a very effective target.

European security services have warned that Saudi Arabia has been using its oil wealth to finance groups all over the world that want to spread the Wahabi version of Islam, not only to countries such as Indonesia but also to Europe and the US.

All this is worrying, but the power of the countries is very much tied to oil prices which has had interesting internal effects recently. When the barrel price of oil fell in less than six months (July–December 2008) from $147 to $37, the geopolitical ambitions of Russia, Iran and Venezuela also fell, and their leaders, the 'petro-tzars' Putin and Medvjedev, Ahmedinedjad and Chávez, found themselves faced with unrest in their own countries. All of the handouts they had given their own people, such as energy subsidies, were based on an oil price of between $86 and $100 per barrel. With the price falling to $40 per barrel, either they or the handouts had to go, which would have caused internal unrest, or they would have had to face rising national debt and inflation. Morgan Stanley has calculated that the Russian economy will shrink by 3.5% in 2009, while in Venezuela it will shrink by 1%. Figures like these don't exactly increase the popularity of political leaders. Rising unemployment and deteriorating economies are leading to a political backlash.

In Iran, many factories are closing, making the president less and less popular. In Venezuela, anti-government protests are intensifying. In Russia, numerous street protests have broken out over tax rises and unpaid wages in the steel and manufacturing industries. In response, the

Kremlin has passed new laws including one that makes participating in 'mass disorders' a 'crime against the state.'

It looks like these oil dictators have only themselves to blame. Other oil producing countries have made sure, often through investments in foreign oil companies, that their houses are in order and can operate efficiently. In contrast, Russia, Venezuela and Iran have made things so difficult for Western oil companies that they have decided to make the best of a bad job and look elsewhere. Russia's recent conflicts with BP and Shell ended with the Russian partners unilaterally redefining contracts and terms of business in their own favour. When oil prices were way up, Chávez re-nationalized much of his country's petroleum industry and introduced sixteen-fold tax hikes for foreign companies; many of which subsequently packed up and left. This has meant that there is no longer enough investment in the maintenance of the plant and infrastructure, and there are far fewer fields being prepared for exploitation. Not only that, but the majority of the oil exporting countries have been far-sighted enough to diversify their sources of income, so that their dependence on oil income has decreased. Again, not Russia, Venezuela and Iran, who felt cushioned by an oil price of over $100 per barrel. That a forward-looking and cooperative attitude would have been to their advantage is made quite clear by the following figures: Qatar reaches a *break even point* with an oil price of $10.18. Venezuela would need a price of $90.

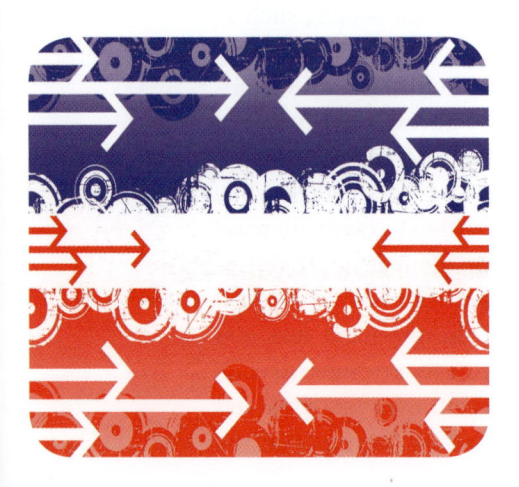

What is the greenhouse effect?

As well as the geopolitical problems, there is of course one other major negative effect linked to current global energy consumption: the greenhouse effect.

The atmosphere around our earth acts as a sort of blanket. The warmth from the sun also radiates out through the atmosphere. Some of this dissipates into space, but some remains trapped in the atmosphere and is reflected back at the earth by clouds and greenhouse gases. The more greenhouse gases we produce, the more warmth is trapped on and around the earth. This creates a self-reinforcing effect. The warming effect causes more water vapour in the atmosphere that in turn retains more heat.

Water vapour itself doesn't cause a huge greenhouse effect. It only has a significant impact because the atmosphere contains such an enormous amount of water vapour; and research has shown that the amount of water vapour is increasing by about 1% every ten years. The most significant greenhouse gases are actually carbon dioxide (CO_2), methane (CH_4) and chlorofluorocarbons (CFCs). The concentrations of the various greenhouse gases are usually shown in ppms, or 'parts per million'.

Nature provides carbon dioxide or CO_2 in our atmosphere, which is lucky for us, because otherwise we'd freeze at night. Without greenhouse gases, earth's average temperature would be minus 18°C (64°F) rather than today's 12°C (54°F). But an excess of greenhouse gases is bad news, because that causes too much warming and that's what we're faced with right now.

The atmosphere of the planet Venus is made up almost totally of carbon dioxide (97%), which makes the temperature of the planet too high for it to be habitable for humans. The easiest way of making carbon dioxide is to burn coal. Large quantities are also released by the burning of other fossil fuels and by volcanoes. Besides acting as a blanket around the earth, carbon dioxide has some other useful functions. Plants need carbon dioxide for the process of photosynthesis. The plant's chlorophyll absorbs the carbon (C) while the oxygen (O_2) is re-released into the air. In greenhouses, carbon dioxide is also used as a fertilizer for plants: if there is more carbon dioxide in the air, the plants grow faster.

Carbon dioxide has a number of other practical applications: as carbonic acid it can be dissolved in liquids, creating the fizz in soft drinks. Because carbonic acid vapour is heavier than air, and will sink to the bottom when released, it is often used in the enter-

part 1. The energy economy, past and present

tainment world to run the 'smoke machines' that you see on TV shows and on the stage.

In 1958 in Hawaii, the American Charles Keeling began measuring the CO_2 concentration in the atmosphere and in that year arrived at a figure of about 315 ppm, which by 2007 had risen to about 380 ppm. The CO_2 concentration for 1958 can be recovered by analysing ice samples. The result: in the last century and a half, the amount of CO_2 in the atmosphere has risen by 35%. This increase can be explained by the use of fossil fuels in keeping our factories in production, heating our homes and running our cars.

Carbon dioxide causes about 53% of the greenhouse effect. Other greenhouse gases are present in the atmosphere in much smaller amounts but they have a relatively stronger effect. Concentrations of methane account for less than 2 ppm and CFCs for only 1 ppm, but these gases account for 17% and 5% respectively of the greenhouse effect cause by humans.

Carbon dioxide doesn't just make the greatest contribution to the greenhouse effect but it will also ensure that the problem will last for many years: CO_2 molecules remain in the atmosphere for a century; in contrast, methane molecules will break down in about ten years. The persistence of CO_2 means that its accumulation will increase exponentially if we carry on emitting the gas at the current rate.

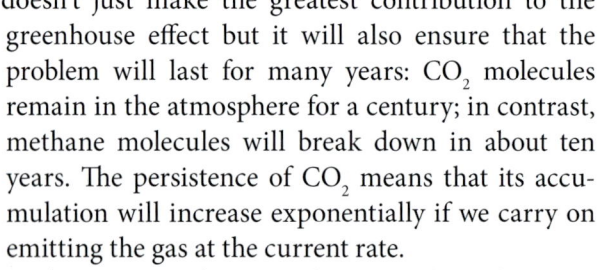

The amount of CO_2 in the atmosphere is around 3000 gigatons at the moment, and to that we are adding around 14 gigatons each year. Actually, the amount of CO_2 we emit is double that amount, 28 gigatons a year, but half of that is absorbed by the oceans and plant life. The CO_2 graphs made by Charles Keeling look like a rising zigzag line, and that zigzag effect in the graph is caused by the cycle of plant growth in the Northern Hemisphere which has by far the largest green areas. In Spring, plants grow quickly and absorb a great deal of CO_2, while in Autumn, they absorb very little.

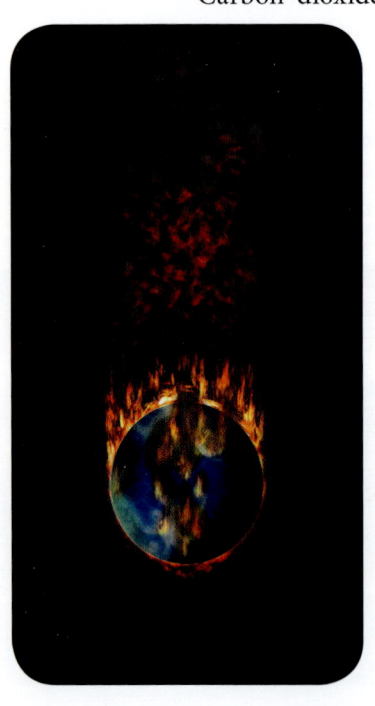

The IPCC has made an assessment of the most important sources of human CO_2 emissions. Industry still accounts for the largest part, at around 40%. In the wealthy countries, industry is becoming ever more efficient, to the extent that in some countries emissions have been falling by several per cent since 1990. However, emissions from the industrializing countries such as China and India are showing a visible increase. In total, industrial CO_2 emissions are rising at the moment at just 1% a year. The next largest source of CO_2 emissions comes from our buildings: heating, cooling and electricity use account for about 31% of emissions, and that is rising by 2% a year, mostly because we live in increasingly larger houses and use ever more electrical appliances. The third sector in the list of major CO_2 emitters is transport, accounting for 22%. The transport sector poses the most problems with respect to emissions, with a growth of about 2% a year. In the wealthier countries this increase is due to the use of ever-larger vehicles, particularly the Sport Utility Vehicles (SUVs), and the huge increase in air transport. In fact since 1990, the amount of fuel used for international flights from Great Britain has more than doubled. In 2005, CO_2 emissions from international flights were estimated at 9 million tons, the equivalent of half of all the emissions from buildings in Great Britain. In countries such as China and India we can expect a huge future growth in the number of cars. If we want to cut back on greenhouse gas emissions, we really have to start looking at alternatives in the field of transport.

So, who are the world's biggest emitters of CO_2? Obviously the industrialized countries emit more CO_2 than less developed countries. The United States had topped the list for CO_2 emissions for many years, but in 2007, China took the lead. The US produced 20% of annual CO_2 emissions, even though they only accounted for 5% of the world's population. Every American emitted four times as much CO_2 as the average world citizen. In comparison, the British produced 2% of global emissions while they accounted for just 1% of the world's population. That is half as much as the average American but twice as much as is sustainable. The reason for high CO_2 emissions in the US is the focus on economic growth rather than on energy efficiency. Plus, over the years Americans have developed an energy-hungry way of life. A town like Las Vegas, where air conditioners hum day and night, neon boards blaze and water flows even though it is in the middle of a desert, is a symbol of the profligate *American way of life*. Americans love big cars and travel enormous distances every year. *Suburbia*, living somewhere that is well away from the workplace, accounts for much of the huge mobility of the average American.

However, as we have noted, another nation has just taken over as leader when it comes to CO_2 emissions: China. The US Energy Information Administration had calculated that this would not happen until 2025 – but by 2007 China had beaten that 'target'. In 2000, China was responsible for 15% of global emissions and that figure will only continue to increase in the coming years.

We need to mention here that we have been talking about the total emissions of countries, which doesn't really say anything about the CO_2 emissions per capita of populations. If we actually look at the emissions per person per year, then we get the following top five CO_2-emitters:

(1) Qatar
(2) The United Arab Emirates
(3) Kuwait
(4) Bahrain
(5) Australia.

In the Arab oil states listed, most emissions are caused by the oil industry and by air-conditioning. In countries such as the US, Australia, Canada and New Zealand, the culprits are mainly buildings (heating and cooling) and the number of kilometres travelled, while in the European countries it is industry and transport that produce the most emissions.

The industrialized world is therefore far and away the largest CO_2 emitter yet research shows that the poorest countries suffer the most from the greenhouse effect. This is partly due to geography: the wealthiest countries generally have moderate climates, where a rise of a few degrees is not disastrous, and indeed in some areas is welcomed. Most of the developing countries are in the tropics or in desert regions or have a prairie climate and are vulnerable in the climatic sense. The major reason why the developing countries suffer more from the greenhouse effect is economic. Because these countries are poor, there is less money available to spend on combating the negative effects of climate change. Not only that, but these countries rely heavily on agriculture – the economic sector most sensitive to climate change. The idea that we are all in the same boat, and can work together to combat CO_2 emissions doesn't really ring true.

In the following chapter, we will look more closely at the different future scenarios that have been suggested, in order to illustrate what a future of falling oil production and global warming might be like.

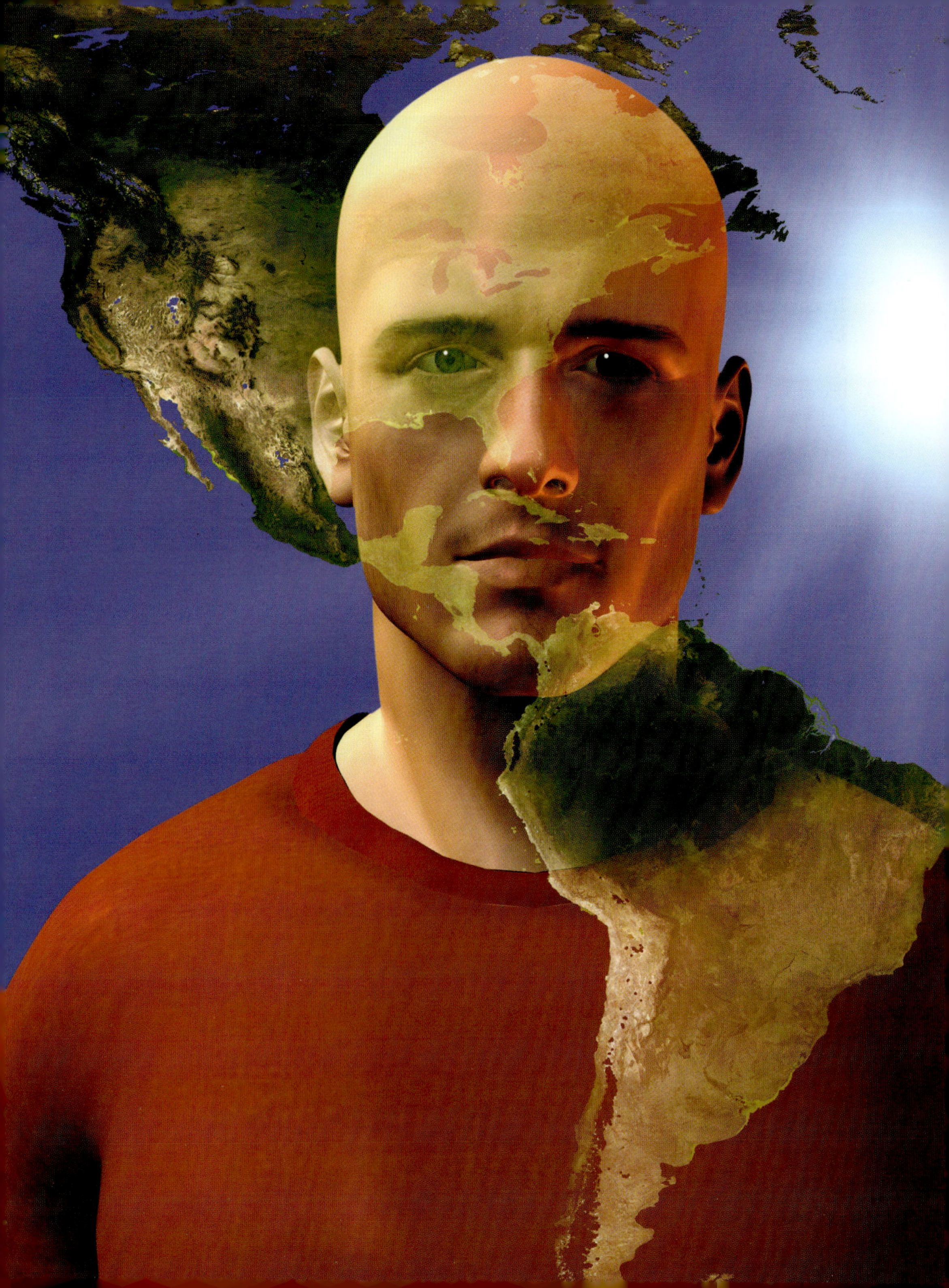

Chapter 3

The future of our energy supplies

In chapter one we discussed three possible scenarios for the future: the Easter Island scenario, the Lutheran scenario and the Ostrich scenario. In this chapter we will look at some current trends and discuss other scenarios including those put forward by the IPCC and Shell; we will examine the predictions made by both climate alarmists and climate sceptics.

Trend 1. Recognizing the real problem of over-population
During a recent climate conference, a Chinese official said that the world should thank China for their one-child-policy. If it hadn't been for that, there would be three hundred million more Chinese than there are now. If the African and other Asian countries had also implemented a one-child-policy, there would be one billion fewer people on the earth – a real plus for the environment. The man was right of course. The birth rate in some areas is simply mind-boggling and that is catastrophic for the environment. Thus, limiting the birth rate must become an absolute priority.

Trend 2. Growing consensus over the approaching end of fossil fuels
When we take everything into account, it looks like the use of fossil fuels will eventually have to come to an end. But even in the greenest of future scenarios, we will still be using them as far into the future as 2050 to supply 80% of our energy. The unpredictable factor in all this is still peak

oil, the point at which demand will outstrip supply. As we said earlier in the book, there is still disagreement as to when peak oil will be reached, but some point between 2010 and 2015 looks most likely. It is clear that the price of oil will rise dramatically, and this could be a death-blow to some sectors. For others it will be the spur to reduce energy use or switch to renewables, thereby creating a more sustainable business model.

Ex-Shell senior executive Rein Willems has stated: 'Oil will run out, and so will gas. It is quite clear that mankind must be more economical in his energy consumption. Everyone affected both within and outside the energy sector must pull out all the stops to develop new sources of energy. I do not foresee one single dominant new energy source, but rather a range of possibilities, from wind energy to nuclear fusion. However, you can be sure that the transition will take decades. Living without oil just won't be possible in the next few decades.'

In 2005, Shell published *Shell Global Scenarios to 2025*, which distils trends in the relationships between the three major players who will control energy developments: governments, industry and ordinary citizens.

In the first, called *Low Trust Globalization,* governments and companies are the chief players. The market economy is the driving force behind developments in this scenario thus companies play a major role. It is however characterized by a crisis in security and trust that governments will have to try to control. Because economic globalization erodes the legitimacy of national status and there is no global consensus between the various governments, it will lead to a flood of new legislation which governments will use to try to restore feelings of trust and security. Lawyers would definitely benefit from this scenario.

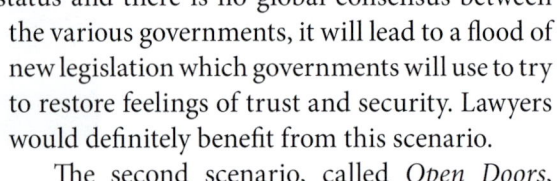

The second scenario, called *Open Doors*, proposes a development steered by industry and citizens who will maintain an open relationship with each other. Together they will create a balance between efficient consumption and trust/security. In this scenario trust will be created by industry itself through certification and standardization. The right of investors, consumers and governments to be heard will be crucial. Terms like 'socially responsible business' emerge within this scenario. It is also a world in which smart codes, global tracking systems and network technology play a major role.

The third and final Shell scenario, called *Flags*, is characterized by fragmented trust: the various social groups trust only others within their own group and governments take refuge in nationalism. Energy efficiency is no match for patriotism, populism and protectionism; globalization will fall out of favour, to be replaced with 'inter-nationalization'.

Trend 3. Towards the increasing influence of IPCC scenarios on political policies

The Intergovernmental Panel on Climate Change, the climate organization of the United Nations, proposes four future scenarios with respect to CO_2 emissions. The IPCC relies on a great deal of scientific research. Unfortunately, the IPCC's conclusions and recommendations are somewhat politicized, much to the annoyance of the scientists who worked on the reports. In spite of this, the IPCC scenarios will be used by governments and other interested parties to develop energy and climate control policies. So whatever we might think about these reports, it would be in our best interests to know what they say. Here are the IPCC scenarios.

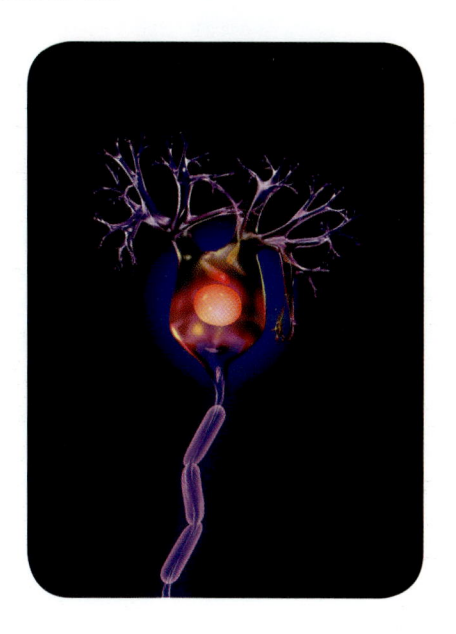

Scenario A1:
In this scenario the world goes through rapid economic growth, the world population increases up to the year 2050, after which it will shrink and new environmentally efficient techniques will be quickly put in place.

Scenario A2:
In this scenario, there is major global diversification, the world population continues to grow and there is low and fragmented economic growth.

Scenario B1:
This scenario is similar to A1 except that the economy increasingly concentrates on services and information and will be less dependent on the consumption and production of materials.

Scenario B2:
This scenario is based on the premise of finding local solutions for sustainability, a continued growth in the world population and an average growth in the economy.

As far as the climate is concerned the best scenario is B1. This is the only one in which CO_2 emissions can be hauled back to 1990 levels. It is the scenario that sees economic growth, coupled with developments in services and information sectors. Other conditions are a decrease in the world population from around 2050 and innovation though new, long-term techniques. The most doom-laden scenario for the climate is A2, which suggests a fragmented global economy and a continued increase in the world's population. In this scenario, CO_2 emissions will rise steadily until in 2100 they will be three to six times higher than in 1990.

How do the IPCC scenarios fit in with the ones we talked about in chapter one? Our Easter Island scenario, that forecasts hell and damnation, fits in best with the IPCC scenario A2. Our Lutheran scenario goes well with the IPCC scenario B1, because it presents both sacrifices and opportunities. Our head in the sand Ostrich scenario has no parallel in the IPCC forecasts.

Trend 4. Towards an accentuation of the Kyoto Protocol
The big problem concerning new legislation for reducing greenhouse gases is the global nature of the CO_2 problem. Tightening up the laws of separate countries doesn't achieve much because CO_2 concentrations don't respect national borders.

The Kyoto Protocol was agreed in 1997 with the aim of cutting back on greenhouse gas emissions. The major industrialized countries agreed that in 2008 emissions, including carbon dioxide and methane, should be cut back by an average 5% to bring them down to 1990 levels. The reduction for each country would differ, depending on their economic resources. A trade in emissions rights was also set up and regulated. The European countries ratified the treaty in 2002 and the Russian government signed it in 2004, which meant that there were enough signatures to set the treaty in motion, which is indeed what happened on February 16, 2005. The treaty will remain in force until 2012. For a long time, the major industrialized nation, the US, opposed the treaty on the grounds that it would greatly damage the American economy. However in 2007, at the major conference of the industrialized nations, the G8 summit, changing public opinion forced them to deal more forcefully with the CO_2 emissions question. With the change of leadership in the White House, there is now a better chance that the US might take on a more active role in reducing CO_2 emissions. A cooperative America is crucial in any international climate control agreement.

In 2007, the Kyoto treaty was followed by the Bali treaty, but its vague wording meant that it had very little effect. The following climate summit held in 2008 in Poznan, in Poland, was also disappointing, at least from an environmental point of view. The crisis had just kicked in and the countries taking part had their minds on 'other' priorities, i.e. their national economies. Some unilateral promises were made. Some South American countries, in particular, took some encouraging steps. Mexico is now aiming to halve its greenhouse gas emissions by 2050, Brazil will actively reduce deforestation and wants to reduce the loss of the forests by 70% in the next ten years, while Peru has indicated that it wants to halt deforestation altogether. However, so many concessions were made to the polluters that there was very little progress made in respect of the original Kyoto treaty.

Internally, the European Union has lived up to the original goal of reducing emissions by 2020. However, peace offerings have been made to those countries that are worried that the 'polluter pays' principle will raise the costs of electricity, and that industries might decide to look outside Europe for better options, for example to Asia. Opt-outs were granted from plans to force large polluters to buy allowances to emit carbon at auction. Poor ex-communist countries that rely on coal for power will be allocated up to 70% of the carbon allowances needed by power firms, for no payment, for a few years after 2013. European heavy industries that face global competition will also get up to 100% of their allowances free initially, if they use the cleanest available technologies. Otherwise they are sure to lose out to competitors outside Europe, because the new super powers such as India and China will definitely oppose regulations to limit their greenhouse gas emissions.

Because of the breakdown in the consensus and the chaotic results of the last climate conference, there are now many people who no longer have any faith in climate agreements. At the beginning of 2009, the Institution of Mechanical Engineers report said: 'The existing Kyoto Protocol has, to date, been a near total failure, with emissions levels continuing to rise substantially.' The report calls for 'realism'.

The Institution feels that we should accept the fact of climate change and expect much higher temperatures, extreme weather conditions and a rise in sea levels that will make many coastal regions uninhabitable. The engineers insist that we should already be adapting construction, including that of houses and infrastructure: 'Towns and cities should be planned to adjust street layouts to correspond with prevailing winds, maximising ventilation and cooling. The location of many power stations may have to be reconsidered, as they are often in coastal areas. And railways were often placed in river valleys to make the most of low gradients, but they should be moved to higher ground.' In other words, engineers should be rolling up their sleeves.

Trend 5. Towards a pioneering role for Western Europe and Japan?
At the beginning of March 2007 Germany, the then chair of the EU, through their spokesperson, Chancellor Angela Merkel, took up the

ecological reins at a summit conference of European government leaders in Brussels. 'It won't be easy but the European Union must start fulfilling its obligations right now and show a pioneering spirit', said Merkel in *The Financial Times*. European leaders committed themselves to a reduction of 20% in greenhouse gas emissions by 2020, compared to the situation in 1990, and a reduction of 30% if the other industrialized nations and the BRIC nations (Brazil, Russia, India and China) also take part. Also, by 2020 at least 10% of all the oil and diesel used in Europe must be made up of bio-fuels. Finally, 20% of energy in the EU must come from renewable sources such as solar, wind and water and the countries must try to attain a total energy saving of 20%. The European climate agreement reached in Brussels was met with scepticism throughout Europe. Although people appreciated the aims of the European leaders regarding sustainable climate control, there were still many question marks about the real interpretations of the measures and the observance of the agreement itself.

The European Union seemed to be seriously addressing the urgency of climate issues. Japan was another example of a country really getting to grips with the need for sustainability. However, priorities have shifted somewhat recently due to the crisis. The climate, it seems, can wait for the short-term problems of the economy to be solved. This phenomenon can be perfectly illustrated by the about-turn made by Angela Merkel between 2007 and 2009. She has given in to pressure from German industry and now seems to be modifying some of the important objectives or even changing her mind altogether. Even though she was known as the 'Green Chancellor' in 2007, in 2009 the British press dubbed her 'Frau Nein' and in her own country she is called 'Angela Mutlos,' which more or less means 'Faint-Hearted Angela'.

Trend 6. Towards growing consciousness of the climate issue

The public has been aware of the greenhouse effect and climate change for a number of years, but few have bothered about it and the average person in the street sees it as a sort of technical problem about which experts such as meteorologists and climatologists constantly disagree. The discussions about the Kyoto Protocol at the start of the twenty-first century brought CO_2 emissions into focus, but what has really made an impact on people has been the extreme weather changes. All over the earth, world records have been broken. Europe has had its mildest winter ever, followed by the heaviest January storms then the warmest April on record. In the US, hurricanes are more severe than ever and tornadoes are suddenly striking outside their normal season. This kind of thing really makes an impact and has had a greater influence than any number of well-researched climatology reports.

The idea that the extremes in the weather could have something to do with our behaviour was brought to our attention in the autumn of 2006, when two publications dominated headlines and TV programmes. Sir Nicholas Stern, economist and former vice-president of the World Bank, issued *The Stern Review on the Economics of Climate Change,* in which he calculated what climate change was going to cost. And the ex vice-president of the US Al Gore, in his book and film *An Inconvenient Truth* presented the general public with impressive images of the potentially catastrophic consequences lying in wait for us as a result of greenhouse gases.

Stern translates the abstract subject of the climate into the clear language of money, which is understood by all. He has calculated that, if we carry on emitting the current rate of CO_2 emissions, it is going to cost the global community €5.5 trillion, or 20% of total global production. This would lead to a deep economic crisis, comparable to or even worse than the crisis of the 1930s. Climate change threatens to be what Stern calls 'the biggest and most sweeping market disturbance ever known'.

Media aligned to both the right and the left made much of Stern's message, although there was criticism of some of his calculation methods. Industry also couldn't ignore the report. His language is utterly devoid of any inspirational or motivational tone, but sticks to a clear profit and loss analysis, the language of business.

Trend 7. Towards the temporary domination of the Great Alarm

This can't be said of Al Gore's *An Inconvenient Truth*, even though it also contains many figures. Gore plays on sentiment, fear and guilt and draws a hellish picture of melting ice, rising sea levels, advancing deserts and approaching super storms, all caused by hedonistic energy consumption. Gore travelled all over the world proclaiming his disturbing message, and with much success. The book was a best-seller, the film by the same name won two Academy Awards and was screened in cinemas week after week. Politicians, including his former crony Bill Clinton, fell over themselves to declare their support for Gore. In his own lectures Clinton is now drawing his audiences' attention to Gore's *An Inconvenient Truth*. The general public seems to be very receptive to this message, which we call the *Great Alarm*. All over Europe and America you can see politicians who are trying to cash in on the fear that has taken root in people's psyches.

Not all are convinced of course. For some time now in the climate debate, dogma has seemed to be hitting harder than healthy reasoning. And usually it's the messenger not the message that is criticized. At the beginning of April 2007 Steven Hayward, director of the American Enterprise Institute (AEI), produced a documentary, entitled '*An Inconvenient Truth... or Convenient Fiction*'. Hayward used the same kind of production methods that Al Gore had used in order to ridicule *An Inconvenient Truth* and to make personal attacks on the filmmaker. Hayward called Gore 'an environmental extremist'. When Gore received his Grammy award in the spring of 2007, reports immediately appeared in the press about his own large scale energy consumption. It seemed that mudslinging was being used as a weapon in the climate debate in the same way it has been used during elections.

Trend 8. Towards climate change as a new religion

At the moment there is a clear polarization of opinion about human impact on the climate. On one side are those who proclaim hell and damnation with tales of climatic catastrophe caused by our evil impact on the environment, while on the other are those 'nothing's-the-matter' types who dismiss climate change as nonsense. Both attitudes are held with something approaching religious conviction, and are propounded with a religious fervour. The problem for the rest of us is the complexity of the issue and the flood of 'scientific' but nevertheless contradictory information with which we are faced.

The 'climate sceptics' accuse the 'prophets of doom' of clinging to prejudices, rather than taking on board the full range of scientific investigation on the topic. According to them, people need a common enemy (the devil in the form of a CO_2 producing human) to fight, to explain guilty feelings (why are some in the world well off while others aren't?) and to justify their holy mission.

In this vein, the former British Finance minister, Lord Nigel Lawson, wrote in *The Spectator*: 'It has to be said that this is not an easy message to get across, not least because climate change is so often discussed in terms of belief rather than reason. It is, I suspect, no accident that it is in Europe that climate change absolutism has found the most fertile soil. For it is Europe that has become the most secular society in the world, in which the traditional religions have the weakest popular hold. Yet people still feel the need for the comfort and higher values religion can provide, and the current climate debate is the best example of a quasi-belief, which is in fact what green alarmism is, where reasoned questioning of its mantras is regarded as sacrilege. But this can be no basis for rational policy-making.'

The German climatologist, Hans von Storch, also draws a parallel between climatic doom scenarios and religion. In *Der Spiegel* he says: 'Unfortunately, many scientists see themselves far too often as priests who have to preach their message to the general public. This is a legacy of the 1968 generation, to which I myself belong.' He feels that climate change is being presented as God's punishment for our sinful, hedonistic behaviour, and that this is why environmentalists dismiss talk of the potentially positive effects of global warming. To admit an upside would be to undermine their catastrophic vision.

The fact that some environmental groups and worried scientists present their views about the climate within a religious framework can be explained in another way. The climate has something of a higher order about it: the weather happens to us, and literally comes 'from above'. The worship of nature is a very ancient practice that carries on today in some religions. Even those of us who claim that we are not religious are still inclined to treat natural phenomena like the weather with something approaching religious fervour.

The image painted by Gore & Co doesn't seem that far removed from the vision of the Apocalypse. In its last report, the IPCC itself called the irreversible changes in our climate 'apocalyptic'. Biblical language and imagery abound in the climate debate. The imagery strikes a chord, because according to the Bible, God regularly punishes man's sinful behaviour by inflicting natural disasters. Psychologists explain our susceptibility to this kind of doom scenario as follows: they are ways of expressing our inner insecurities and they create the illusion of control. Just like the Old Testament 'punishment prophets', the climatologists from the IPCC call on us to repent of our sins so that we will be spared the rising waters of the ocean, the extinction of species, starvation and all of the other negative scenarios. They create the illusion that climate change can be prevented, if we will just make the right sacrifices. We are not saying that their climatic observations are incorrect but we feel that making a religious crusade out of it all is counterproductive, because it causes a polarization that prevents the parties involved from joining forces to find a solution.

Trend 9. Towards banning cow farts

Grist to the mill for all those who dismiss the hooha round CO_2 emissions as mass hysteria are the stories about the massive contribution to higher concentrations of greenhouse gases made by cow farts and cow dung. Excuse me, cow farts? Indeed. The digestive systems of cows (and other quadrupeds such as pigs) actually do release methane, which makes a significant contribution to greenhouse gas emissions. Methane is one of the strongest greenhouse gases, twenty times more significant than CO_2. According to a recent UN report, the cow is the biggest polluter on the planet. The report states that consumption and other uses of animal products accounts for 18% of greenhouse gas emissions – this at a time when meat consumption is increasing world-wide. In countries such as China, India and Brazil, the consumption of red meat has risen by 33% in the last few decades, and it is expected to increase by 50% between

2000 and 2050. The production of one pound of beef results in 11 times as much greenhouse gas as the production of the same amount of chicken, and 100 times as much as the production of a pound of carrots. In the large agrarian and meat-producing countries such as New Zealand, Australia, Brazil and Argentina, agriculture accounts for more than 50% of CO_2 emissions. In a country like the US, that figure is only 7.4%, but that is because emissions from others sectors such as industry and transport, are especially high.

So: do we have to get rid of the cow as well as our sacred cow: the car? Should we reduce the bovine population by eating as much beef as we can in the shortest possible time and then switch to a vegetarian diet? Well, no. According to a British study, the methane produced by cows could be reduced by 70% if the amount of organic sugars in their diet were to be reduced. That means feeding cows on fresh grass rather than sugar beet. And in Australia, scientists have developed a vaccine that could reduce the methane produced by cattle by a fifth.

Still, the Dutch branch of the environmental organization Friends of the Earth regards a decrease in livestock as part of the solution to the problem. In their report published in March 2007 called *Boeren met Toekomst (Future of Farming)* they said: 'An environmental levy of 85 eurocents per kilo of meat and a halving of livestock are inevitable. This is the only way the cattle farmer will have any kind of future.' The environmental levy has to make the 'hidden costs' incurred by the present day meat sector more transparent. 'At the moment, such issues as the greenhouse effect, loss of biodiversity and the pollution of drinking water are not reflected in the price of meat', says spokesman Wouter van Eck. With an estimated income of 700 million euros, Friends of the Earth in Holland hope to stimulate the conversion of farmers. The environmental levy (van Eck: '10 cents per chicken fillet, fifteen cents per fillet steak') also has to apply to meat from abroad, to take into account any competition from that sector. What the full plan for the conversion of farmers entails, van Eck doesn't say. Meanwhile, some farmers are getting together to try to find solutions themselves. They are exploring the potential for converting the methane in manure into electricity without creating any CO_2 emissions at all; what's left over can be used as fertilizer.

Trend 10. Towards a new language of climate change

The way we talk about climate problems has a huge impact on public opinion. What do we mean by 'greenhouse effect', 'climate change', 'global warming' or 'climate crisis'? Those four terms have totally different emotional impacts. 'Greenhouse effect' is a technical term implying something negative. 'Climate change' sounds different but is still relatively neutral and implies that some degree of control is possible. 'Global warming' is more alarming because it's more concrete, and finally with 'climate crisis' we get the feeling of something final. It's no surprise then that Gore talked about a 'climate crisis', while the American ex-president George W. Bush stuck to the term 'climate change'. 'Climate crisis' gives the impression that immediate action is necessary while 'climate change' doesn't sound quite so urgent. Researchers, who were monitoring the terminology used in *The New York Times*, concluded that between 2004 and 2006, the term 'global warming' won hands down. It appeared twice as often as 'climate change'. It's these subtle changes in terminology that not only mirror public opinion, but also influence it to a great extent.

Another phenomenon that we have seen in publications about climate change is the indiscriminate adoption and even exaggeration of data. To illustrate: in 1997, the English professor Norman Myers produced a report called *Environmental Exodus*, in which he predicted that one of the major dramas in the coming decades will be the rising number of environmental refugees. Organizations, including the Red Cross, the UN environmental organization UNEP and the Stern reports we have already quoted, adopted Myers' figures. Some of them are still gilding the lily, including the British aid agency Christian Aid, which expects at least one billion environmental refugees before 2050. Many other scientists feel that this is just rousing public feeling. Stephen Castles, professor of the National Migration Institute in Oxford, states: 'A great deal of suffering will be avoided if governments could just plan for changes to the environment. Mankind is resourceful. If the climate changes, man will come up with ways of dealing with it. But this message just doesn't suit the environmental lobby. Using a politically sensitive subject like migration and juggling the figures just to shock people is immoral.'

Trend 11. Towards a temporary displacement of the climate crisis by the crisis

In the first half of 2008, while we were still reasonably healthy economically, there was a broad band of public consensus about the need for far-reaching and often painful measures to put the brakes on global warming. There were countless initiatives for limiting our CO_2 emissions. Suddenly everything had to be 'green', even products that were obviously not environmentally friendly at all. Industry started searching furiously for ways of manufacturing their products in a more sustainable way. People all over the world were starting to think about how they could contribute. They thought about clean technology when buying a car and had started being more careful with energy consumption at home. Governments too were doing their bit. They introduced initiatives like banning high-energy light bulbs and taxing air travel. Slowly but surely we were all heading in the right direction. Then the crisis hit the world in September 2008 and we all started feeling the effects of an economic recession. Suddenly everyone was looking for the cheapest solution instead of the most affordable green solution.

The current focus on the economy is going to last for quite a while. People want to save their own skins before worrying about the collective good. This attitude will mean that sustainability is no longer the decisive factor in many situations.

It's high time for us to ditch the old economy and create a new clean economy. If we can resist panicking, and instead focus on transition and innovation we should emerge from the crisis stronger than ever.

In conclusion
The IPCC, the aforementioned UN think-tank consisting of 2,500 climate experts, put forward some alarming figures in their February 2007 report (even though these figures were less shocking than those contained in their previous report). For example, the range of projected temperature increases of 1.4°C to 5.8°C by the year 2100 has been lowered to a range of between 2°C and 4.5°C. The same applies to the rise in sea levels. In the previous report this was projected to be 9cm to 88cm during this century, but is now estimated at between 14cm and 43cm. This allowed governments to take their eyes off the ball, although we must point out that in their latest prognoses, the IPCC did not take the melting of the polar caps into account, as Gore did in *An Inconvenient Truth*. They justify this by saying that there are no models to predict what effect all that melting ice will have on ocean levels. In any case, action must and will be taken, as we will see in part two.

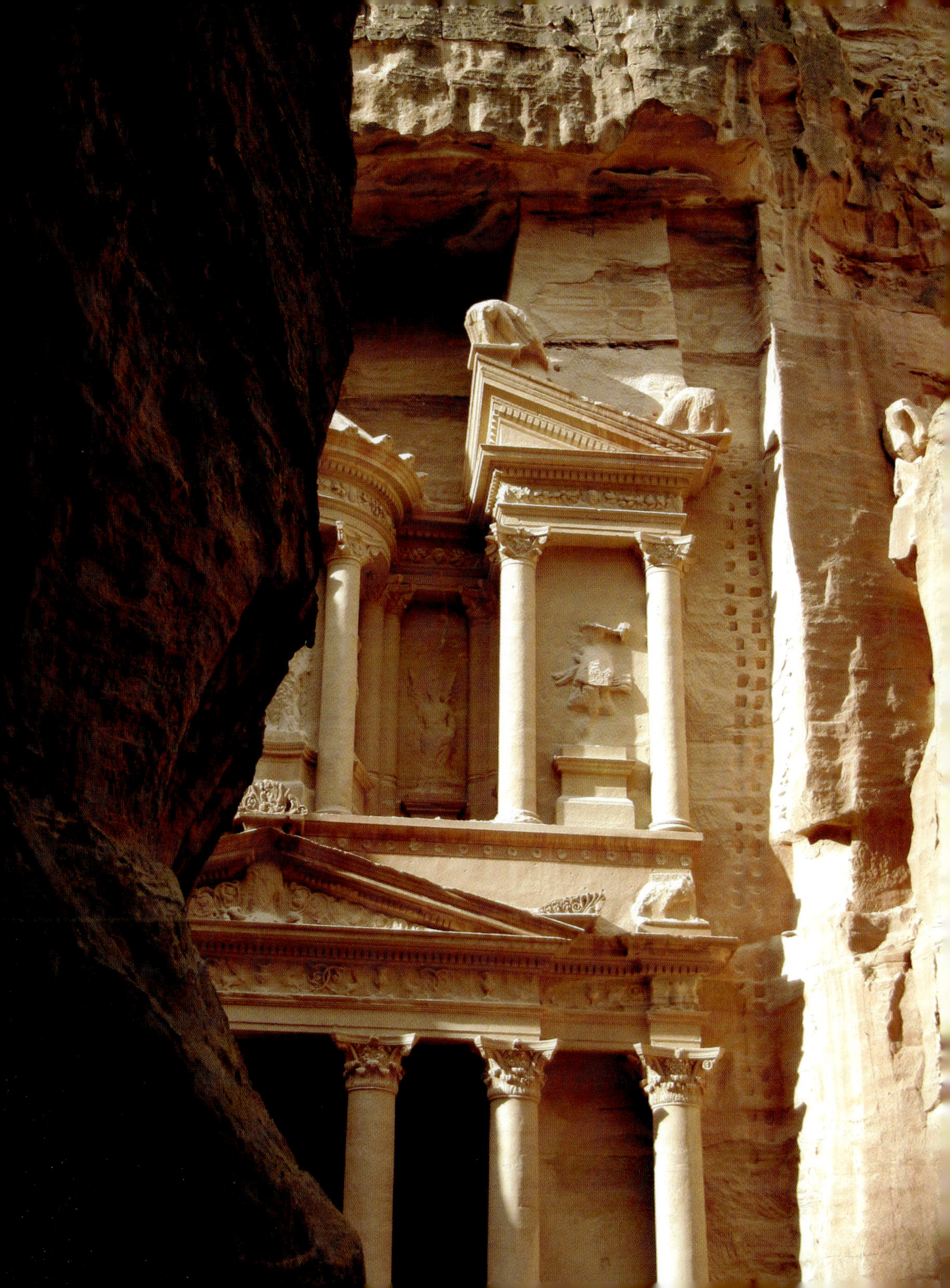

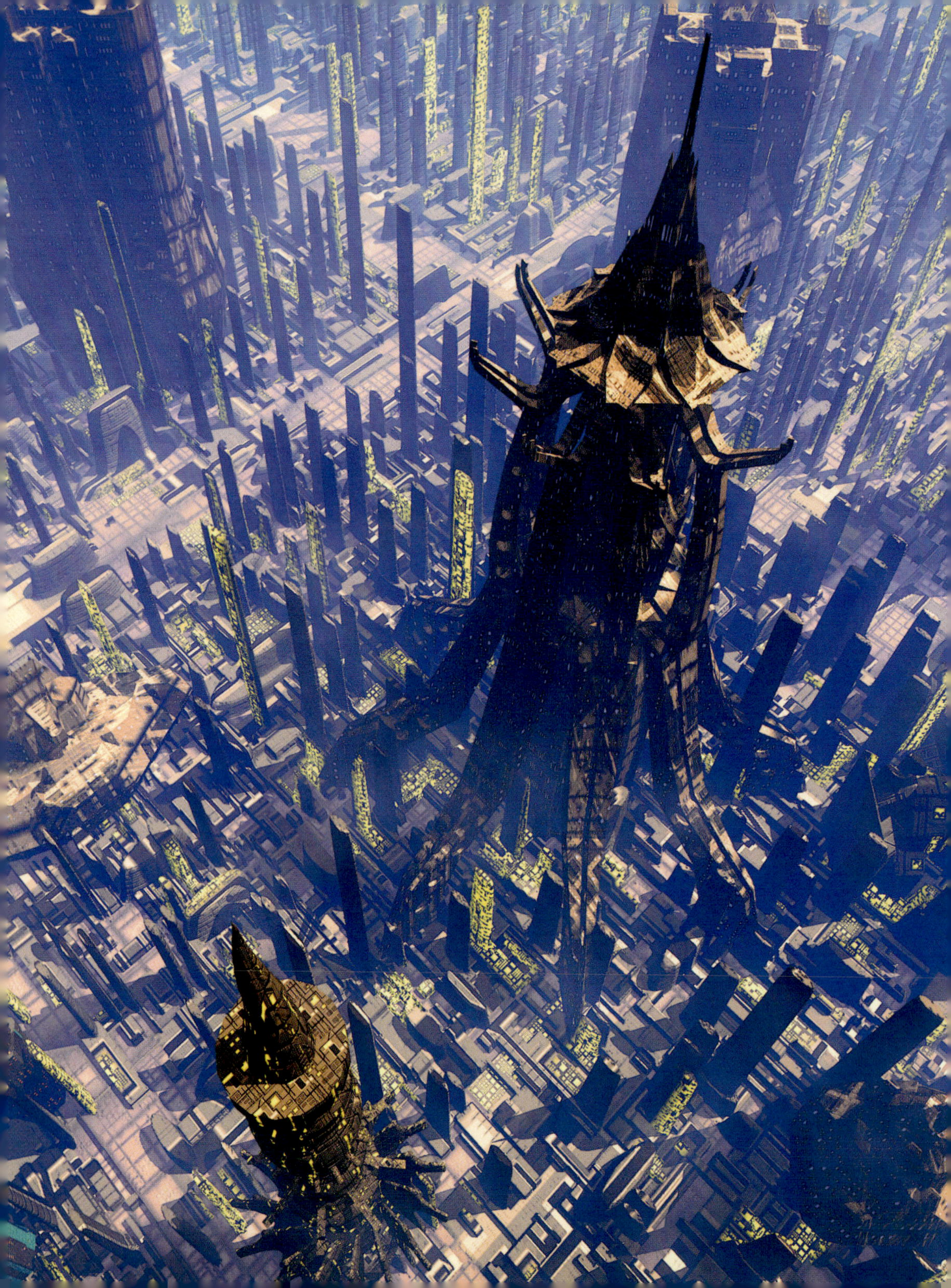

part 2

The new energy economy: outlines and trends

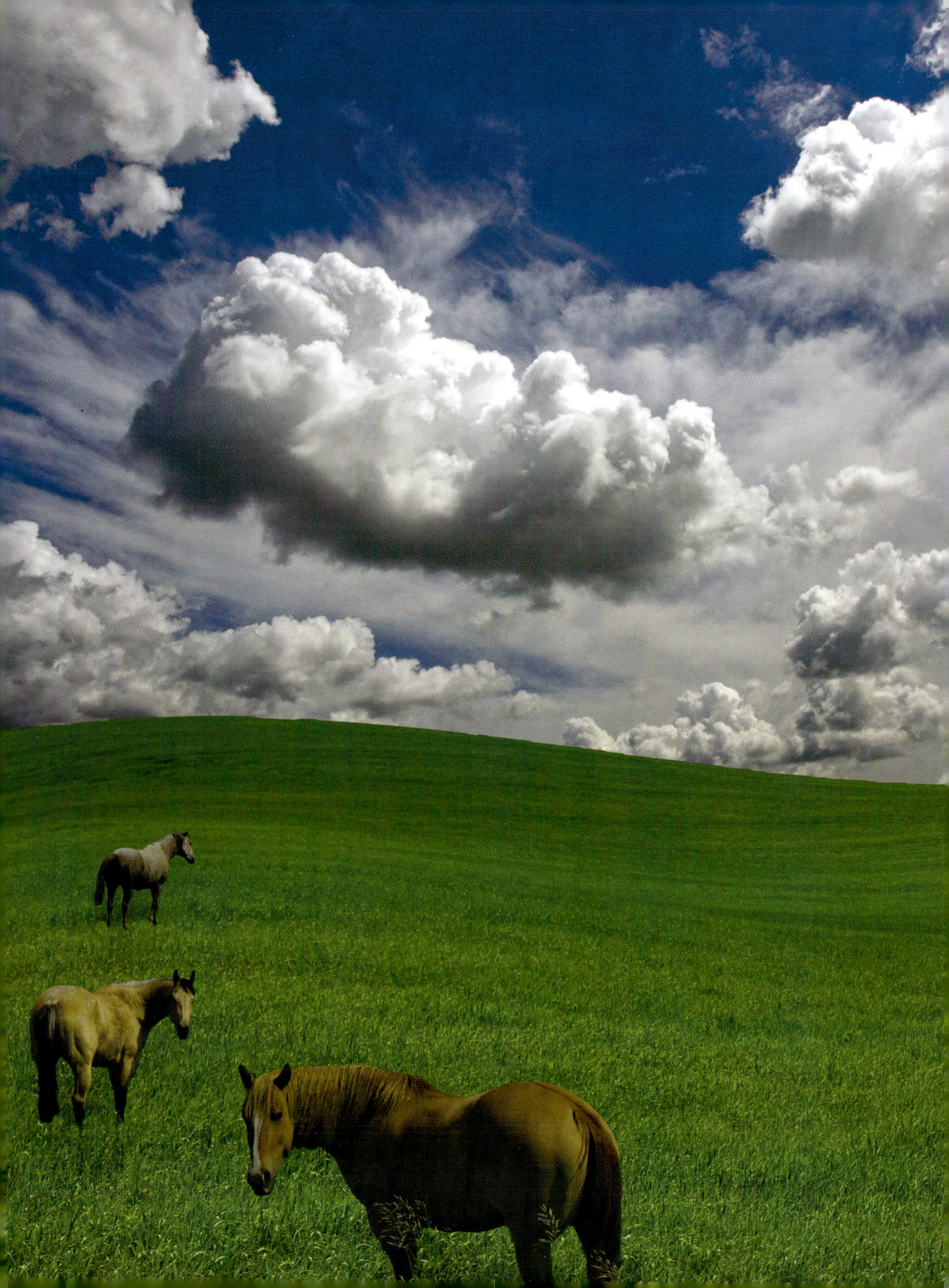

Megatrend I

Towards new energy policies

It will already be obvious that governments all over the world deal with the question of climate change on different levels. The reasons why politicians and leaders act as they do varies. In some cases they mean well and want to take responsibility for controlling the climate. Hippie era ideals about communing with nature have influenced some politicians. In other cases, an apparent climate consciousness is just a thin, purely opportunistic veneer covering a desire to improve popularity, or justify tax increases.

What is certain is that after a long period of governments taking a back seat, our leaders now want to take control in certain areas. Climate change and the measures that will be needed to learn how to survive afford governments and government bodies more legitimacy for realizing these ambitions. At the beginning of the twenty-first century, governments and politicians gave vent to their ambitions in various ways.

It seems that European citizens have very different opinions about the role that they expect their governments to take with respect to environmental issues. Authoritative, long running research by European Values Studies shows that when faced with the statement: 'I would be prepared to give up part of my income for the environment', the Germans, French and English were not very enthusiastic, while the Danes and the Dutch were prepared to make personal cut backs. In 1999, only 32% of Germans reacted positively, of the French 46.2%, of the British 48.8%, while among the Dutch and the Danes this figure was 74.6% and 78.8% respectively. To the proposal that 'the government should make the effort to combat environmental pollution', 70% of the Germans reacted positively, 84.1% of the French, 77% of the British, and only 23.2% of the Dutch and 30% of the Danes. Evidently the Danes and the Dutch see environmental problems as more of a personal responsibility, while the Germans, English and particularly the French prefer to pass the responsibility to government.

The reasons for these striking differences can perhaps be found in the religious backgrounds of these nations. The Netherlands and Denmark are the most Protestant nations on the list, and Protestants place more emphasis than Catholics on personal responsibility and are less inclined to rely on hierarchical authorities.

The outlines of an era of new energy policies are already starting to form. We see six trends making up the megatrend of new energy management and government action for the new energy economy.

Trend 1. Towards combined global and regional government initiatives

Politicians are beginning to realize that while local or national energy management might be useful and necessary, we will get nowhere without global and regional cooperation. Climate change affects the whole world and CO_2 emissions are a global problem. Scientists in Germany and America have found that the air pollution above their countries originates, in part, from China. It is already evident that politicians from all parties – both those for and against globalization – are getting together in cross border networks and joint ventures to deal with with CO_2 emissions. Sometimes these joint ventures have existed for some time and are formal, such as that of the G8 countries, the seven richest industrialized countries plus Russia. At their summit in 2007 in Heiligendamm, they agreed that a 'significant' limitation of greenhouse gas emissions was necessary. However, the eight could not agree about the scale of compulsory limitation.

Some of these international networks are newer and less formal, such as the Clinton Climate Initiative (CCI) which was launched in 2006 by the American former president Bill Clinton. This is a joint initiative by the Clinton Foundation and the Large Cities Climate Leadership Group (C40), to realize concrete quantifiable reductions of CO_2 emissions in cities with more than three million residents. Cities consume 75% of the world's energy and produce 80% of its greenhouse gas emissions. This extensive network has concentrated on finding practical and quantifiable solutions in the battle against climate change. New York, Philadelphia, Los Angeles, Chicago and Houston are the American cities taking part. In China, Beijing, Shanghai and Hong Kong are involved. London is the only British city belonging to the Large Cities Climate Leadership Group. C40 membership compels London to take action and offers extra opportunities to work effectively on a global scale. Within the C40, London functions as an example of an industrialized city that is striving towards the integration of port, industry and city. Other C40 cities include: Bangkok, Berlin, Bogotá, Seattle, Melbourne, Lagos, Rotterdam and Stockholm.

Trend 2. Towards more ambitious and quantifiable government aims in respect of CO_2 reduction

Politicians have always found it difficult to formulate quantifiable, measurable objectives for their policies. Committing to objectives opens governments to assessment and criticism if targets are not met (even though 'success' depends on many factors). Formulating fine objectives without any quantifiable aims is therefore easier. This also applied to targets for the reduction of CO_2 until quite recently. If quantifiable objectives were formulated, they were modest, so that the risks were limited, and there was scope to be more successful than expected. This was the case with the 2005 Kyoto treaty, in which 141 countries agreed to tackle global warming by reducing greenhouse gas emissions.

This is now changing. Government objectives with respect to energy policies and CO_2 reduction are getting tougher and more ambitious. The quantitative objectives are aiming higher. The European Union is standing by a tough, binding objective to emit 20% less greenhouse gases in 2020 than it did in 1990. In Asia and other regions, the authorities are also agreeing on more quantifiable CO_2 objectives. China is currently being forced to deal with smog problems in Hong Kong, because the pollution is so bad that businesses are threatening to relocate.

There are various ways in which governments can make good on their agreements about the climate. For instance, we have the European Union trade in emission rights that might now also be adopted by Obama's new American administration. But the easiest and cheapest way of reducing CO_2 emissions is to put a price tag on them. In other words: a tax on CO_2.

Gilbert Metcalf, an economist at Tufts University (US), has calculated the costs and consequences of a carbon tax for America. In *Technology Review* he says: 'The best way to levy a carbon tax would be to tax fossil fuels as they come out of the ground. You can levy the tax where it is most convenient: for coal at the coal mine, for oil at the refineries, etcetera. It's pretty easy to catch all the fossil fuels with a small number of tax payers. Administratively it is very easy.' Of course, the impact of the tax will eventually reach the consumer. According to Metcalf, a $20 tax per ton of carbon dioxide, would add about 15% to the cost of electricity for the average American.

Trend 3. Towards energy confrontations and energy power politics

Western governments are stimulating the development of alternative energy sources – an unpopular trend among the countries that are dependent on their fossil fuel export revenues including the oil producing countries represented by OPEC. This is why OPEC is becoming more openly hostile towards the West, is looking more to the upcoming economies in Asia, and is refusing to increase oil production. This is their lever for keeping the oil price high.

But if the oil price rises too high, it will further motivate the West to reduce dependency on the oil and gas cartels.

Dubai and other Emirates have recognized that the world's energy economy will have to change and have responded by diversifying their economies and greatly decreasing their dependence on their oil income. Others should take note. In the long run there will be no other way for these countries to stay afloat.

Trend 4. Towards the end of liberalization in the energy arena

Since the 1980s, when Ronald Reagan and Margaret Thatcher came to power, economic liberalism has been more acceptable than ever. As part of this trend, the energy arena was privatized. Until then, governments had retained a monopoly over energy. Energy companies belonged to the governments and generally operated locally or nationally. In the 1980s that all changed. Governments sold off their energy companies and a wave of mergers and reorganizations followed. This created energy giants, like the well-established German E-ON, which is now the largest energy company in Europe. In other countries, state energy companies were set up for geopolitical ends, like the Russian Gazprom.

Unease has grown in England about the dependence on energy from, for example, Russia. Incidents such as the poisoning of the spy Litvinenko by the Russian Secret Service in a London sushi bar did not help. The British government has capitalized on this. They have considered adapting merger laws to prevent a takeover of the energy group Centrica by Gazprom. Gazprom has warned the EU not to thwart its international ambitions.

Gazprom is very keen to take over European energy companies and is working towards the expansion of infrastructure in Europe with the goal of controlling gas from extraction to supply. Should we worry about this? Some people think not. According to them: 'If you own interests in each others' countries, you will think twice about hurting them'. Peter

Vogtländer, chairman of the Dutch Energy Council, has said that it is 'logical' for Gazprom to cast its eyes towards Europe. 'This is one way for them to secure sales of Russian gas', says Vogtländer.

Since 2005, work has been carried out on the North Stream or NEGP, a pipeline running from Saint Petersburg along the floor of the Baltic Sea to Germany. The section ending in Northern Germany should be completed in 2010. This pipeline will then supply about 55 billion m³ of gas per year, nearly half of Germany's annual gas consumption in 2005. Gazprom has a 51% majority share in the project. The rest is divided between the German energy companies Wintershall (BASF) and E-ON, which both own a 20% share, and the Dutch Gasunie with 9%. Eventually the North Stream will extend to England via the Netherlands and Belgium.

'It should have been obvious that even according to the greenest energy scenario for the future, we would still be 75% dependent on fossil fuels for the next few decades', says Rein Willems, the former chairman of Shell Holland. 'It therefore makes sense for governments to get over their aversion to Russia and others, and to think in terms of what is practical, if they want to secure the energy needs of their people, who are after all their voters in the middle term.'

That may be true, but we live in ever more emotional times, and politicians can't afford to ignore the growing desire of large numbers of citizens for energy nationalism.

There are many examples of this trend. The Spanish government tried to block the takeover of the Spanish company Endesa by the energy giant E-ON. The European Commission did not support the Spanish government. Since then an enormous row has broken out involving not only the big European energy companies but also politicians. This is the prelude to the last big push towards consolidation in the energy arena in Europe. The fighting is taking place at the highest levels and politicians are heavily involved. The Italian energy company Enel announced that they were considering a takeover of the French Suez, whereupon France announced that Suez would merge with Gaz de France in order to frustrate Enel's overtures. France was promptly accused of protectionism.

Meanwhile, the European Commission is looking at the coalescing of the big energy companies with mixed feelings. They quite rightly want more players, more competition, so that the consumer will have more choice and prices will stay down. The European Commissioner for Competition, Neelie Kroes, said that she wants more jurisdiction in respect of looking into mergers between energy concerns, although she does encourage the emergence of pan-European concerns, for example in the steel sector.

Whatever the case may be, in the next few decades there will be more mergers and takeovers in the energy sector, and energy companies will increasingly want to spread their risks. Whether these takeovers will be of any value to shareholders, customers and politicians remains to be seen. Upscaling does have certain economic advantages when it comes to the purchase of raw materials. But when it comes to the maintenance of the networks (high tension cables and gas pipelines) the advantages are limited. Risk-spreading is a very interesting element of all of this.

Energy companies want more nuclear energy as well as more coal fired and gas powered generating plants. If gas prices are high, as they are now, a company could switch to coal, or vice versa.

Analysts expect that the wave of takeovers will also spread to Great Britain and the Scandinavian countries. These markets are relatively fragmented at the moment. The question is whether the same four or five big concerns (EDF, E-ON, RWE, Enel and Suez) will dominate the market there, as they are doing in other countries.

Is this the kind of competition that Brussels wants? A new wave of regulations will wash over the EU. There is the fact that Russia has invested far too little in its gas production over the last few decades, while Europe has already taken this into account. Europe still hasn't made up its mind about the use of nuclear energy and coal fired power stations. Heavy investment in nuclear energy is inevitable; Finland is already doing it. But the old nuclear power stations must be replaced in the next few years by the new generation of nuclear power stations and that is going to be expensive. There is no money to pay for this unless new investors such as pension funds, hedge funds and venture capitalists enter the arena. If this doesn't happen then there is going to be a big problem: very high gas prices and too little electricity. The battle going on at the moment between energy companies is being played out in particular by those concerns that supply gas and electricity. They are a vital part of the whole energy chain. This chain starts with oil and gas companies such as the British-Dutch Shell, Saudi Aramco and Gazprom. They pump unrefined oil and gas and sell it on. Two thirds of the oil moves though the transport sector. Moreover, gas is used to a large extent by energy-intensive companies including steel makers and chemical factories. Households also use a great deal, particularly for heating homes, bathing and showering. Their gas is delivered by the energy companies that purchase their supplies from the big gas suppliers like Gazprom or Gasunie. Companies also use gas as fuel for their power stations.

Upscaling and concentration in the energy market are therefore on their way while at the same time countries with a large internal market will try with more or less success to hold back cross border mergers. Governments play a vital role in this process. They could either support and stimulate these kinds of changes in the energy sector, or they could oppose them. The role of the EU here will be crucial. Creating energy nationalism goes hand in hand with energy globalization, and energy politics will be played out on several fronts at the same time.

Trend 5. Towards public–private partnerships and new, unexpected coalitions in the energy market

In future there are going to be 'coalitions of the willing' set up between governments and businesses in many countries. These *public–private partnerships* (PPPs) will take various forms. In England you have the public–private Carbon Trust Fund. In some instances it is a strategic alliance, looking towards the transition to a renewable energy economy, with a target of 2050, that seems to be the magic year when many agree energy transition will be feasible.

In other cases it will be about government subsidies for the development of new sources of energy. This will happen with the development of nuclear fusion. Nuclear fusion is not the same process as nuclear fission, which is used in nuclear power stations. In nuclear fusion, light atomic nuclei fuse into heavier ones. This is the energy source of the sun and the stars, the largest energy sources in the universe. ITER, the nuclear fusion reactor that will be built in Cadarache (France) will cost billions and will be financed by a large number of countries. That means endless negotiations. Technically speaking, the reactor could have been built fifteen years ago and of course that should have happened. The world desperately needs an unlimited source of energy that doesn't emit greenhouse gases. In China they understand this very well; they have already started their own programme to build something that could steal ITER's thunder. The ITER-group, which includes Japan, has a technical head start but that could all change. Will nuclear fusion be the energy source of the future? It could all go wrong of course, and it still requires a great deal of monetary investment before it reaches fruition. But we have to try, because there really is no serious long-term alternative. How long will it take? Thirty-five years, say the experts. Until now, governments have been financing these kinds of initiatives but they are no longer so keen. In the future, new financiers like venture capitalists, as well as more public–private cooperatives must support nuclear fusion.

Trend 6. Towards more expensive, reliable energy, more energy efficiency and the stimulation of alternative sources of energy

Governments want us to reduce our energy consumption. They will do this by making the energy that we are used to consuming more expensive, in the hope that we will then use it more economically. Energy will become more expensive in all kinds of ways, and some products, such as the incandescent light bulb, will be banned altogether.

The German government has announced that it is going to tax cars in a different way. In Germany cars are taxed according to their cylinder capacity, but in the future the tax will be based on their emissions. In the spring of 2007, the Australian government announced that traditional light bulbs would henceforth be banned in Australia. The entire country has switched to the energy-saving light bulb. Every little bit helps. Even something as simple as the energy-saving light bulb? Yes: research shows that banning the light bulb will lead to a modest 2% energy saving. The traditional light bulb does have undeniable drawbacks, the main two being its relatively short lifespan and its low efficiency. An energy-saving light bulb lasts up to fifteen times as long and uses much less electricity than an incandescent light bulb, which only yields 5% to 10% of light for the energy it consumes, the rest being converted to heat. The efficiency of the fluorescent lamp could be as much as 65%. An energy-saving light bulb is in fact nothing more than a curved or pear-shaped fluorescent lamp thus its efficiency rating is much higher.

You could argue about whether or not the energy-saving light bulb really is environmentally friendly. A used energy-saving light bulb is (because of the mercury vapour and other compounds in the tube) defined as chemical waste. And the heat from a traditional light bulb could be said to count towards heating costs. But the old slogan 'if you won't do it for the environment, do it for your wallet' still applies. Energy-saving light bulbs use about 75% to 80% less energy compared to traditional light bulbs and half the energy of fluorescent and halogen lamps. Energy-saving light bulbs still cost more than traditional light bulbs, but according to Greenpeace, an energy-saving light bulb saves €7.90 per bulb per year, and taken over six years, that adds up. However, you have to use them everywhere. The bulbs in the toilet or the boiler cupboard would never yield a return on the purchase price because you don't use them very often. And you are not able to put energy-saving light bulbs in a chandelier. The much-lauded LED lamps, a big seller from Philips, can also save on energy consumption.

LED lighting is more expensive than energy-saving light bulbs, but could still signal the future, partly due to the fact that they are so much more flexible than energy-saving bulbs. LED lights offer a range of colours, are dimmable and programmable. They use one-tenth the power of traditional light bulbs and last up to twenty times as long. But their price remains high. An LED that could replace a $1 incandescent light bulb or a $2 compact fluorescent bulb now costs about $60. So until volumes go up and prices fall, they will mostly be used in commercial settings. Philips expects that in 2011, twenty per cent of its lighting sales will come from LEDs. The company is using demonstration projects to promote its vision of the future of lighting. The London Eye Ferris wheel has been retrofitted with LED products and Philips also has a bid on a project to light the Empire State Building.

The trend is for both local and national governments to give high priority to energy management, and the cheapest way of reducing greenhouse gas emissions is to tax them. Air travel will have its eco-tax and cars a slurp-tax, measures that will definitely hit the pockets of ordinary citizens. Sometimes governments see this kind of pollution tax as an extra source of income, but if we all want to take a step in the right direction, then measures like this are inevitable. We simply have to fly less and use our cars less, at least while these activities emit so much CO_2. If governments invest tax money in the development of renewable energy sources, and aren't too quick to spend it on the old energy economy, then we really will be taking a step in the right direction.

Owners of petrol-guzzling cars in London, or to be more precise: cars that emit more than 225 grams of CO_2 per kilometre, are taking the brunt of Greater London Council's new determination to go green. Since October 2008, they have to pay at least 34 euros per day to drive in the centre of the city. Previously, the charge was 11 euros per car per day. It has been estimated that 33,000 high-emission cars drive around the centre of London every day. The law would perhaps have been easier to swallow if a resident's discount had still been in force but it was discontinued. This means that the annual cost will hit the pockets of even the wealthiest car owners.

In conclusion

In the near future old and new energy management will move closer together. How do we ensure that energy remains accessible, clean and cheap and how do we ensure the independence of energy sources? How do we handle energy being used as a geopolitical tool and what will we do about the energy nationalism that will follow in the wake of a wave of nationalism and regionalism that will break over the world and threaten globalization? These are interesting times for politicians and leaders, who need to take a strong lead and show their citizens how important the subject of energy really is.

Nilas

A powerful metaphor for leading change on thin ice

Position: 84° 56' 38" N / 74° 01' 12" W
Temperature minus 28° C; April 7 1997

The magnificent ice flowers that are forming on the surface almost make you forget that the sea is actually still in the process of closing its hungry jaws. The ice between the ice flowers is jet black, fresh and treacherously thin.

The first time I was confronted with the same type of ice was when I joined Simon, an Inuit hunter from Resolute Bay, Canada. Reluctantly pricking his ice pick into the ice, he stepped onto the first couple of metres. Then, he told me something that I would never forget, 'This ice is called Nilas. It is hardly a day old. It is strong enough to walk on, but definitely not strong enough to stand on'. He decided to turn back and discontinue the hunt for the polar bear ahead of us.

This time we haven't brought heavy snow scooters and it is up to me to decide whether our team will be able to ski across the thin fleece of ice. I mustn't tempt fate but should also not waste the opportunity. It is going to waste valuable time to look for an alternative route. Let's give it a try.

I sit down and carefully put my skis on the thin ice that is roughly one metre below me. Slowly I put my weight onto my skis... I see a ripple, which moves away in a subtle wave like motion. It feels a bit like getting onto a waterbed. Shivers are running down my back, but my instinct tells me it should be OK. Carefully I take a couple of steps. Now I have to bring down my sledge carefully. I could end up swimming and ruining everything for the others if I simply drop it with its full weight.

I turn around and pull the sledge halfway over the edge of the ice sheet. It is now balancing precisely on its tipping point. Carefully I move the nose of the sledge towards the thin ice. Then it slowly slides down. It grinds to a halt without breaking the surface. The ice is strong enough….

On May 20 1997, after a 70 day journey, we reached the Geographic North Pole. We travelled by ski and on foot, crawled over pressure ridges and crossed open water in our floating sleds. In my mind I still hold vivid pictures of the landscape we lived in for over two months. This expedition has given me an inspiring and appropriate perspective on this icy wilderness and our relation to it.

In 2004 I went back to the Arctic Ocean to test some instruments and protocols for an expedition that was to involve both adventure and scientific research. Before performing a single measurement, I immediately knew that the North Pole had indeed changed significantly. The ice was not sticking out above the water anywhere near as much. Pressure ridges were less extreme but more prevalent. The ice was clearly less robust, frequently fractured into a maze.

In 2005 and 2007 I returned again. Only a few months after that last visit, the world community of polar and climate scientists was shocked to see that summer-melt reduced the ice cover to an absolute, record-breaking minimum. Existing climate models had not foreseen the dramatic loss of sea ice. The debate on when the Arctic Ocean would see only seasonal sea ice cover, was put in a different context from that moment on. Scientists now expect that the Arctic Ocean may well be ice free in summer within a decade. Only four years ago this was described as something that might happen over the course of a century. Whatever the outcome might be, we are ahead of schedule.

Imagine the North Pole without permanent ice cover. Please do me a favour after reading this column and take five minutes to let this sink in, and think about what is at stake. Spend five silent minutes thinking about the fact that we are changing this unique planetary feature, a habitat to the polar bear, the territory of indigenous people, a wilderness without comparison and replacement.

In almost all aspects global climate change is ahead of schedule and previous anticipation. Imperfect climate models are partly at fault. Current models have difficulty in dealing with the complexity and interconnectedness of mechanisms. But let's not get confused, the trend is clear: temperatures are rising and will continue to do so even if we stop carbon emissions today. In fact, we have a significant warming in the pipeline due to the lagging effects in system Earth. More warming is already locked in.

The current scientific debate is all about whether we can still manage to avoid dangerous climate change by keeping the global temperature rise below 2°C. The answer to that question lies not in better climate modelling but in policymaking, entrepreneurship and leadership. The best science we have tells us that business as usual and current political ambition levels will not result in the global temperature rise staying below 2°C.

The bitter reality is that our carbon emissions are growing by 3% per year and are therefore also ahead of the worst case scenarios that were used for policy making.

We are currently consuming 84 million barrels of oil, 8 billion cubic metres of natural gas and 8.5 million tonnes of coal per day in order to meet our energy needs. Despite the economic crisis, demand will continue to grow. This will bring us within four decades to a serious depletion of available stocks and a total of 1 trillion metric tons of cumulative carbon emissions since the beginning of the industrial revolution. Today we are halfway towards passing that threshold, something we cannot do without provoking dangerous climate change. I apologise if this line up of facts and scenarios has made you depressed. It's a realistic picture of the challenge ahead. There is really no question whether we should make a transition towards a carbon-free economy.

So far I have used many words telling you we MUST change. Perhaps I have even instilled fear. But as someone who has skied and crawled to the Geographic North Pole, I know that fear will not bring us where we need to go. It might be a trigger to get moving but we need inspiration to be able to sustain our efforts.

I am sure that *Living without oil* will inspire you to think of what we can WIN if we have the courage to create a new reality. As this book illustrates we already have a set of solutions to get going on a long and challenging journey. The good news lies in the fact that it is not only the Arctic landscape that has changed. The societal landscape has changed too; for the better, that is. There is a growing coalition of inspired business leaders and conscientious citizens leading us along the path of change. In that sense the metaphorical analogy with Nilas ice is striking, 'Strong enough to walk on but definitely not strong enough to stand on'. Let's accelerate on the fragile sheet of ice that has formed over the last years. Let's facilitate the willing and set rising standards for the reluctant, those who think change is merely an option. It is not. The journey into unknown territory has begun, inspiring as it is.   ☐

Marc Cornelissen is a polar explorer and co-owner of icentials, a bureau for collaborative and innovative sustainability programs (www.icentials.com).

part 2. The new energy economy: outlines and trends

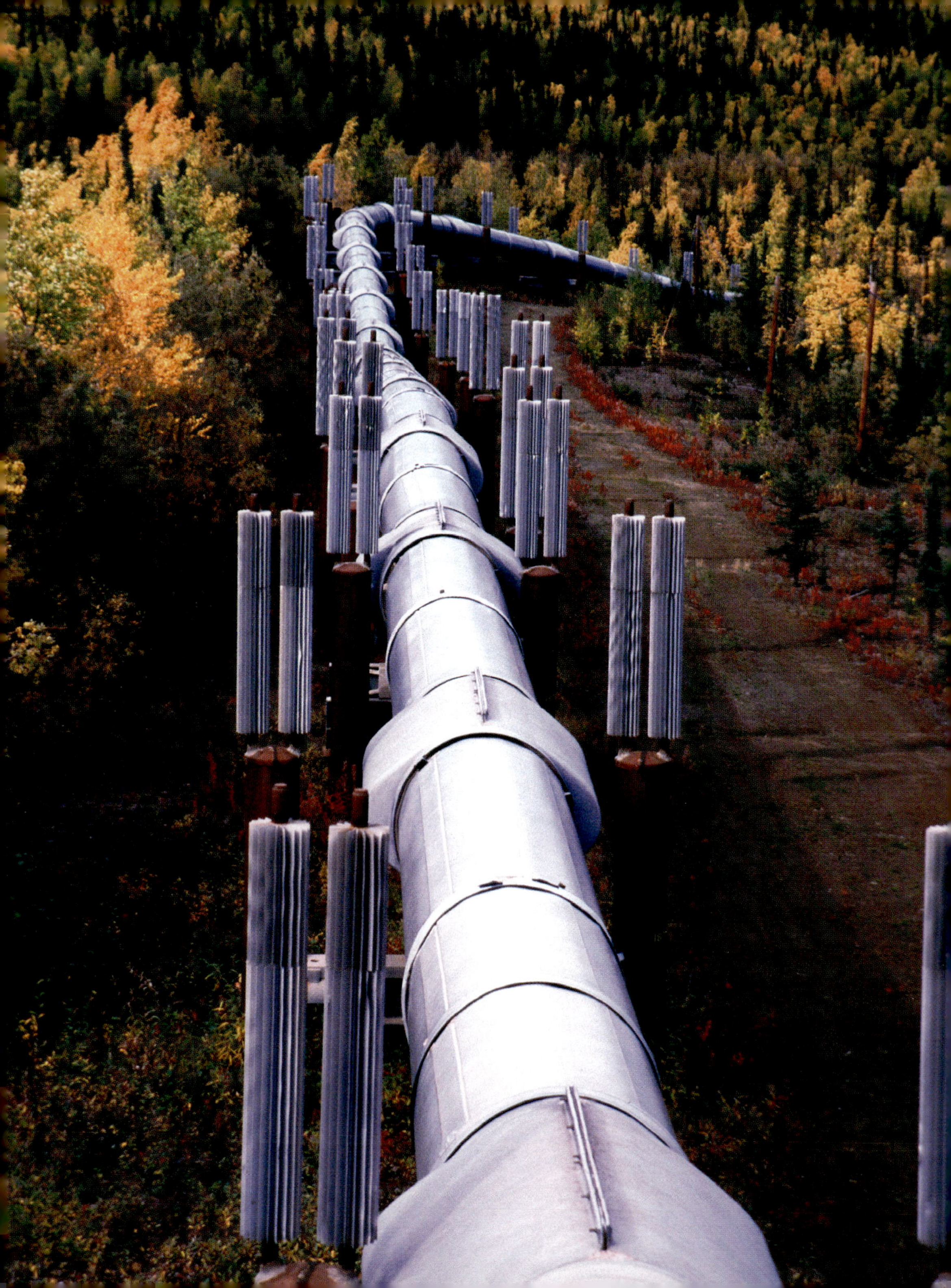

Megatrend II

Towards the greening of industry

A good business-person can sense commercial opportunity. A new energy economy will rise in the coming transition years and many an entrepreneur can feel it coming. Consumers are more conscious of the environment than ever and look at products and services through 'green glasses'. In an age when the consumer is so aware, businesses and brands have to meet their demands. If they want to survive, then the greening of industry is the only option.

Many businesses are doing their utmost to take real steps towards a green future; others are adopting a wait-and-see policy. In 2008, a report entitled *Corporate Governance and Climate Change: Consumer and Technology Companies* was released by Ceres, an alliance of investors and environmental movements. The report assesses sixty-three of the largest businesses across the globe on their approach to climate change. Companies are rated on several fronts: bringing down greenhouse gas emissions; becoming more energy-efficient; and providing leadership at the highest levels for climate-change initiatives. The results rank companies in eleven industry sectors, including apparel, big-box retail, technology and real estate. IBM, Tesco and Dell topped the list, while Burger King, Tim Hortons and Abercrombie & Fitch were at the bottom. More than half of the companies scored fewer than fifty points out of a possible hundred. Ceres expected high scores from industries such as leisure and real estate, whose operations use a lot of energy, creating a more urgent need for environmentally friendly policies. But with 27, 27 and 17 points respectively, the travel & leisure, real estate and restaurant sectors had the lowest average scores of all the sectors reviewed. Real estate developers and property managers in particular could benefit from lower energy costs. Buildings indirectly account for about forty per cent of greenhouse gas emissions in the USA. The Ceres study was carried out at the request of corporate investors from the Investor Network of

Climate Risk, a group of seventy-five investors that manage more than $7 trillion.

Companies of all shapes and sizes will have to adapt their products and services in the near future. This will happen in various ways. The potential home builder or renovator can now opt for renewable materials, seamless insulation, solar panels on the roof, renewable electricity suppliers, solar boilers, a heat pump for ground water and if that isn't enough, the work can also be financed with a green mortgage. The most wildly different products are being extolled as being 'green' and that isn't necessarily just window dressing, because businesses know all too well that consumers aren't stupid. In addition, governments are demanding ever stricter environmental controls, and CO_2 emissions are being taxed ever more heavily so that if they want to survive, they have to 'go green' with their manufacturing processes and their products.

Businesses are doing more than ever before with regard to energy management. They are trying to reduce electricity use in their offices, to change their employees' driving habits by offering company bicycles and are buying more economical company cars. More and more companies are allowing their staff to work from home to save energy and in a world of international companies, a new function has been created: the *sustainability officer*. They are expected to make sure that the energy consumption in their companies is reduced as well as being responsible for the exploitation of the green image of their brands.

Some companies have chosen to go for a more original approach to achieving greener futures, such as Ben & Jerry's. In 2005 the American ice cream maker set up the Climate Change College, at the suggestion of polar explorer Marc Cornelissen and with the support of the World Wildlife Fund, where a select group of young people receive part-time training to become climate ambassadors. Via e-learning modules, workshops, lectures, advice and as the cherry on the cake, a trip to the North Pole, the students are groomed to create and launch their own climate campaigns. The Climate Change College began its activities in the Netherlands and in England, and in the next few years it will be 'rolled out' to many other European countries. Cornelissen explains: 'A couple of years ago the Spanish and Portuguese branches of Ben & Jerry's didn't really see global warming as a social problem, but since then they have had a change of heart. It could be that the College will also start up in the United States in the future, because there also times are changing and awareness is growing.'

The megatrend for the greening of industry has the following five subtrends.

Trend 1. Towards harmonizing environmentalism and profit orientation
In these times of more flexibility in the employment market, we are seeing more and more self-employed enterprise – people who are self-employed but have no personnel. The first objective for any business is to make, and continue making, a profit. That isn't going to change, but many of these new entrepreneurs seem to be very sensitive to the environmental impact of their products. Social responsibility in business is still on the way up, particularly in those just starting out as entrepreneurs. While idealistic entrepreneurs were rather airy-fairy in the past and quickly found themselves overwhelmed by the harsh world of commerce, we now have a new generation of entrepreneurs who really know how to link idealism with pragmatism and how to sell their idealistic visions. For the idealistic entrepreneur of the 1980s and 1990s, earning pot loads of money was simply *not done*, but that's changed. Young entrepreneurs want to achieve sustainability and earn money at the same time, and now they are sailing *with* the tide because the market for green products is definitely 'cool'. It's only in the alternative energy market that a world-wide growth of over 50% is expected in the coming ten years. The largest growth is expected in the bio-fuels sector, in fact, more than 80%. Wind and solar energy technology will grow at 60% and 70% respectively, and in the development of fuel cells, a growth of around 15% is expected up to 2016. But as soon

as the fuel cell has been perfected, its market will grow very rapidly. And then we have the enormous market for green consumer products. The new market will mean good pickings for the really bright entrepreneur.

Trend 2. Towards the 'green is cheap' rule

It seems that the current green wave is less opportunistic than that of fifteen or twenty years ago. This was when the consumer first came face to face with green logos, but then it tended to be just a marketing ploy, which only served to tarnish the green image. Green still implies expensive, but the connection with green-means-expensive isn't right. When a manufacturer produces an energy saving product, then they are actually reducing their own costs, thus the product should be cheaper. Many shoppers still see the environment-friendliness of products as just another sales ploy. They first look at the price, quality and the look of a product. If young entrepreneurs with an environmental mission make sure that their products are in keeping with current consumer behaviour, it will stand them in good stead.

Future entrepreneurs will be able to get green messages across much more easily. They should remember that the consumer is far more likely to be attracted by optimistic messages than by anything that smacks of negativity. Customers will much sooner buy a product labelled with pictures of a gushing waterfall or an Arcadian landscape than one offering fancy messages proclaiming fewer damaging chemicals. Shell once introduced a cleaner petrol that they called Shell Pura, a product which didn't really take off. They later brought out a similar product under a different name – *Shell V-Power* – this time emphasizing how good it was for engine performance, while also claiming that this petrol was better for the environment: and we went out and bought it en masse. In a few years' time, when laws have been passed to reduce CO_2, non-green products will be taxed and 'buying green' will automatically be cheaper.

Trend 3. Towards the standardization of the 'green seal' of approval

It looks as though the world's population is going to go on consuming more and more in the coming years. The middle classes are growing world-wide, particularly in fast-developing countries such as Russia, Turkey, China, India and Brazil where there is a growing group of consumers with money to spend. Consuming less is apparently unrealistic, so we have to make sure that the products we do buy are less polluting, and if at all possible, climate-neutral. On that point, the consumer needs help, because how much CO_2 is emitted in the production, distribution and disposal of a product is not always obvious.

There are currently a number of 'green' labelling schemes but none that are internationally recognized. An internationally recognized green seal of approval, which would show the environmental footprint of products, would be a real plus for the consumer. When the public is better informed, the environmental footprint of a product will be a factor when people are making their shopping choices. We already know that certain products cause pollution, but even the most ordinary of articles can have high environmental costs without us even being aware of it.

Fruit and vegetables are an example. Supermarkets seem to go out of the way to clock up as many transport miles as possible. Sometimes vegetables are flown in from distant parts of the world because they now offer the widest possible selection year-round: Israeli strawberries in November, apples from New Zealand at Christmas and Kenyan green beans in January. Even home-grown vegetables travel many miles between the greenhouses and fields before they reach the shops. They go from the farmer to the cold store to the washing area to the packaging plant to the distribution centre, and these places can sometimes be miles apart. In addition, most supermarkets wrap the fresh produce in as many different layers of packaging as possible. Just add up the environmental damage done by one humble green bean or a simple head of lettuce. In Great Britain the SustainGroup researched twenty-six random foodstuffs and calculated that together they had travelled 241,000 kilometres, almost six times round the earth. Most of these kilometres are travelled by air.

And while we're on the subject of supermarkets: their energy bills are high, no surprise really when you think that they are centrally-heated or air-conditioned every day, often with the doors wide open. And in the store itself, there is an ongoing battle between heat and cold: open freezers operate day and night to keep the contents at minus 18°C, while the area next to the freezer is warmed to at least +20°C to make sure that the customer feels comfortable. In addition, most supermarkets are badly insulated halls, with no external windows and an absurd level of lighting. The result: where an average government office would use 64 kilowatts per m² for heating, an average European supermarket will use 185 kwh/m². And as far as electricity is concerned, it's much worse: the government office uses 39, and the supermarket 275 kwh/m².

Supermarkets also tempt customers to use their car to do their shopping. The owners do this deliberately to increase the average size of the weekly shop, choosing out of town industrial parks for their new branches, and offering plenty of parking spaces. The British Ministry of Transport has reckoned that twenty per cent of car journeys made by in Britain were to supermarkets, and shopping by car accounts for twelve per cent of all the car miles in England. Where supermarkets are built involves an interaction with local planning laws and available sites, so it isn't necessarily feasible to simply demand more local shops but there is a call for retailers to reduce their energy costs. Especially in new build units, better insulation, closed freezers, more targeted lighting and similar measures would save a great deal of energy.

Currently, new smart technology is being developed that will take the energy efficiency of supermarkets and other shops to a whole new level. The Dutch company Besam has designed the 'smart air curtain'. We are already familiar with the standard air curtains at the entrances of shops: warm air is blown down from the ceiling, forming a barrier between the inside and the outside. The new, smart air curtain is connected to the electric doors and will operate when the doors open. It measures the force of the wind outside and adapts its airflow accordingly. According to Besam their system will halve in-store heating costs.

Trend 4. Towards CO_2-neutral financial services
In the financial service sector, banks and insurance companies are increasingly focusing on a green image, even though, because of the crisis, their current priorities are liquidity and profit making. This is why the financing of many costly energy projects has been suspended – the projects might be profitable in the future but right now the banks don't want to part with their money.

Most people don't immediately think of banks and insurance companies when they are considering CO_2 emissions, but the investment decisions made by banks can have big implications for the growth of companies. Banks have to ask themselves whether they should invest all those savings in polluting businesses, as well as in the clean ones.

We are now seeing the development of CO_2-neutral investment. In addition, the current social emphasis on the reduction of CO_2 and the expected warming of the climate present other kinds of opportunities. The sectors that take part in the energy swing will ultimately be the winners, and will become highly attractive investment objects. Examples of such growth sectors are the bio-ethanol business, wind and solar-energy generation, waste disposal, water management, CO_2 trapping techniques and catalytic agents. These industries could have a double advantage: first of all, they have their environmentally friendly image and secondly they will create a growing market. Imagine the potential profit for a banker or investor.

But there are also less obvious businesses that are going to profit from this focus on the climate and the need to reduce greenhouse gases. Consider pharmaceutical companies that create vaccines and medicines against diseases that will undoubtedly manifest themselves in places that used to have a moderate climate, such as Lyme's disease carried by ticks or mosquito borne malaria. Jackpot!

Besides investing in obviously green businesses, banks have another option, and that is the CO_2 off-set programme. This is where banks offer their clients 'green credit cards'. When you use them to make a purchase, the CO_2 emissions of whatever you buy are automatically off-set by the bank. Visa has embraced the concept of the 'green credit card' on a worldwide basis with the ClimaCount.

Richard Piechocki, issue manager for Dutch Rabobank, estimates the current potential of green financial products and services at about fifteen per cent of the market, based on the size of the group of trendsetters. Besides the trendsetters you have an even larger group of trend followers, who will ensure the steady increase of green financial products in the coming decades. Also, insurance companies and pension funds are making more green investment choices – questionnaires indicate that their clients find 'responsible' investment extremely important.

The big, corporate investors are, in the coming years, going to find that the environmental consciousness of businesses will play a large part in investment decisions. One example of an influential international platform that supplies this kind of information is the Carbon Disclosure Project (CDP), a collaboration of corporate investors who collect the appropriate information about greenhouse gas emitted by companies on a world-wide scale. The investors jointly sign a request for the issuing of data which, when completed, will be sent to the companies. The aim of the project is to keep the investors up to date about the risks and opportunities that climate change will bring, and to tell industry leaders about the serious concerns of shareholders and investors over the impact that these issues will have on the value of the businesses.

So far, five CDPs have been filled in. The first questionnaire was sent in May 2002 to the Fortune Top 500's largest companies by thirty-five of the major investors. In contrast, the request for information for the five CDPs that were submitted in February 2007 was supported by 280 corporate investors with a joint capital of $41 trillion; this time, the questionnaire was sent out to more than 2400 companies. The results of the data requests can be seen, free of charge, at http://www.cdproject.net/responses.

Reporting about carbon dioxide will become the norm in the future, although it's in its infancy at the moment. We think initiatives from investors will provide a stimulus for changes in the law.

Trend 5. Towards the expansion of emissions trading
Since the Kyoto Protocol, a number of means of achieving the required CO_2 reductions have been proposed. One of these is the emissions trade that came into practice in January 2005 within the European Union. In the United States, a proposal for a similar system is at the centre of the Obama administration's energy policy. Emission rights are the rights to emit a certain amount of greenhouse gas and can be obtained by investing money in carbon off-set measures such as creating wind farms, planting trees or investing in research into the new generation of solar cells. The businesses in industrialized parts of the world that have started carbon off-set programmes often involve initiatives in developing countries.

Up until recently, it was mainly the big greenhouse gas polluters such as the steel, cement and chemical industries that were forced to make use of the emissions trade in order to comply with new CO_2 standards. However, gradually more and more sectors will adapt to this kind of carbon off-set programme on a voluntary basis to boost their image. The aviation sector for example will start emissions trading in 2011.

Emissions trading expanded enormously between 2005 and 2007. According to the World Bank, in the first nine months of 2006, $22 billion (US) in emission rights were traded. The share of the purely voluntary trade in emission rights was very small, about one per cent of the total trade, but when the financial crisis is over, that will rise steeply. At the beginning of 2008, experts expected that in 2010 the voluntary trade would multiply but because of the current economic situation these figures have had to be adjusted. The price of emission rights has fallen through the floor since the start of the crisis: in August 2008 it was still at €23 per ton CO_2, in February 2009, the price fell to €8. Such low prices are simply not good enough to promote 'going green' and could even mean a complete collapse of emissions trading, because it becomes cheaper to go on polluting. A guaranteed price fixed by governments could be one solution to this problem. Colette Lewiner, global energy leader at Capgemini consultancy, says this in *Newsweek*: 'The carbon price volatility has hurt long-term investment in renewable energy. When the price is so low, it plays no role in investment decisions, for example decisions concerning lower CO_2-generating power plants.' For clean tech investors who had been banking on high carbon prices to subsidize costlier but eco-friendly technologies, 2009 doesn't look promising. Market analyst firm Point Carbon now forecasts Europe's 2009 CO_2 price will be a mere €12 per metric ton, down from an earlier estimate of €22. During 2010, analysts reckon that the price will only climb to €19 – still less than the €25 threshold above which green tech starts to become more cost-effective. Hopefully this setback will only be temporary, and when the economy picks up again, the price of emission rights will increase once again.

Even so, there is still a dark side to the trade in emissions that we feel we should mention. European countries that found it difficult to comply with the obligations set out in the Kyoto Treaty started buying back companies' emission rights, rights that they had given to the companies free of charge. In this way they met their climate objectives but didn't actually do anything for the climate.

Also, the unscrupulous CO_2 traders who give the business a bad image need to be reined in. Because it is a tempestuous, fast growing market, there are a lot of CO_2 cowboys who want to make a fast buck out of this green gold fever. They don't stick to the rules, they make no use whatsoever of CO_2 reduction programmes to assess their own effectiveness and even sell fake off-sets. What also seems to happen on the 'free market' is that emission rights are sold more than once, because unlike in the mandatory trade, there is no central registration system. If the world of emissions trading doesn't improve and demonstrate its credibility, we will have to return to systems that are better controlled such as an eco-tax, and even then we have to ask if we can trust governments to spend our tax money on CO_2 reducing projects. Who decides whether or not to build a new motorway?

In conclusion
In brief, five trends form the megatrend of 'greening' trade and industry. Greening will become a major issue at all levels of business in the future as businesses take steps to keep up with the greening of the consumer. The environment is big business and one of the world's oldest laws has never been more appropriate: *money makes the world go around.*

The alternative from FreshDirect

I was in my local supermarket not long ago and saw some chicken pies in the freezer sporting large stickers: thirty-five per cent off. We all know what that means: that the meat has reached its sell-by date and has to be sold. Of course there will always be customers who think 'great, I'll take that bargain'. But you should ask yourself why it's in the reduced section at all – especially when you realize how much energy it cost to get it there in the first place.

If you ask supermarkets you will rarely get a straight answer. But Joe Fedele – a former supermarket boss in New York – is really honest about it. He says that all the portions of sliced meats lie around in storage bins under bright lights for a long time before being eaten. Quite apart from the energy issue, it doesn't do much for the taste. Fedele thought up a new concept. Every day, he buys fresh goods at markets, meat factories, and fish markets and he stores them for as little time as possible in twelve climate-controlled rooms, with temperatures varying from minus 40 °C (for ice) to +21 °C (for tropical fruit). He sells his wares through a fantastic website (www.freshdirect.com). Whatever his customers order before 12 o'clock at night will be delivered the next day between 2pm and 11.30pm. So what you get is *really* fresh. Fedele has elevated 'fresh' to an art form. If you order coffee in the evening, you will get it the next day fresh-roasted and ground according to taste (eight grades ranging from fine to coarse ground) delivered to your door in any quantity you want. You can order more than twenty kinds of salmon, which they will clean, marinate (a choice of seven different marinades) and even cook for you. They have recently started supplying line-caught fish. If they don't catch anything then it's tough luck, but if they do you'll have a fish caught just two days before you eat it. Now you might be thinking that all this will come with a hefty price tag but that isn't the case. FreshDirect is fifteen per cent to thirty per cent *cheaper* than supermarkets! Not only that, the company makes more profit (margin) than a supermarket. How do they do it?

This is the bonus of thinking outside the box. FreshDirect has no shops, no shop staff, no distribution centres, no long-distance transport requirements, no stock levels, no unsold goods, in short, they have rejected everything that our supermarkets are so proud of. FreshDirect is a much more economical concept. Thus, energy saving and freshness go hand-in-hand. Some people say that they don't like this way of doing things. They go to the supermarket because they enjoy the experience. That may be so, but I think it's only a matter of time before it becomes the norm here too. It's no coincidence that FreshDirect has over 100,000 regular customers in New York, that during peak hours there are 18,000 customers visiting the website *at the same time*, that there are 33,000 orders delivered every day and the turnover in 2006 was $240 million.

I recently read an article by a local estate agent who said that people looking to buy apartments in New York usually first ask if FreshDirect deliver to that block. If not, it's harder to sell the apartment. There's also the story of the FreshDirect delivery-man who was accosted by a passer-by who wanted to know if he was in their street because FreshDirect had started making deliveries there. So much enthusiasm from potential customers is rare. What makes FreshDirect special is they have seen the *im*perfections of the usual way of working and know how to improve what can be offered using *new* technology. ☐

By Professor Dr. Marcel Creemers

Professor Dr. Marcel Creemers is programme manager at NYVU Executive MBA, an internationally accredited MBA course, orientated towards food and finance, a collaboration between the University of Nyenrode and the University of Amsterdam.

Addressing the challenges of climate change and clean energy
In the future chemistry and biotechnology will play a major role in addressing the challenges of climate change and clean energy. Actually they already do. Life Sciences and Materials Sciences specialist DSM has built its 'Vision 2010' strategy on addressing these challenges.

The chemicals industry has long been perceived as part of the climate-change problem instead of the solution. The 'average' global citizen considers the chemical industry to have only limited relevance to improving society. The time has come for a fundamental perception and paradigm shift. Chemistry, especially based on its more recent fertile marriage with industrial biotechnology, is well-positioned to get a firm grip on the challenges posed by climate change and the quest for clean energy. Climate change, greenhouse gases and dwindling oil and gas reserves call for a transition to the use of renewable resources. Innovative solutions through a combination of biotechnology and chemistry will lower costs, reduce CO_2 emissions and provide for new functionalities.

White biotechnology
White biotechnology, or industrial biotechnology as it is also known, refers to the use of living cells and/or their enzymes to create industrial products that are made from renewable feedstocks in a production process that typically requires less energy and creates less waste than other methods. Nevertheless these products perform as well as or better than products created using traditional chemical processes.

Not to be confused with red biotechnology (health-related applications of biological technology) or green (agricultural) biotechnology, white biotechnology is widely regarded as representing the next evolutionary step towards a sustainable and environmentally-friendly chemical manufacturing industry, which itself creates the building blocks that comprise every man-made object and applications that range from bio-fuels to pharmaceuticals, food nutrients, chemicals and other materials.

White biotechnology is not new. Indeed, biotechnology has been used in industrial applications for the creation of food ingredients, beverages, vitamins, washing powders and other products for many years. However, recent scientific advances in the fields of genomics, molecular genetics,

Asperigillus niger
Enzymes
Citric acid

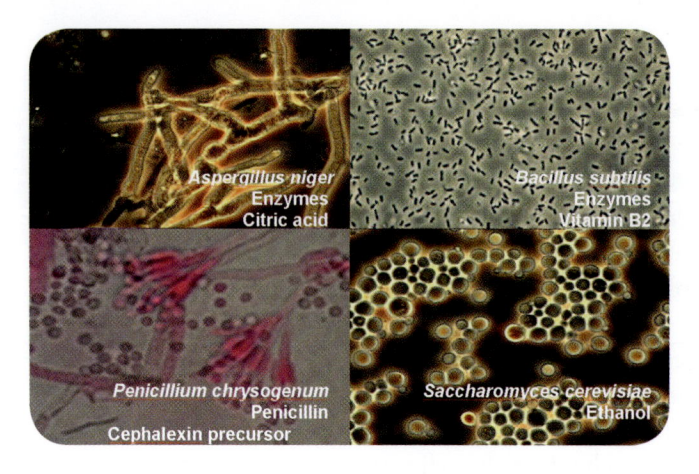

Bacillus subtilis
Enzymes
Vitamin B2

Penicillium chrysogenum
Penicillin
Cephalexin precursor

Saccharomyces cerevisiae
Ethanol

metabolic engineering and catalysis, coupled with advances in enzyme and fermentation technology as well as external factors such as soaring energy prices, renewed environmental concerns and energy security fears, have combined to make white biotechnology more important than ever. Our knowledge of white biotechnology has evolved to the point where today products derived from white biotechnology often display better performance, score higher on sustainability parameters and are more commercially viable than products created through traditional chemical processes.

White biotechnology today

White biotechnology works by turning living cells into micro-factories that, by using biomass derived feedstocks rather than traditional petrochemicals, create a variety of materials with better energy efficiency, increased productivity and better safety and environmental characteristics than could have been otherwise achieved through traditional means.

White biotechnology is already delivering measurable results in reducing industry's reliance on non-renewable raw materials, and also in reducing its carbon footprint. DSM, for example, is set to produce succinic acid – a platform chemical used in numerous applications – using white biotechnology for the first time in 2009. By using a fermentation process that relies on micro-organisms, the result is a 40% reduction in energy requirements and an actual positive impact on CO_2 levels. This is first of all due to the fact that sugar, which is produced by plants that capture CO_2 from the air, is used as a starting material. Next to that, additional CO_2 is used by the micro-organisms during the production process.

With its collaboration partner Roquette, DSM will open a demonstration plant for bio-succinic acid in France in 2009. This plant is expected to begin producing succinic acid at an industrial level within two years.

DSM also applies white biotechnology at one of its antibiotics plants in the Netherlands, with the result that the firm has been able, through advanced fermentation technology, to replace a complex thirteen-step chemical process with a biotechnological process, leading to energy savings of 65% and a halving of raw material costs.

Today, DSM is the global leader in white biotechnology excluding bio-ethanol, with a fermentation network comprising 14 plants worldwide with a total fermentation capacity of appr. 30 million cubic metres per year.

Second generation: the future of white biotechnology

White biotechnology is already delivering considerable savings, both financially and environmentally, by reducing or eliminating our dependency on non-renewable fossil resources and reducing greenhouse gas emissions from production. However, application of white biotechnology on an industrial scale, especially for voluminous products such as bio-ethanol, is limited by the fact that it, to some extent, also relies on scarce resources: sugar and starch. With dependency shifted from one commodity to another, the resulting scenario could lead to an unsustainable demand from industry for sugar and starch that would have catastrophic effects on food and other crop prices.

Today, as an outcome of wide ranging research by industry, academia and knowledge institutes, significant progress is being made in the formulation of second-generation technology which enables the recovery of sugar from waste biomass from food crops or the production of high yielding energy crops from non-agricultural land. This technology goes a long way to ensuring that it will be possible to meet demand for bio-fuel – with the correct regulatory and governmental assistance – without a large impact being made on food prices or food production.

DSM is working with a number of international partners including the US Department of Energy to overcome the challenges posed by white biotechnology and is well positioned to play a leading role in the development of second generation technology to meet the perceived demand for bio-fuels and other bio-based applications. The company has already invested hundreds of millions of euros in this area and has placed its ambition to be at the forefront of a technology which it believes will transform the nature of manufacturing industry and society at large, at the very heart of its business.

Innovation induced by climate change

Next to the white biotechnology program, DSM has set up a dedicated Climate Change Induced Innovation program to tap into the opportunities following from global climate change and energy developments. The objective of this group is to realize added value derived from innovatively responding to these global macro drivers, as chartered in the DSM Vision 2010 strategy. Climate change induces a wide variety of changes within sectors such as renewable energy, food, animal feed and transport. Chemistry and biotechnology offer solutions to respond to these changes and thus create added value for the company. Exploiting the opportunities offered by climate change takes place in the context of DSM's strengths in life sciences, materials sciences and synergies between these domains. Climate change is both a concrete, proven business opportunity and a means to further substantiate DSM's sustainability agenda.

Biogas

Within the Climate Change Induced Innovation program, DSM is working on increasing the efficiency and performance of biogas plants. Biogas is produced by anaerobic fermentation of biodegradable materials such as biomass, manure or sewage, green waste and energy crops. It can be used to generate electricity and as a low-cost fuel for any heating purpose. Biogas can also be upgraded to natural gas quality.

Driven by climate change and alternative energy initiatives, the market for production and optimization of biogas-related processes will become significant in the coming years. DSM has developed a service concept for optimizing the biotechnology of biogas plants. Based on a thorough analysis of the production process, DSM offers agricultural and industrial biogas plants tailor-made advice and a product mix to improve the biotechnology process and to increase the performance of the plant.

Bio-based materials

In response to the global transition from oil-based materials to bio-based materials (i.e. renewable materials), DSM is furthermore working on the development of a portfolio of bio-based performance materials. The company has developed EcoPaXX™, a bio-based, high performance engineering plastic for various demanding applications, for instance in the automotive and electrical markets. Approximately 70% of EcoPaXX™ consists of building blocks derived from castor oil as a renewable resource. Castor oil is a unique natural material and is obtained from the

part 2. The new energy economy: outlines and trends

Ricinus Communis plant, which grows in tropical regions. It is grown in relatively poor soil conditions, and its production does not compete with the food-chain.

EcoPaXX™ has been shown to be 100% carbon neutral from cradle to gate, which means that the carbon dioxide which is generated during the production process of the polymer is fully compensated by the amount of carbon dioxide absorbed in the growth phase of the castor beans.

DSM also developed resin materials for the bodywork of one of the Formula Zero racing karts. Formula Zero is the world's first zero-emission motor racing championship. Seventy per cent of the kart's bodywork is manufactured from biorenewable materials, which boast a considerably smaller carbon footprint than traditional, non-renewable-based materials. DSM is planning a broader launch of this technology into the commercial car market.

A marked difference for our future

Innovation through the combination of chemistry and biotechnology will make a marked difference on our future and will not only provide business opportunities, but perhaps more importantly will be an expression of the chemical industry's responsibility in helping to preserve a safe and sound planet for the generations to come.

Helping to fight the global problem of 'hidden hunger'

As the world's population is growing, providing people nutritious food, while keeping tropical rainforests in good shape, requires a lot of creativity and innovation. The world population is expected to grow from the current 6.5 billion people to 9 billion people in 2050, while in the same period land equivalent in size to the African continent will be lost to the sea, due to climate change. Feeding people properly, with less arable land at the disposal of humanity, will become a major task. Since agriculture is the main user of oil, and oil prices are expected to soar as well, this task becomes even more important. Therefore, next to working on addressing the challenges of climate change and energy, DSM is committed to addressing the problem of micronutrient deficiency – or 'hidden hunger'– a problem that affects an estimated 2 billion people across the world.

Whilst the world has focused much of its attention on treating communicable diseases, too little emphasis has been placed on the fight against chronic diseases – which are significantly influenced by diet. As the world's largest suppliers of vitamins, carotenoids, micronutrient premixes and other health ingredients, DSM is committed to raising awareness of the issue of hidden hunger, in partnership with others such as the World Food Programme (WFP), to create better understanding of the real impact of hidden hunger, so that greater attention is given to addressing this serious global public health issue and ultimately the lives of millions can be improved.

DSM is supporting the World Food Programme both with its expertise and its products with the objective of improving the food basket that they provide to the most needy and the most vulnerable across the globe.

In addition, the company is building knowledge and understanding of hidden hunger, through sponsoring the non-profit humanitarian initiative Sight and Life, the mission of which is to encourage better scientific understanding of the impacts of hidden hunger and, through working with others, trial approaches to address specific micronutrient deficiencies.

DSM is able to create food supplements that ensure that those in need get the right mix of micronutrients, in the right way. DSM refers to this menu of solutions as 'tailored food solutions' as they have been developed with the needs of a specific target group of the most vulnerable in mind.

Some examples include:
- MixMe. In many developing countries across the world the staple food, that generally makes up the greatest proportion of diet of the most vulnerable, is low in key vitamins and minerals. The DSM solution: a single dose MixMe™ sachet of vitamins and minerals, that can be used at home sprinkled over food just before serving or eating, provides an individual with the full Recommended Daily Allowance of all essential micronutrients as recommended by the WHO. To date, approximately a quarter of a million people across Nepal, Kenya and Bangladesh have been supplied with DSM's MixMe™ via the WFP food basket programme: improving nutrition – improving lives. The programme's aim is to meet the micronutritional needs of at least 80% of WFP's beneficiaries (75 million) in 2012.

- Iron deficiency and malaria. DSM has found a new way to resolve a longstanding nutrition problem, using its enzyme expertise to provide iron to those suffering from iron deficiency, without increasing the incidence of malaria.

- NutriRice. Rice serves as the staple food of more than half the world's population, yet rice is low in a number of critical vitamins and minerals. The DSM solution: NutriRice made from broken rice kernels (a byproduct of normal rice production) and enriched with vital vitamins and minerals. The broken rice kernels are milled, a specially formulated premix of vitamins and minerals is added and the mixture is run through an extruder, resulting in fortified rice kernels that can be added to normal rice at a ratio of 1:100 without affecting the taste or colour. The final white rice product provides a highly nutritious meal unlike normal rice. DSM is currently working with the WFP to provide NutriRice to groups of people in the Indian province of Orissa.

It is time for the world to take notice of 'hidden hunger' and time for real actions to start focusing on and addressing the crisis. Adding vitamins and minerals to staple foods that are eaten every day by vulnerable populations does not require health care systems, costs a few dollars per person per year, and requires little or no change in consumer behaviour.

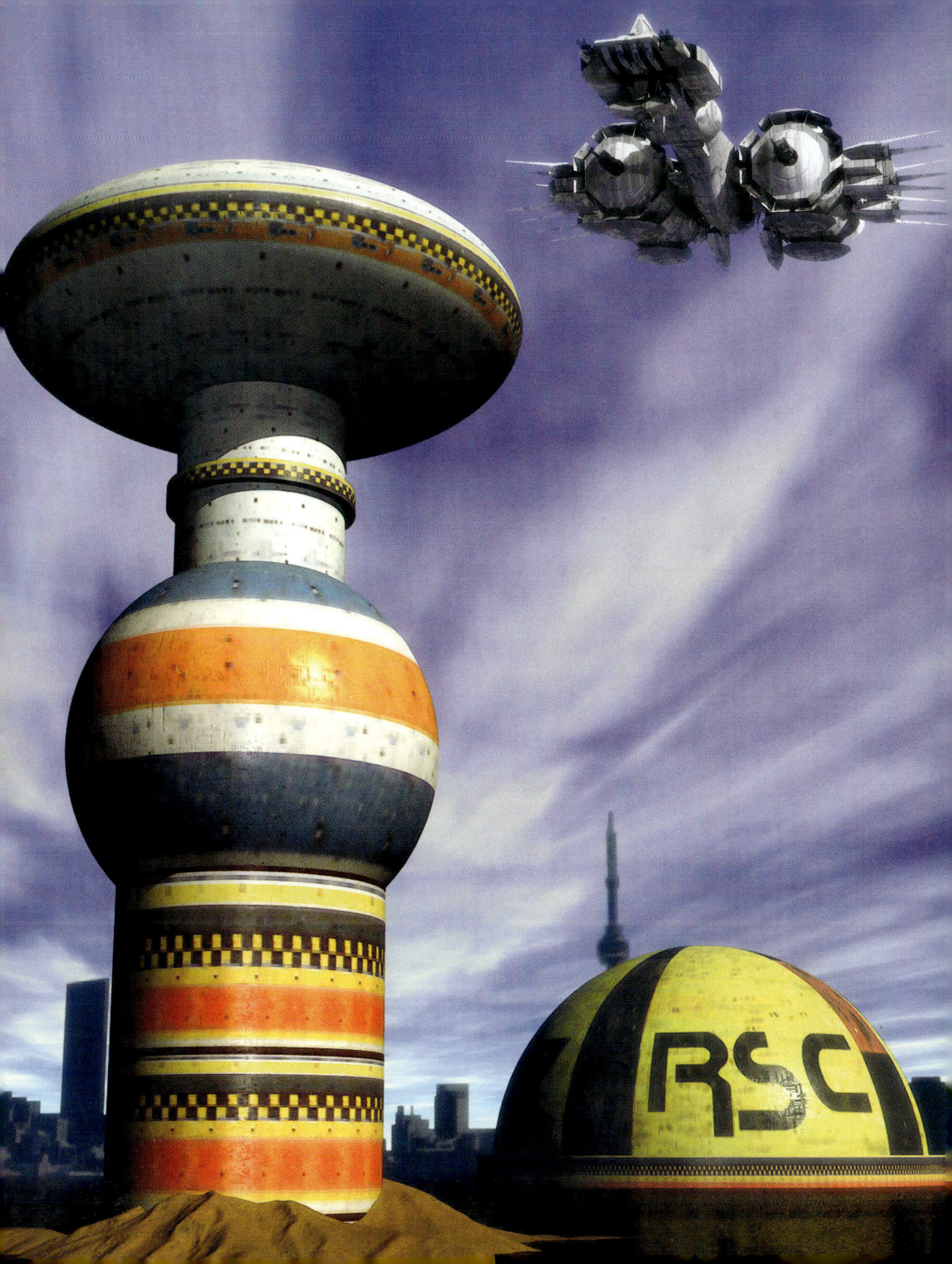
RSC

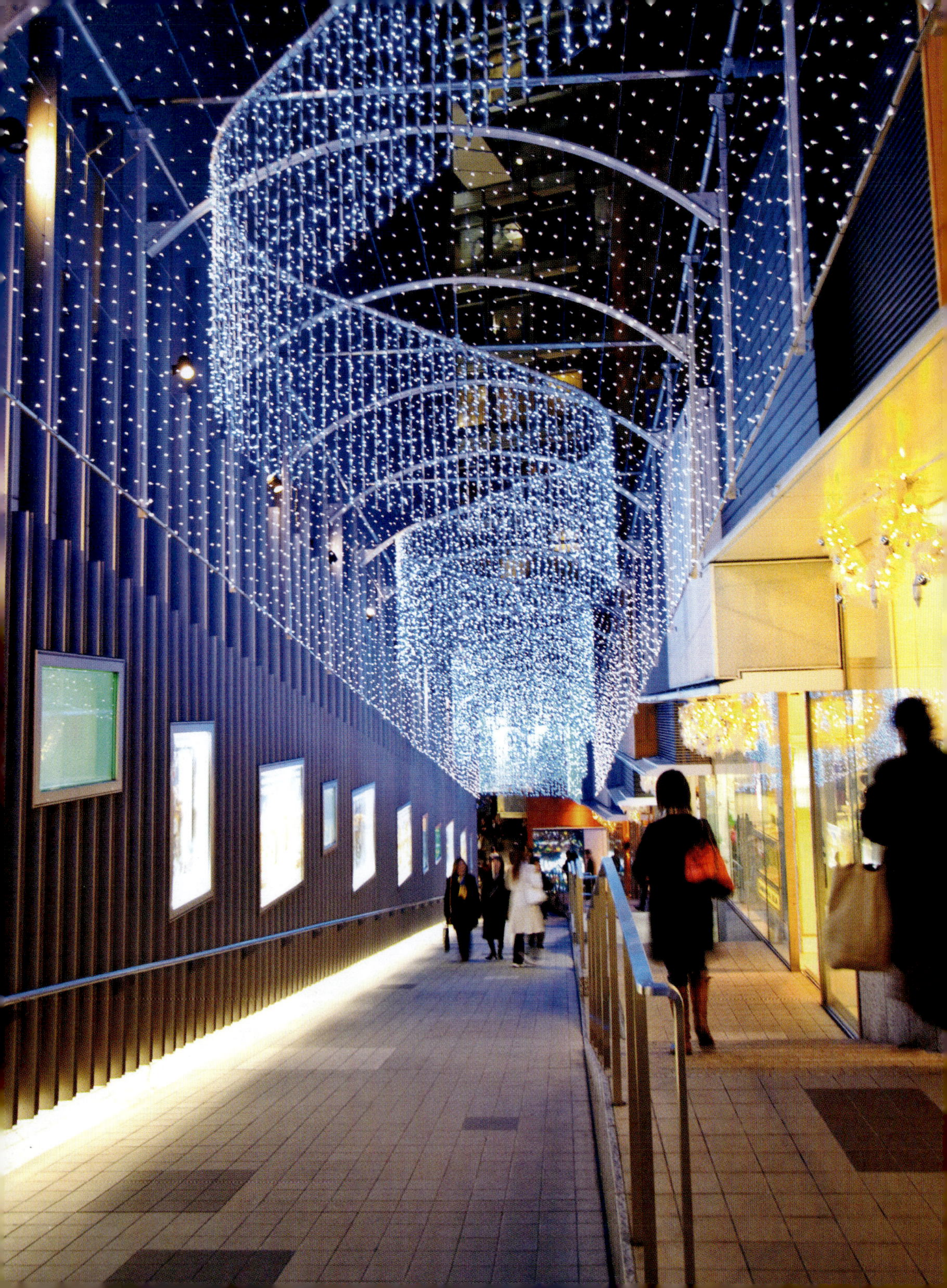

Megatrend III

Towards the greening of consumers

Some of the 'clean' environmental alternatives that will become available in the future are the result of innovative technology. This technology, often financially subsidized by governments, is first introduced in trade and industry. However, consumer energy management also has a considerable influence on CO_2 developments. Private individuals are taking more and more energy initiatives – a development that fits with the trend of an active citizenship. As we noted earlier in this book: in May 2007, McKinsey produced a report that cited an anticipated global growth in the demand for energy of 2.2% year on year until 2020, more than half (57%) of this growth being generated by consumers. This shift to the consumer sector is related to the transition from an industrial to a service economy. In the coming years, as far as energy production is concerned, much of what is to be gained is in the hands of consumers. Therefore, we need to make environmentally conscious behaviour more attractive. Environmentally friendly products are nearly always cheaper in the long term than environmental pollutants, and in addition governments are now starting to tax powerful contaminants. This is not only being done for the sake of the planet and generations to come, but also (perhaps particularly) to line their own pockets.

Technology can also help us to become more energy conscious: there are new *prepaid* energy meters on the market, which encourage energy efficiency through awareness of consumption. This is in fact a step back in time; in the past, meters were fed with coins. According to experts, such meters can result in energy savings of between 5% and 10%. And even if the environmentally conscious behaviour of one single individual is but a drop in the ocean, we, as consumers, have considerable economic influence when we go shopping with environmental awareness.

Even so, public interest in environmental issues sometimes seems to be nothing more than a thin masquerade. With the economic crisis in full swing, people are now more concerned about their jobs and homes than about CO_2 emissions. In January 2009, after Barack Obama was sworn in as president of the United States, the Pew Research Center carried out a survey on the concerns of Americans. Out of a list of twenty areas of concern, 'global warming' came last as a priority. Only 30% of those questioned felt that this was a *top priority*, compared to 35% in 2008. 'Protection of the environment' was an issue that climbed strongly up Pew's list of priorities during 2006 and, in 2008, also fell considerably. Only 41% felt that it was a top priority, compared to 56% in 2006. Americans are, however, concerned about their energy supplies. This concern was placed at number 6 in the list of 20, with 60% of those questioned declaring it a top priority. In short, people want to be sure that they have electricity and that they can drive their cars – many people don't really care about the climatic impact of their actions.

Social scientists say that environmental concerns are often the first to fall by the wayside when more immediate threats surface.

Trend 1. Moving towards the increasing input of analytical democratic citizenship on environmental measures

Serving one's own interests is a familiar concept. However, we live in a time in which serving the communal interest is a dominating cultural value (at least in the West: in the East, solidarity is based on and at the same time restricted to the family system). We hold these values in such high regard that we have institutionalized them into our political systems. We are all part of a calculated citizenship – the common interest is overseen by government, and the individual retains the right to brush as many crumbs from the communal biscuit onto his or her own plate as possible. In terms of climate problems, this means that we expect governments to set rules and laws that will secure a green world (our ecological legacy), after which we reserve the right to disregard or circumvent such government regulations. With that in mind, we must recognize the reality of calculated citizenship.

No one will stop buying flashy cars on their own initiative. They are already more expensive and less practical, and that doesn't deter people who want them. When purchasing a car people make a choice based on performance, ease, impressionability and sometimes economy. The car is not called our holy cow for no reason. People are susceptible to status and ego – as long as public opinion accepts the choice to drive a 'gas-guzzler', any actual change in our behaviour will have to be enforced by governments, in the form of an eco-tax for example.

The price of energy is one of the most important controlling elements that we have in this matter. In Japan energy is very expensive because of extra taxation: twice as expensive as in the United States and one and a half times as expensive as in Belgium. The effect of this higher price is that energy consumption is proportionally lower in Japan – twice as low as in the United States and one and half times as low as in Belgium. Our well-being needn't be affected as a result of increased energy prices; it would simply spur greater efficiency.

Trend 2. Moving towards more economical households

In Great Britain, a wide range of measures has been implemented to improve domestic energy efficiency and to reduce carbon emissions from the domestic sector. One important approach is the Energy Efficiency Commitment (EEC) which was founded in 2002. It is a commitment by energy suppliers to support households in using energy more efficiently.

In the UK, the domestic sector accounted for 30% of total energy consumption in 2001, which is almost as high as the transport sector's consumption and higher than that of industry and services. Most (40%) of domestic energy consumption is used for

part 2. The new energy economy: outlines and trends

space heating. Additionally, almost 30% of the UK's total carbon emissions are from the domestic building stock and more than 50% of these emissions are caused by central heating. There is a lot to be gained by focusing on residential energy consumption. Insulation helps of course, as do lower thermostat settings. With regard to electricity consumption, there's a lot of room for economizing at home. Using more efficient light bulbs (low-energy light bulbs and LED lighting), turning off machines that are not being used (for example telephone chargers – standby energy is money burnt) and using more efficient appliances. Take the clothes dryer as an example. Among household appliances, it is far and away the champion in electricity consumption: if you must have a dryer, at least get one with an A-rating. These aren't just more environmentally friendly, but are cheaper in the long term. And with the predicated warming of the earth's climate, drying laundry will become easier using the old-fashioned washing-line.

Even so, a couple of points need to be made with regard to such savings. According to SMR Research, conservation efforts made in the past, like increased home insulation, have failed to prevent massive energy waste – not because they were bad ideas, but because they have been overwhelmed by a demographic counter-trend: the decline in household density, driven mainly by single-person household formations. In the United States, consumer energy usage per capita is 29.6% higher today than it was in 1960, based solely on the sharp decline in the number of people per household. From 1960 to 2007, the average number of people per household in the USA declined from 3.33 to a record low of 2.56. In the same period, the number of single-person households grew by 350%. In 2003, 26% of all US households consisted of just one person, compared with 17% in 1970. This increasing trend in single-person households is also visible in other parts of the Western world. It is a trend which will only continue to grow over the coming years due to the ageing population. Amongst older people, there are now more widows and widowers. The divorce rate, expected to remain high, also results in many single households. In Great Britain, government figures indicate that by 2026, 38% of all households in England and Wales will be single-person households. A lot of these singletons are well-off, making them the biggest consumers of energy, land and household goods. They consume 38% more products, 42% more packaging, 55% more electricity and 61% more gas per person than one individual in a four-person household! The government could encourage people to live more space-efficiently. For example, an occupancy tax could be introduced which would be charged based on the number of people and habitable rooms in a house, to encourage people to live in smaller properties. A relocation package could be introduced to encourage lower-income households to move into smaller homes.

Over the past couple of years, there has been much focus on the insulation of old, draughty houses. A good thing too, but it is the size of the house that determines how much energy is needed for heating. Given that we live in ever bigger houses, the gain made from insulation is immediately lost. The Consumer Expenditures Survey of the previously mentioned American research agency, SMR Research, calculates that in the last twenty-five years the average size of new homes has risen by 34.2% in the US. It can only be hoped that the trend for living in larger houses has in the meantime reached its pinnacle. There will be a critical boundary where 'greater' no longer automatically means 'better'.

Trend 3. Moving towards the popularization and conservatization of environmental awareness

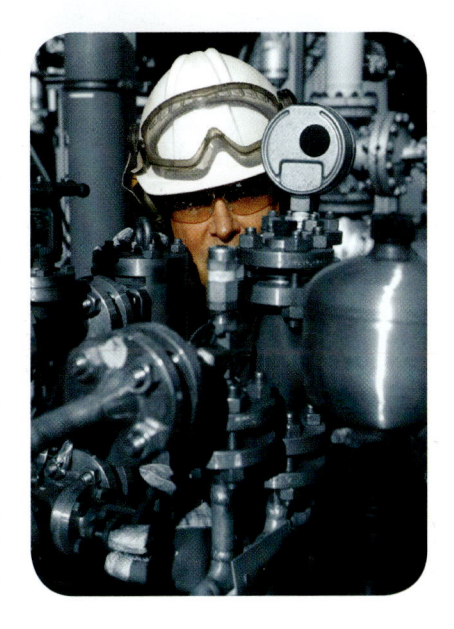

Over the past year, the need to change energy consumption habits has dawned upon some of the world's population. Reports on melting polar caps and desert formation, some on European soil, have made many appreciate that we not only need to talk about the environment, but that we actually need to do something about it. This realization first occurred in Japan and Western Europe; however, it now seems that the American population is 'converting'. These aren't just the alternative types from the Democratic camp; Republican America is also starting to show a greater environmental awareness. A significant sector of Republican grassroots supporters are conservation evangelicals – in total about 30 million people. Preacher Joel C. Hunter, committee member of the influential National Association of Evangelicals, expects that a large number of these grassroots supporters will expand their activism in the fight against greenhouse effects in the coming years. The conversion of religious America to 'green evangelism' indicates a major shift in public opinion, given that for a long time most Americans disregarded reports on the greenhouse effect and global warming. In order not to isolate himself from his voters, former president George W. Bush changed his tone during his last year in office. From the start of his presidency, Barack Obama has indicated that one of his priorities will be the fight against global warming.

Trend 4. Moving towards a greater need for energy information

Many individuals think that the reduction of their CO_2 emissions will be achieved by restricting direct energy consumption: driving less, improving domestic energy efficiency and so on. They tend to forget that the items they purchase from shops also have embedded CO_2 consequences. One product may be produced and distributed with a lot less energy than another. Consequently, a vegetarian lifestyle is much more environmentally friendly than a meat-eating one, as the production of meat requires a lot of energy and also emits greenhouse gases. A strict vegetarian diet results in a 7% reduction in CO_2 emissions. However, if the vegetarian consumes industrially manufactured meat replacements, then they are responsible for 4% *more* emissions than the average meat eater.

Another example: in the majority of companies, you'll find people who, with the best intentions in the world, are anti-plastic cups. They argue that single use cups are bad for the environment, and suggest the reintroduction of mugs. However, the manufacture of earthenware mugs requires a considerable amount of energy and every time the mugs are washed more energy is used. In fact, it doesn't really make much of a difference to the environment whether you use a plastic cup or a mug.

Many people have good intentions with regard to the environment, and aim for a reduction in their energy consumption. However, as these examples demonstrate, it can be difficult to make the 'right' decisions. An environmentally conscious lifestyle demands a considerable amount of knowledge and thus requires information. Motivated by governments who prescribe environmental laws, and companies who want to be conspicuous in their energy efficiency, we will receive more and more such relevant information.

Trend 5. Moving towards a shift from symbolic to effective environmental measures

We are inclined to link energy saving and environmentally friendly behaviour to issues such as sorted waste disposal, the rejection of plastic bags in supermarkets and the use of low-energy light bulbs, However, many of these measures seem to have become no more than symbolic. Getting into your car to drive to a shop to buy a low-energy light bulb is counter-productive, and the separation of your household waste for recycling doesn't have any positive effect on your CO_2 emissions. Turning off telephone chargers and stand-by buttons on appliances reduces CO_2 emissions by 1.5% per household; exchanging a normal car for a hybrid model reduces your emissions by 4% and car-sharing delivers savings of 5.5%. To make a real difference, we will also have to take carbon off-setting measures, expand renewable energy use and reduce air travel.

The Dutch newspaper, *de Volkskrant*, calculated that the carbon off-set of every new purchase via the previously mentioned Visa ClimaCount quickly provides a carbon emission reduction of 27% in subsequent use of the product. Switching to a green energy supplier results in a 14% CO_2 saving and forgoing intercontinental flights results in a reduction of 12% in CO_2 emissions per household.

If a household organizes its energy management in these three areas, it can reduce its CO_2 emissions by three-quarters. Moreover, in comparison to what many people think, there is barely any reduction in one's comfort or luxury. The switchover to a green energy supplier costs only a little more and yields the same results as a conventional energy supplier.

Trend 6. Moving towards the emergence of environmental pressure groups and environmental terrorism

When a Dutch public TV channel announced that it wanted to broadcast the 'climate sceptic' Channel 4 documentary, *The Great Global Warming Swindle,* it resulted in disapproving reactions and even threats from some environmental activist groups. In future, such reactions will be seen more often. Some environmentalists profess their beliefs with a strong, almost religious passion, and wouldn't shirk from using threats or even violent direct action to make their points.

Trend 7. Moving towards a greater popularity amongst ad agencies of the environmental theme

Energy efficient! CO_2-neutral! Green freshness! The advertising world knows only too well that the greater public has environmental guilt awareness. They are playing on this. Sometimes, it yields some very amusing adverts, sometimes some really ridiculous ones... what is an environmentally friendly car? At the 2007 Cannes Lions International Advertising Festival, the principal guest was Al Gore, the prophet of the green gospel. Even within advertising circles, Gore has achieved a sort of pop star status, as his message means that there is money to be made. The girls and boys of advertising translate his gospel into the (beautifully packaged) message: there's nothing wrong, you can carry on consuming as much as, if not even more than before, so long as you do it in an environmentally 'caring' way.

Ten years ago, we wouldn't have seen durability used as a sales pitch. In future, we will see this more often, as well as more detailed publicity campaigns that inform us about a green future. MTV launched the Switch campaign (www.mtvswitch.org) in 2007, to 'promote environmentally friendly lifestyle choices amongst the young'. A little taster of the typical advert copy from the campaign: 'OK, so you love shopping. That's great. Switch isn't going to tell you that you've got to hug a tree or that you've got to be an environmental warrior but we're cool if you want to. The only thing that we'll ask you here is to make small changes in the way you shop. Changes so small, that you won't even mind.' Everything is permissible for a better environment, even the little white lie that lower CO_2 emissions won't hurt.

Trend 8. Moving towards a glorious future for green feel-good events and green charities

Al Gore's visit to the advertising festival at Cannes in June 2007 was the prelude for the Live Earth concert series, with its kick off on 07-07-07. This date was chosen with particular attention. Traditionally, the number seven is the number of God. With this, the previously mentioned religiousness of the environmental movement is underlined once again. Live Earth was a series of concerts held in various world cities, broadcast on TV across the world attracting hundreds of

part 2. The new energy economy: outlines and trends

millions of viewers, particularly young viewers. Via this mega-event, the green message was rammed down their young throats, and an environmentally conscious future was drilled into their uninfluenced youthful spirits. Today's pop stars pose with an 'environ-mentality'.

It isn't only pop stars who parade the climate issue, politicians do it too. When the British Prime Minister, Tony Blair, was interviewed about what he was planning to do after he stepped down as leader, he told the BBC reporter that he 'wanted to do something truly useful'. He continued: 'Climate change is definitely something that I'm interested in. I'll continue working on it, even if I'm not prime minister.' After Al Gore, it seems to be a trend amongst political leaders to climb the environmental barricades once their political careers are over. Those with good intentions will also mobilize more frequently on the subject of CO_2 reduction and a sustainable environment. Now that the generous donors are tired of aid programmes for poverty stricken and war-torn regions, the environment is an ideal new objective which barely needs any explanation as the topic regularly fills newspaper columns and current affairs programmes on radio and television.

The young and the old are the age groups that show the greatest environmental awareness. According to research carried out by the Dutch research organization, Intomart, midway through 2007 on children between nine and thirteen, it seems that no less than 84% are concerned about the environment. Of these children, 59% are afraid of climate problems. A large percentage – 67% – want to do something about the climate problem, but don't know what. Nevertheless, a large percentage – 62% – do not shower any less to help the environment. Of the children, 22% do take this into consideration, and 16% don't know. Additionally, turning off the television and computer after use is not yet second nature for many of those worried children. With all the reports on the climate, 43% pay more attention to energy consumption. For 32%, all these alarming reports have no influence.

The over-fifties environmental concern is based on a sense of guilt about the highly polluting activities that their generation allowed for many decades. They are keen that their grand-children have a better world.

In conclusion

Consumers will play a key role in the implementation of sustainable energy consumption and the realization of a CO_2 neutral world. They have power in numbers, and with their purchasing power they can make or break companies. There seems to be a definitive turnaround in the global citizen's environmental awareness. It is in the rich countries that there is the most concern with regard to climate change; however, the fact that riches lead to environmental taxation hasn't eluded people in upcoming economies such as India and China.

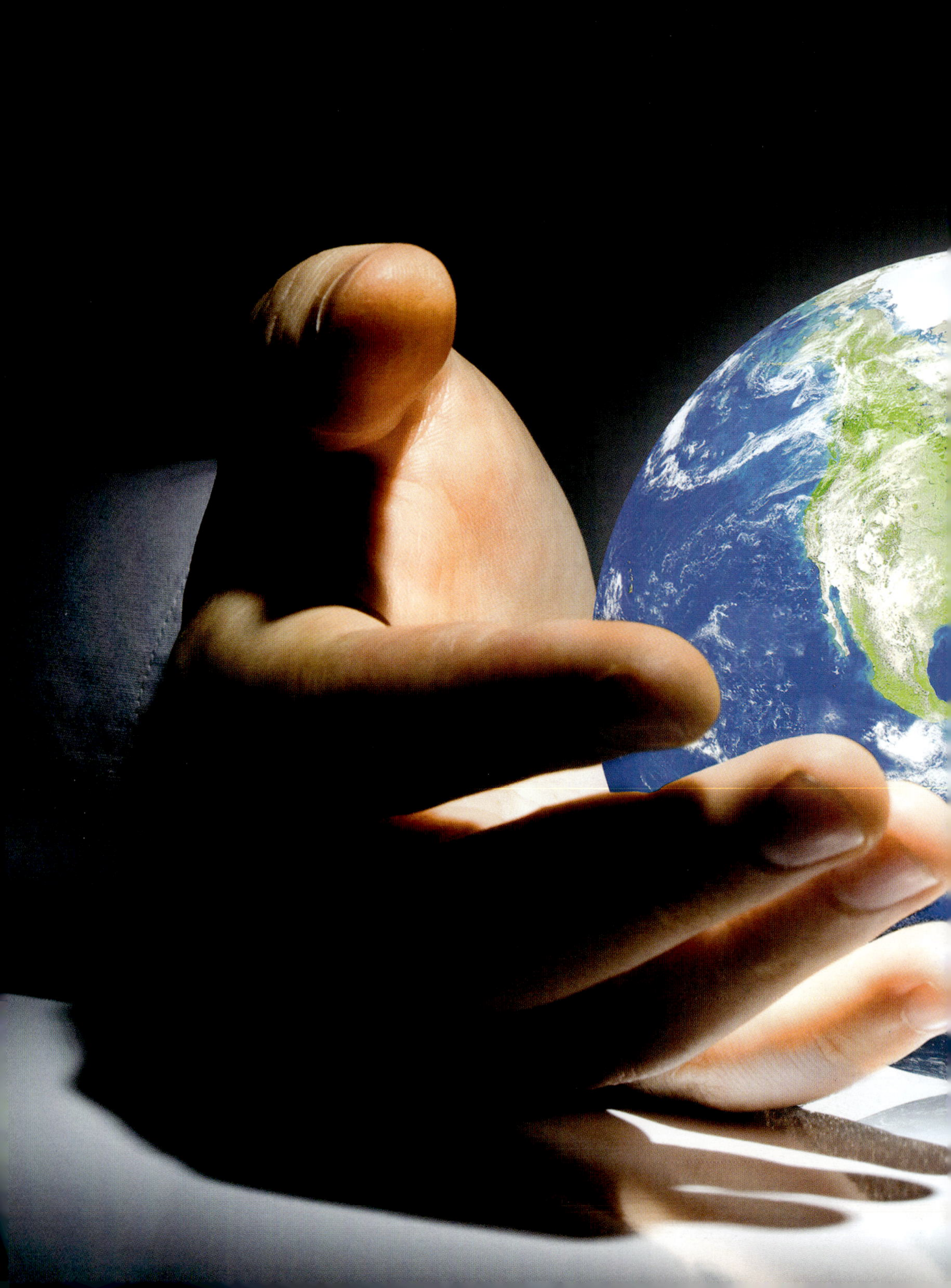

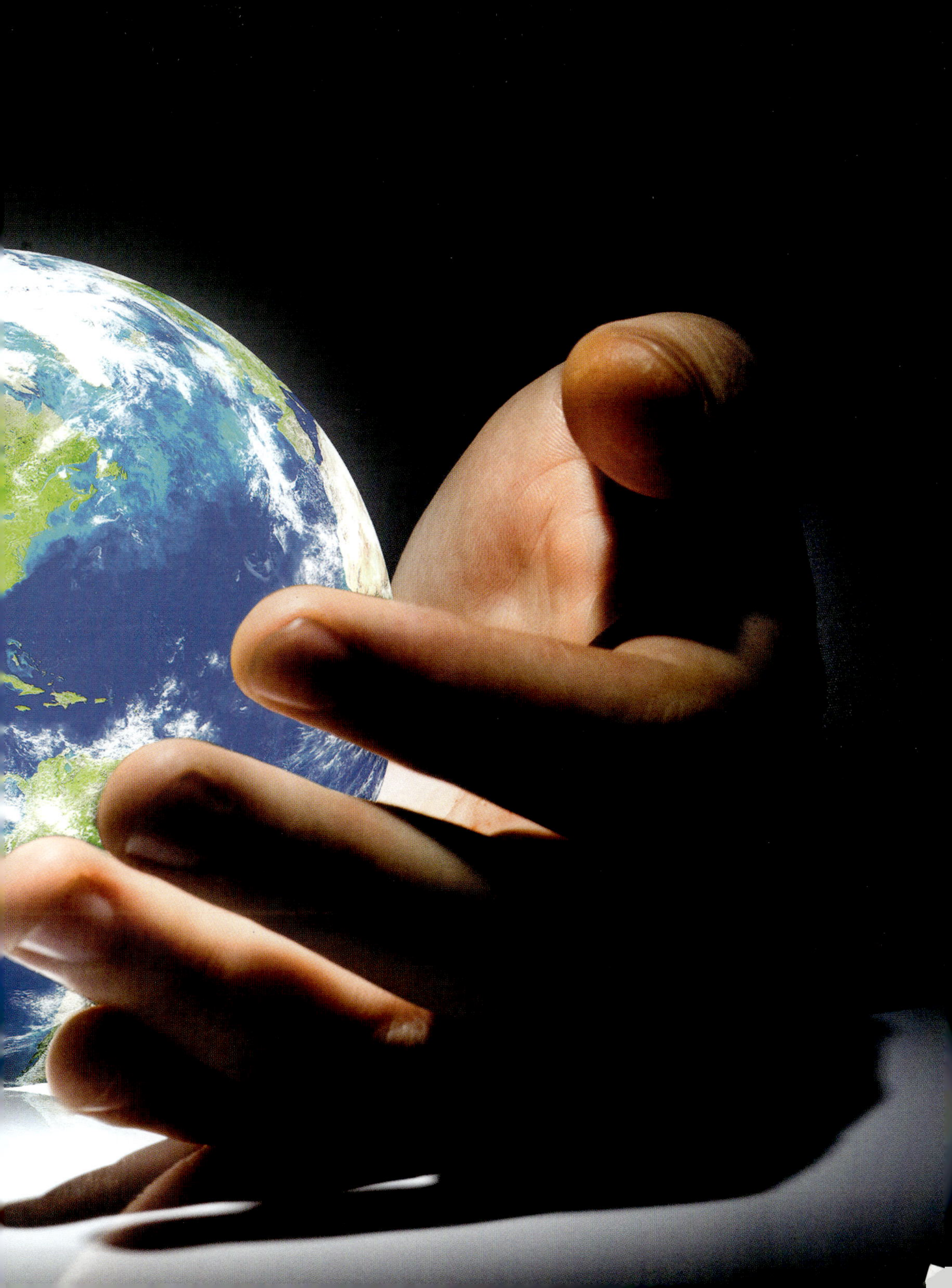

Moving towards more eco-sleeping

According to the famous Max Planck Institution in the German city of Munich, people get their best ideas when they sleep. Mr Singer was a good example. This tailor invented the sewing machine in his sleep. When he awoke in the morning, he started to draft what he had dreamt about. This finally became the Singer sewing machine. And the start of the Singer brand for sewing machines all over the world. Mr Singer forgot to patent this, so unfortunately he did not become rich. Yet the idea of people inventing their best and brightest ideas in their dreams, was set. According to the scientists of the Max Planck Institution, people can steer their dreams and their ideas, by steering their sleep. If you organize a good night's sleep, and if you surround yourself with items related to the issue you want to dream about or want to come up with a good idea about, chances are that you'll succeed.

Designing the ultimate eco-bed

Designer Frans Segers has been designing and producing one of the best lines of sleeping facilities in the world for years now. His company Lavital produces luxury, bespoke, state-of-the-art ecological boxsprings and mattresses and natural beds and organic bedsystems. These beds provide responsive solutions to the urgent needs and evolving life-style concepts such as sustainability and health-conscious living. Whereas Vital beds utilize natural materials such as organic cotton, wool, flax and horse hair in products, the vast majority of beds manufactured today contain numerous petroleum-based materials (e.g. foams, fire retardants). The disadvantages of oil are becoming more and more visible. From an energy security perspective, we have become more and more dependent. Frans Segers says: 'The continued use of oil brings further damage to our environment. Finally, there is increasing concern that oil- and petrochemical-based products pose a potential threat to personal health and well-being. Therefore I only want to make beds which are adjusted to your personal characteristics, wishes and requirements. After all, no two people are the same. Latex or foam products are unfit for use in beds, in my opinion. These sponge-like materials cannot ensure an optimal air circulation and can heat up uncomfortably during the night. Moreover, they pulverize because of the natural salts the body produces, resulting in degeneration and a shorter life expectancy for the mattress or top mattress. Foam products are synthetic, not durable and are produced with toxic chemical processes. For instance to become a latex mattress, sulfur and ammonia are used. In the sleeping advisors jungle your personal characteristics, such as length, weight, proportions and sleeping position are not taken into account. Everything is mass-produced. Very often technically contradictory sleeping systems are offered. For most people this is a confusing situation, because how is one to know what distinguishes a good bed from a bad bed?

part 2. The new energy economy: outlines and trends

I wanted to start a firm which distances itself from this type of sales, and I succeeded. We want to offer top quality beds and let our customers fully experience the luxury of a custom-made bed. We have an unconventional vision, casting a new light on old beliefs and the distribution of faulty information in the bedding business. Lavital fights for consumer objectivity and awareness.'

Innovation rooted in history

'Our personalized boxspring shows we constantly strive for a higher quality, comfort and no-nonsense concepts for our customers,' says Frans Segers. 'We believe in an honest product, tailor-made beds and, above all, no mass-production. Enterprising is in our blood. The Segers are an old tanners family from Antwerp. Following in my forebears' footsteps, I was trained and educated in the ancient skill of tannery and fur working. Designing, innovating, pioneering and producing traditional, high-quality, long-lasting natural products is my passion. I understand that every person is unique. I understand that only natural materials are virtually everlasting. This was my mission when I established myself in the Dutch village of Zwaag. My first establishment of the leading personalized bed workshop and store was built here. Having grown so much the first workshop had become too small; in 2004 we moved to premises five times the size of the previous accommodation.'

Disposal of mattresses

The disposal of petrochemical-filled mattresses is an increasing global concern. The combustion of petrochemical mattresses (about 1 million each year in The Netherlands alone) represents an environmental concern, both from the perspective of greenhouse gases being emitted as well as the disposal of petrochemical waste residues which are produced. In addition, the intensity of the process itself can create furnace-related problems (burst lagging, clogged airflows). In addition, sheer necessity, countless mattresses are dumped and sent to landfills annually, with disastrous results and posing even greater risks for our environment.

There is more to a mattress than meets the eye. Yet, too often, simple standard-sized mattresses are installed in yachts and boats, that moreover tend to be of questionable quality. Lavital is specialized in custom-made luxury yacht bedding. The craftsmen of Lavital gained several years of valuable experience while working for a luxury superyacht shipyard, specialized in yachts built wholly to the specifications and quality standards of highly discerning and often very demanding clients. At this stage, berth requirements as regards size and quality can usually be tailored to the specific bedsystem needs of the owner. Once these requirements have been evaluated, Lavital can advise the client on the choice of mattress that is optimally suited to that client's personal situation.

Natural beds

Lavital recently came with a hand-made sleeping system, with an affordable outstanding eco-quality. These so called Natural beds provide a unique opportunity for those who appreciate a sleeping environment that distances itself from everything that is synthetic and harmful to the environment. The flexible spring system is enriched with unbleached organic cotton, organic wool, organic flax and horse hair. The one hundred per cent organic cotton mattress-cover is also developed under ecological and fair-trade conditions. A completely pure and natural, compostable and recyclable composition guarantees unprecedented comfort and an extremely sustainable sleeping environment.

The future of organic sleep

According to Frans Segers, 'Sustainable, pure organic sleep is automatically better for energy use and CO_2 emissions and thus the environment. Living concepts based upon this idea have a sustainable future, I believe.'

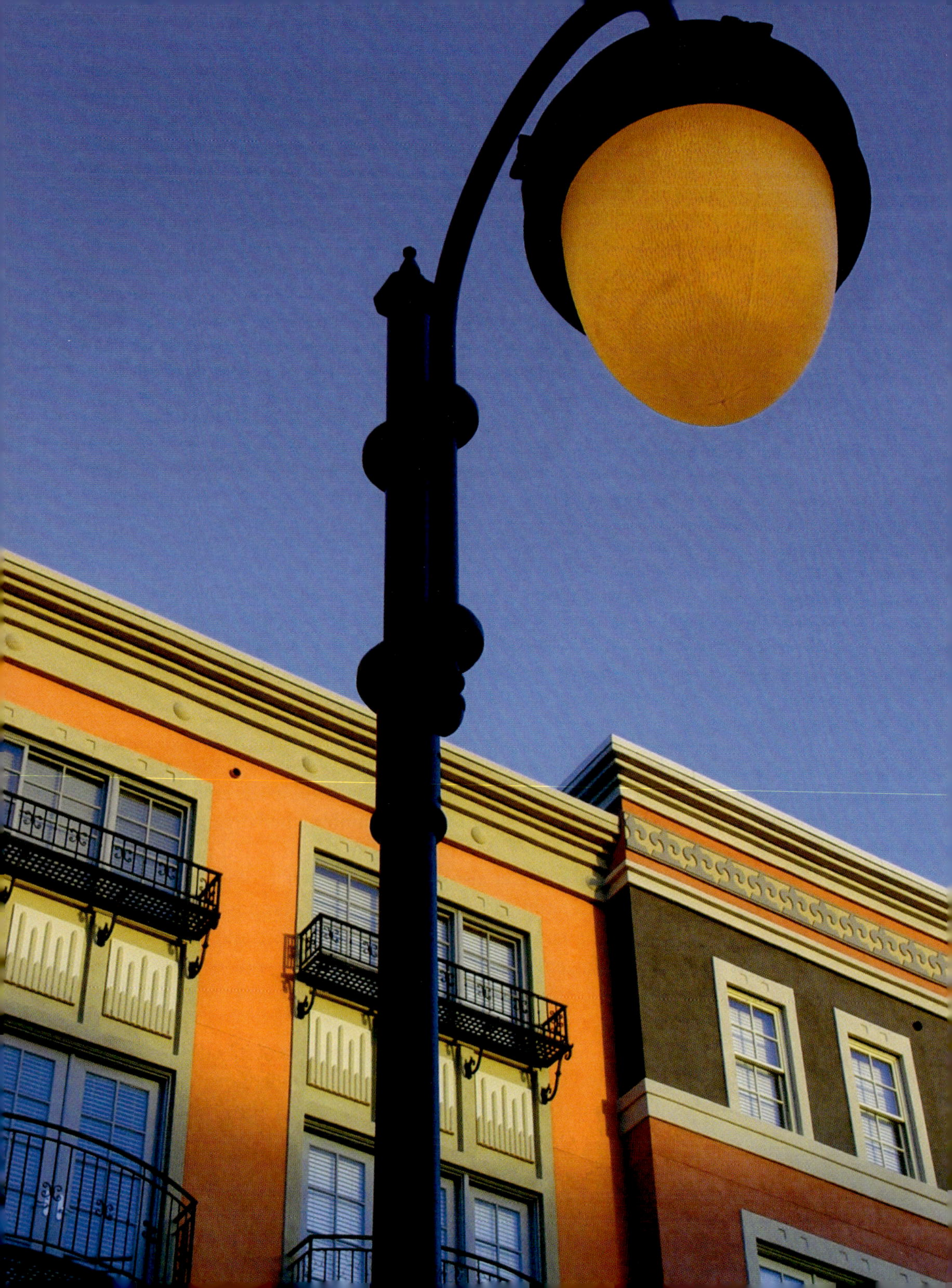

Megatrend IV

Towards new transport innovations

Clogged up roads, and traffic jams that seem to grow year on year are a familiar feature of modern life. Yet, how many of us choose to get out of our car, and take a train instead? Very few. In spite of the traffic misery, the car still has so many advantages that people tolerate the delays. For many, the car is, after all, one of the few places where they can still enjoy some privacy. For many, a journey in the enclosed space of a car feels safer than one on public transport. The number of cars will continue to increase over the coming years, even if our road usage changes. Due to an ageing population, the majority of adults will no longer work; consequently they will not be travelling during peak hours, but during off-peak hours. This will result in a smoothing of traffic volume fluctuations, with fewer peaks and troughs. Yet with more cars, we can expect traffic jams all day long.

Until the economic crisis began sales of cars were growing annually in the industrialized world; after a slump this growth will quickly pick up again as the crisis dissipates. On top of this, there are more and more car owners in developing countries such as India and China. Globally, the private car remains one of the most important status symbols. When someone in India moves up into the middle class, one of the first objects purchased is a car. And everywhere else in the world, you see the same. When you drive though a South African township, you'll frequently see a Mercedes proudly parked beside a hut built of corrugated iron sheets and old boards. Such images illustrate our priorities.

Reducing the number of cars seems to be a vain pursuit, but fortunately designers and engineers both in and outside the car industry are busy developing cleaner and more efficient cars. In the not too distant future, there will be cars on the road which are beautiful as well as luxurious, fitting in with the consumer's need for status while being very fuel efficient (possibly 1 litre:50km). Currently, there is the Volkswagen Lupo, in itself an ugly biscuit tin, but it does do 1:30. If VW were to put the Lupo engine into its successful Golf models then something useful would have been given to the world. The Lupo technology could then be sold to other car-makers, and before you know it, half the world would be driving around in an energy efficient car and Al-Qaeda would have a lot less income from oil. What's Volkswagen waiting for?

A quick note about the word hybrid: hybrid technology means a technological hybrid, a combination of different techniques. We use the phrase for both the specific Toyota technology as used in the Prius, and to describe innovative combinations of car and aircraft technology.

The megatrend for car innovations and other car use consists of various sub-trends, which are described below.

Trend 1. Moving towards an accelerated changeover to cleaner cars due to the crisis

One of the industries which suffers most under new environmental measures is the car industry. In the nineties, European car manufacturers agreed, of their own free will, to reduce the CO_2 emissions of their cars to 120 grams per kilometre by 2008. However, it seems that the industry was a long way off achieving this objective. After much bickering, The European Commission introduced more restrictive measures. In 2004, a European car emitted an average of 163 grams of CO_2 per kilometre; a figure that, according to EC directives, will have to be reduced to a maximum of 120 grams per kilometre in 2012. That means an emissions reduction of 20% in the coming five years. How this reduction is to be implemented is not yet clear, but the objectives are in place.

Of course, there were a lot of objections to this measure from the car industry, in particular the German car industry. German cars are well-known for their performance: people buy them for their size, luxury, power and speed. However, the better the performance, the more pollution the car emits. Thus, German cars are generally 'dirtier' than French or Italian cars. The average new Porsche produces at least 300 grams of CO_2 per kilometre. Mercedes, BMW and Audi are all first class polluters. Protest from these costly brands was to be expected. What was surprising was that the manufacturers of smaller cars, those which are closer to the 120 gram CO_2 emission per kilometre mark, such as Fiat, Peugeot and Citroën, also pulled the emergency cord. The reason for this is that the profit margins on smaller cars are a lot lower, according to manufacturers, too low to warrant developing further technology.

Christian Streiff, member of the board at Peugeot-Citroën, suggested that car based pollution could be reduced by two-thirds simply by removing the oldest 20% of European cars from the roads. Older cars are the greatest polluters, so why are such measures not implemented? The answer to this is, for the most part, political. The owners of the banned vehicles would refuse to vote for any politician or party that introduced such a rule. Formulation of general objectives is popular with politicians; however, if measures will lead to protest or their own unpopularity, they prefer not to get involved. They're usually more concerned about repercussions at the next election. Such behaviour is part of democracy. Even in India, 'the largest democracy in the world', necessary measures are not taken out of fear of losing voters. A good example was the row over the heavily polluting, noisy three-wheel motorized rickshaws that drive around every Indian city in considerable numbers. The Indian government signalled that it would take action against the rickshaws and the Indian Supreme Court decreed that, as of January 1, 2009, all auto rickshaws which used toxic, adulterated fuel were to be banned. Owners of such rickshaws would have to change to cleaner fuels, such as compressed natural gas (CNG). Calcutta, a city with more than 60,000 auto-rickshaws, was declared to be the dirtiest city in India in 2008, and that really means something in India. The city has the highest rate of lung cancer in the country, and 70% of the inhabitants have bronchial conditions. Even so, hordes of auto-rickshaw drivers, incited by the Communist Party, took to the streets, set buses on fire and brought traffic to a standstill in protest at the measures. As a result, they managed to have the High Court order shelved by the Indian government until further notice.

During George W. Bush's second term of presidency, few measures or laws to stimulate a changeover to cleaner cars were implemented in the United States. According to the politicians in Washington that was a matter for the car industry. However, the car industry didn't want to put a lot of money into R&D for cleaner cars; they preferred selling ever bigger and even more expensive SUVs. In their book *Two Billion Cars: Driving Towards Sustainability,* Daniel Sperling and Deborah Gordon write about this: 'Huge SUV-profits allowed the Detroit automakers to ignore fundamental corporate weaknesses,' including 'the lack of investment in fuel economy and alternative fuel technology'.

Since 2006 the sales figures for Japanese hybrids have risen in the US. However, US manufacturer sales were still going well, so there was no problem. When oil prices snowballed in 2008, more Americans began to choose smaller and more efficient cars and the car city of Detroit began to feel the repercussions of many years of underinvestment in fuel efficiency and innovation. When the crisis followed at the end of 2008, the entire car industry collapsed. Car sales in the United States, which were worth a good 16.5 million cars, had fallen to 10.5 million by 2008. January 2009 was the worst January sales month for the entire car trade since 1963! The figures for the 'Big Three' from Detroit were terrible: at General Motors, sales fell by 48% in comparison with January 2008, at Chrysler by at least 55% and at Ford by 40%. Even European and Asian cars experienced a considerable fall in US sales: Toyota fell by 32% in January 2009 compared to January 2008, Honda by 28%, Mercedes-Benz by 43%, Lexus by 28% and BMW by 16%. The sales of clean cars such as hybrids fell as well, but the greatest blows were dealt to the 'heavy boys' of Detroit.

The shares of these car makers tumbled, and they were in serious trouble. At this point they knocked on the government's door. Since there are 1.6 million US jobs – including American suppliers and dealers – at stake across the Big Three, the car industry had the government's full attention. Some economists estimate that their bankruptcy would create up to 2 to 3 million unemployed workers across the globe. General Motors also owns Saab in Sweden, Vauxhall in Great Britain and

Opel in Germany. In December 2008, GM and Chrysler received loans amounting to $17 billion. The car makers had to show future viability otherwise the loans would be recalled – this presumably means cleaner cars. Fortunately, Obama's government has put considerable emphasis on restructuring the car industry to make it more sustainable.

Additionally, an American High Court verdict of 2 April 2007 will have repercussions for the car manufacturers. The court decided that the government body that deals with environmental pollution measures – the Environmental Protection Agency – may pass judgement on the CO_2 emissions of cars. Such a judgement opens the way for individual states to reduce their CO_2 emissions standards, meaning the American car industry will have to begin producing cleaner cars.

Whether the promised loans will be enough to save the car industry is another question. In February 2009, GM indicated that it needed another $16 billion, and announced that it would also have to dismiss 1 in 5 employees. In total, that would mean 47,000 employees, and that is only the beginning. GM also started looking for buyers of its European brands.

There are people who no longer believe in a fundamental change within the Big Three. At the end of February 2009, *The Wall Street Journal* wrote: 'The shrinking of GM and Chrysler are inevitable; the only questions are how long it takes and how much it will cost. President Obama will help himself, taxpayers and the economy if he forces the hard decisions as soon as possible... Bankruptcy increasingly looks like the least painful choice.'

After the American government promised loans to the dying car industry, other Western countries could no longer opt out: in December 2008, the Canadian government rushed to the aid of its car industry, which, in fact, consists of branches of the American car makers, with $3.3 billion. In January 2009, the British government credited its car industry with £2.3 billion in aid. Spain and Italy followed suit with similar measures. The French government also decided to assist its car industry in February 2009 to the value of €6 billion. The immediate cause was the threat of mass dismissals amongst French car manufacturers, amid fears that production would be transferred to low-wage countries in Eastern Europe. Presently, one in ten French people work directly or indirectly for either Renault or Peugeot-Citroën. In exchange for government aid, the French car industry had to promise that there would be no dismissals on home territory and – a gesture towards public opinion – that management would no longer pocket fat bonuses. When bankruptcy was threatening Opel the German government decided that as the car maker had 25,000 employees and elections were coming up, they risked extreme unpopularity if they didn't take any measures. The funding offered is estimated to be worth €3.3 billion, with Opel hoping to get €2.6 billion from Berlin and the rest from regional authorities.

All these aid programmes were initially about safe-guarding jobs. An important point, not only for the workers involved, but also for the economy as a whole. Even so, the restructuring of the car industry will have to see greater emphasis placed on the switch to cleaner technology. Old, polluting industries such as the car industry must only be bailed out if they guarantee that they will remodel themselves into sustainable industries. If this opportunity is missed, the car industry will suffer when the economy improves and the subsequent rise in the price of oil makes it more important for the consumer to buy a fuel-efficient car.

The current recession is deeply unpleasant; however, such economic crises offer new opportunities. This is a chance for companies to play an important role in the sustainable energy economy of tomorrow. In short: the current economic crisis creates the momentum for an accelerated switch to sustainable and energy efficient technology.

Trend 2. Moving towards hybridization of car engines and more fuel-efficient vehicles

It isn't just new government measures and the economic crisis which have forced car manufacturers to produce green cars. The consumer is now more conscious of the effects that cars have on the environment. Celebrities such as Cameron Diaz and Leonardo DiCaprio have also had an impact by talking publicly about their reasons for driving hybrid cars. Back in 1998 at the Detroit car show – the largest car show in the world – gas guzzling off-roaders such as the Hummer stole the stage; in 2009 it's all about sobriety and the crowd jostles around electrical car prototypes. Even the new, energy slurping Formula 1 monster from Honda is no longer embellished with glossy images of speed and power, but with images of the earth, and there is an accompanying website on which you can sign ecological petitions. Communications departments across the car industry have already made the switch to a green future. Now, it's just a question of the heart of the industry.

Toyota was ahead of the curve when it began development of the hybrid engine in the early 90s, when oil prices were still low and before a widely felt need to reduce CO_2 emissions existed. It now seems like a stroke of genius, even if the original development costs ran to billions of dollars.

The hybrid engine is a combination of either a petrol or diesel engine and an electrical engine. This creates considerably lower CO_2 emissions particularly in traffic jams. When in heavy, city traffic, the hybrid automatically switches over to the electric engine, which emits zero CO_2 emissions. Hybrid engines exist in different versions, with one or two electrical engines. One disadvantage is that the battery packs are large, which means that there is less luggage space; in the future they will be much smaller.

European and American car manufacturers did initially see potential in this technology but gambled on other alternatives; they saw the hybrid as a temporary solution. The German car manufacturer BMW launched the hydrogen car, technology that looked viable at the time. While the Europeans and Americans put their energy into hydrogen and bio-fuels, the Japanese conquered the world with their hybrids. Even the Germans have praised Toyota. *Der Spiegel* has commented: 'The Japanese car manufacturer which once suffered from a reliable but boring image is suddenly world leader, both environmentally and technologically. Toyota actually has earned Audi's car slogan: "Vorsprung durch technik".'

The American and German car manufacturers now see that they miscalculated in not applying hybrid technology. Porsche boss Wendelin Wiedeking realized this in 2005, when he contacted Toyota. Wiedeking wanted to purchase hybrid technology from the Japanese company to use in the gas guzzling Porsche SUV Cayenne as quickly as possible. The deal fell through because Wiedeking only wanted to purchase the hybrid components. The Japanese would only cooperate if they could produce the whole system for Porsche.

In the meantime, the Germans haven't succeeded in developing a good hybrid of their own. The greatest problem is the power train chosen by the Germans. Whereas Toyota chose a complex engine/clutch combination with two engines, Volkswagen/Porsche employed only one electrical motor between the internal combustion engine and the gearbox. This electrical engine has to perform several functions: it must act as a generator; it has to power the car when it's only running on electricity and it also serves as a starter for the petrol engine. The biggest problem up until now has been developing a smooth transition between the electrical state and the combined electrical/combustion state. Mercedes-Benz and BMW have condemned the 'cheap solution' attempted by VW-Porsche. Along with America's General Motors, they have designed a more complex and satisfactory hybrid system.

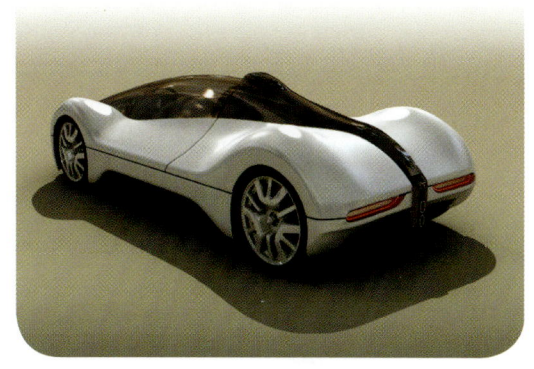

There is also good news from France, even if it sounds pretty implausible: a car that drives on compressed air. The French company MDI, belonging to the Formula 1 boffin Guy Nègre has been working on this for the past fifteen years. The prototypes were driven in the summer of 2007. In 2009, Indian Tata Motors will start selling cars that run on compressed air. Nègre's company, MDI, will also introduce air-cars to the market in France in 2009. In the United States, Zeropollution Motors has a licence to produce compressed air cars for the American market from 2011.

In a normal combustion engine, there's an explosion which pushes the pistons down into the cylinder. In the 'air-car', the same thing occurs but with compressed air and at much lower temperatures. The car is made from much lighter aluminium and is, as a result, a lot more efficient (1:50). The sales price is around 4,000–5,000 euros. The car travels to a speed of around 70km per hour on compressed air and produces no harmful exhaust fumes. Above this speed, it automatically switches over to petrol and uses only 1 litre per 50km. Nègre has produced the world's most efficient petrol engine, and the first car to run on air.

In addition to this, existing petrol and gas engines will become more efficient. The German company Daimler has developed BlueTec technology, which allows both petrol and diesel cars to run more efficiently. Toyota has launched the comparable valvematic system. The hybrid, BlueTec and valvematic technologies can also be brought together, making energy consumption of 1:50 for an average car possible.

part 2. The new energy economy: outlines and trends

The number of people driving hybrid cars to boost their image will increase over the coming years in different market segments. Hybrid cars will become more attractive and will be more closely associated with their driver's sense of status in more expensive market segments. That 'feel good' feeling that they create without sacrificing luxury, appearance, comfort and performance make them the winners of the future.

Lexus' green flagship is the LS 600h, which was first shown in Europe in 2007 at the Salon d'Automobiles in Geneva. The car is 70% cleaner than similar cars from the luxury segment, such as the Mercedes S-class or the BMW 7 series. The LS 600h is jam-packed with innovative technology. There are in-built cameras to keep an eye on whether the driver is about to fall asleep and, if necessary, the car intervenes. If you don't keep to your lane on the motorway, or if the car detects an obstacle, this Lexus takes over. The car can even reverse park itself. It is a little miracle. In the US, the Lexus is the top brand in the luxury segment, but it has yet to attain this position in Europe and Japan.

The American Union of Concerned Scientists annually publishes a list that classifies car brands according to their 'greenness'. Japanese and other Asian car manufacturers topped the 2005 list by a mile. First was Honda, whose models are relatively clean and energy efficient; just behind them was Toyota, chiefly due to the increasing sales of the hybrid Prius; third in line is Hyundai-Kia; and fourth was Nissan. The first European car manufacturer in line is Volkswagen. American car manufacturers Ford and General Motors conclude the list, with DaimlerBenz at the bottom. In the measure of average CO_2 emissions per car, number 1 – Honda – is cleanest by 22% while Mercedes-Benz is a full 15% dirtier!

It seems that the American consumer is finding such statistics increasingly important: in March 2007, Ford's sales fell by 9%; those of GM fell by 7.7%, whereas Toyota saw an increase of 12% because of the Prius hybrid. Between 2002 and 2007, sales of the Prius increased from 28,000 to 400,000 units per year. However, hybrids haven't escaped the economic crisis. Due to lower oil prices and tight household budgets, the market for hybrids has been hit extra hard. In November 2008, sales in the US were 53% lower than in November 2007. On average, these hybrids have two drive systems and cost $4000 more than similar petrol cars. With oil prices over $100 per barrel, it was possible to recoup the purchase price within a couple of years; however with oil prices under $50, you would have to drive a hybrid for eight years or more to reach that point. As long as petrol and diesel don't increase in price, there is no motivation to change to a hybrid that is much more expensive.

Trend 3. Moving towards a limited use of hydrogen
Hydrogen technology is another possibility for the future. Various car manufacturers such as BMW and Daimler have invested in the development of this type of engine. They see hybrid technology as an interim answer, whereas the Japanese consider it to be the final solution. Caught unawares by Japanese global success, the leading German car manufacturers are currently busy developing hybrids. Recently, the interest in hydrogen cars seems to have declined considerably.

There are two different concepts for the hydrogen car. The A-type hydrogen car is the simplest. A car like this burns the hydrogen, which is stored in an extremely cold tank, in much the same way as petrol is burnt. For this, you need large quantities of hydrogen, which needs to be kept very cold, otherwise it evaporates immediately. However, hydrogen as such doesn't occur in nature and needs to be manufactured and in order to do this, energy is required. Frequently, natural gas is used as the base material. As a result, CO_2 emissions are greater than when the (relatively clean) unaltered natural gas is used. This A-type hydrogen engine has numerous disadvantages and will consequently never make a major breakthrough. Just consider the transportation of large tanks from the 'hydrogen factories' to petrol stations, all being kept at extremely low temperatures. On top of that, it can only be pumped through great big, fat pipes.

On the other hand, there is the B-type hydrogen engine. This is in fact an electrical engine that runs off a hydrogen fuel cell. Via an electrolysis process, the hydrogen is converted into electricity. This B-type is thus an electric car.

In the ideal future situation, the rapidly evaporating hydrogen will be compressed into little 'pellets' which can be 'pumped' into a car, where they are then 'unpacked' and electricity can be generated in the fuel cell using the hydrogen. Once the engine is running, it can't be switched off. So as soon as the car is in the garage again, it can be connected to the electrical grid. Any remaining electricity that is produced would flow back into the grid. There is currently no satisfactory method of 'packing or unpacking' the hydrogen and the fuel cells are still very expensive. There is also no distribution network for hydrogen. Consequently, hydrogen is not yet ready for mass consumption.

At the moment, Daimler is working on a second generation B-type hydrogen engine. In this new batch, a number of the previously mentioned drawbacks to hydrogen power have apparently been solved. Several years ago, Daimler anticipated that there would be as many hydrogen cars as hybrids by 2012–2015. Other car manufacturers thought this prediction was a little too optimistic. They estimate that the first hydrogen cars for the consumer market will roll off the assembly lines by 2015. In the meantime, Mercedes has been collaborating with BP on hydrogen issues.

BP is to provide hydrogen stations in the US and Europe. The latest news on the hydrogen front is that the US Government has stopped funding research into fuel cells for cars. Cars powered by hydrogen fuel cells, once hailed by President George W. Bush as a pollution-free solution for reducing the nation's dependence on foreign oil, will not be practical over the next ten to twenty years, the energy secretary has said.

Rein Willems, former chairman of Shell Nederland, says: 'Hydrogen can be cost-effective within the not too distant future. Think of the applications in forklift trucks, buses, trams, rubbish trucks and the like, that are only driving short distances around cities. The hydrogen stations need then only be placed in and around the cities. The result is a dramatic reduction in CO_2 emissions. The first hydrogen – A-type – buses are already in use. Converting the entire fleet to hydrogen is easy!' The American department store chain Wal-Mart already uses forklift trucks running on B-type hydrogen. They only need to install a hydrogen pump on the company premises.

From a so-called Well-to-Wheels analysis carried out by the Dutch ECN (Energy Research Centre for the Netherlands), it seems that fuel cell buses are considerably cleaner than conventional diesel buses. The most important benefit is the reduction of air polluting emissions, in particular nitrogen oxides and particulates. However, these are emitted during the production of the hydrogen. Even so, the net emission of greenhouse gases is about 30% to 40% lower than with diesel. For the discharge of nitrogen oxides and particulates, this percentage is higher.

Taking the approach suggested by Rein Willems of converting public transport and urban maintenance vehicles to hydrogen would create immediately visible results; and because everyone involved is looking for quick success, this seems a very likely development. For average car users, hydrogen will not be acceptable as quickly. There are still too many disadvantages.

Trend 4. Moving towards new generation bio-fuels

Bio-fuels such as bio-ethanol or bio-diesel are created from organic materials. Nearly any plant with an oil-bearing seed can be used for the production of bio-diesel, including sunflower, rapeseed, oil palm and soya. Bio-diesel can be mixed with conventional diesel or can be used pure. Bio-ethanol is made by fermenting the sugars from plants such as maize, sugar beet, sugarcane or wheat. Bio-ethanol can also be used either blended or pure. However, engines need to be adapted if more than 10% bio-ethanol is used.

Bio-diesel produces the same amount of energy per litre as normal diesel; however, a litre of bio-ethanol only produces two-thirds the amount of the energy that one litre of normal petrol does. The biggest advantage of bio-fuels is that they produce much lower CO_2 emissions – up to 60% to 80% less. If however the whole production cycle is taken into account, the savings are much less. In addition, dependency on oil producing countries is reduced. Some countries, such as Brazil and the United States, are already considerably advanced regarding the implementation of bio-fuels.

The greatest objection to bio-fuels is the increased pressure on the food market. The switch to bio-fuels has meant high food prices. It is now a case of choosing between corn in your petrol tank or in your taco. As motorists have more money and power than the poorest of the poor, the majority of the world's maize will end up in fuel tanks. It's the same with wheat. The American Ministry for Agriculture calculated that wheat consumption increased in 2006 by 20 million tonnes. 14 million tonnes were used for bio-fuels, which left 6 million to supply the growing need for food in the world. A further comparison shows that cars are greedier than the mouths of the poor. The amount of grain that is required to fill the fuel tank of an SUV (95 litres) could feed a person for a year. To fill up that same tank every two weeks for a year would use enough grain to feed twenty-six people for a year. A study by the International Energy Agency (IEA) indicated that to replace 5% of European petrol and diesel consumption with bio-fuels, 20% of all farm land would have to be used. If we used all our farm land, we would have only met a quarter of our fuel demands. We would be left sitting in a traffic jam, feeling very hungry. Even in the United States, if all maize was turned into ethanol, only 12% of the car fuel requirement would be met. The situation in Brazil is completely different, ethanol produced from sugar cane doesn't conflict with food production at all. Brazil has been promoting the use of their ethanol for years.

In the meantime, laboratories are working on second generation bio-fuel technology. Where the first generation could only use the most valuable parts of the plant such as the corn cobs and the wheat grains, the second generation can convert the remaining parts of the plant into alcohol. This is because normal yeast, which is not capable of fermenting the tough cellulose of the plant, is now being replaced by specially developed enzymes. These are important organisms for the human race. Thanks to these enzymes, straw, grass or wood cuttings can all be used as a base for bio-fuels. This is a development which no longer threatens the food supply and which suddenly phenomenally increases the volume of potential raw materials.

European guidelines require that by 2010 about 5.75% of petrol will be made with bio-fuels. In addition, there are plans to increase the European guideline to 10% by 2020. In spite of criticism, there still seems to be a rosy future for bio-fuels. It's the same in the United States. The government wants to produce five times more ethanol by 2017. Nevertheless, there are those who maintain that ethanol is only an interim solution. It will eventually make way for the electric engine.

However, according to the McKinsey research agency, half of all the petrol and diesel used by car traffic in the world could be replaced by 2020 by bio-fuels which are produced in a sustainable way. They say that there is sufficient arable land in the world to produce four billion tonnes of raw materials per year for the manufacture of bio-fuels. McKinsey estimates that this could be done without deforestation and without affecting food production. Bio-fuels are cost-effective when compared to an oil price of $70 to $80 per barrel.

If bio-fuels are combined with efficient BlueTec technology and the hybrid engine, the car of the future could probably return eighty kilometres to one litre of fuel. Co-creation and looking for combinations where you wouldn't normally look are the keys to the future.

Using genetic manipulation, the American biotechnologist Craig Venter is working on the development of a new type of bacteria that produces oil. Venter has given himself and his team five years to achieve this. Venter's oil producing 'creatures' could be the saviours of humanity, even if there are lots of critics who expect his vision to remain nothing more than a dream. If Venter is successful in his mission, then that litre of oil, which will allow you to drive fifty or even eighty kilometres in your super-efficient car, will come from Venter bacteria. Oil companies will use farms, which keep these bacteria working, for the production of oil for the human race. Here, religion enters the fray: recently the Pope reported that the development of new 'creatures' is up to God, and that man may not intervene in creation in such a way. And animal activists could also get stuck into this mêlée with a new objective: the liberation of the oil producing bacteria from this new bio-industry.

Trend 5. Moving towards cars with plugs: the plug-in-hybrids

The electrical engine is a clean technology with a lot of future potential: on arriving home, you simply plug the car into the garage socket to charge overnight. The old image of a boring electric car styled like a golf buggy no longer applies. This is evident in the newly designed versions of the electric car. The American company Tesla have launched a completely electric sports car – the Tesla Roadster. The 248 bhp electric engine allows the Roadster to accelerate extremely quickly: up to 100 kilometres per hour in four seconds.

In fact, the electric car is not a new idea. At the start of the previous century, a quarter of the cars produced in the US ran on batteries. However, with the development of the Model T Ford that ran on petrol, combustion engines and fossil fuels became the standard by 1908. It now looks as if the cleaner electric car is making a come-back. At the Detroit Auto Show in 2009, many car brands presented their plans for the development of electric cars. Chrysler indicated that it is ready to start production in 2010. Toyota is a little more reticent. They indicated that their version of the electric car will be driving around the US by 2012.

One disadvantage of the current generation of electric cars is their limited range. On a full battery, the Tesla Roadster can drive around 400 kilometres, which isn't far. After 400 kilometres, it's not just a simple matter of quickly charging up the batteries, as you would fill a fuel tank. The car has to be attached to the energy supply for as long as it takes to charge it again – several hours at the least. The alternative is, of course, the hybrid.

There are two main types of hybrid cars. One where the petrol/diesel engine is used to charge the batteries as well as to drive the wheels (like the Prius) and one where the petrol/diesel engine is purely used to generate electricity. This type of hybrid drives only on the electric motors.

If the battery of the car can be charged via the mains socket, it's called a 'Plug-in-hybrid' regardless of the drive system. The next logical step is, of course, the fully electric car.

In order to give the electric car a greater range, new and improved batteries will have to be developed. Currently, lithium ion batteries work in exactly the same way as when the battery was first invented back in 1800: via a chemical reaction. With computer and chip technology, we have become used to seeing equipment double in capacity and speed every two years. However, with a chemical reaction as is the case in a battery, you are restricted by the laws of physics. Boosting the capacity of batteries is progressing at a rate of about 8% per year. Even so, a lot of energy needs to be put into the development of better batteries. In the United States, the amount of money which has been pumped into this industry by venture capitalists has, according to the Dow Jones Venture-Source, risen from $4.3 million to $200 million between 2002 and 2008.

It is likely that growth will continue as the American government has a special interest in this industry. Obama's Congressional Stimulus Bill includes tens of billions of dollars in loans, grants, and tax incentives for advanced battery research and manufacturing, as well as incentives for plug-in hybrids and improvements to the electrical grid, which could help to create a market for those batteries. President Obama indicated that he wants to have a million electric cars in the US by 2012. The Americans are serious about this.

For Asian car brands, it is important to be able to purchase batteries for electric cars – the hearts of such cars – closer to home, and work is underway to improve batteries there too. Analysts indicate that as yet, neither American nor Asian battery developers have come up with anything that is good enough; after all, we need batteries that are powerful, safe, reliable and affordable. These days, the majority of lithium ion batteries are still made in Asia. And the expectation is that wherever the batteries are made, will also become the centre of the (electric) car industry.

But even here we are faced with shortages. Meridian International Research, an independent consultancy specializing in renewable energy, is not convinced lithium is the answer. To achieve the required cuts in oil consumption, a significant percentage of the world's automobile fleet of one billion vehicles would have to be electrified in the next decade. Ultimately, all production, currently 60 million vehicles per year, would have to be replaced with electrified vehicles. But there are insufficient economically recoverable lithium resources available to sustain electrified vehicle manufacture in the volumes required, based solely on lithium batteries.

'Depletion rates would exceed current oil depletion rates and switch dependency from one diminishing resource to another. Concentration of supply would create new geopolitical tensions, not reduce them', their report states.

Charging station infrastructure could also be developed so that electric cars could 'fill up' along the way or change their batteries. Shai Agassi, CEO of Better Place, is planning to establish such an infrastructure with his company. The US, Israel and Denmark have already shown interest in his concept. The idea is that people buy the car but not the batteries. They remain the property of Better Place, and the client then pays a mileage rate. This business model distinguishes Better Place from other potential infrastructure constructors. Agassi in *Newsweek* explains: 'Our goal for Israel and Denmark is mass-market access by 2011. In 2010, we will have a systems-wide test where we have about 100,000 [recharge] sites installed, a few thousand cars, a few switch stations on location, the software in place, and people driving and paying on customer contracts.' In other ways too, the governments of Israel and Denmark have shown that they are serious about the move towards cleaner, electric cars. In Israel, a car owner pays 60% more tax on petrol than on electricity. In Denmark, the difference is 180%. Such measures will point us in the right direction.

One of the major players in this field could well be China. China has a fast growing number of cars and little oil of its own. In McKinsey's report 'China's green opportunity' the company states: 'Suppose that China began to adopt electrified vehicles widely starting in 2015 and ramped up the rate of adoption to 100 percent of new vehicles by 2020. Our analysis shows that demand for imported oil might fall 30 to 40 per cent. China could emerge as a global leader in this industry by leveraging the country's low-cost labour supply, its fast-growing vehicle market, its success in rechargeable-battery technology, and its substantial investments (both made and committed) in R&D for electrified transport.'

There are sceptics who doubt the anticipated breakthrough of the electric car. Menahem Anderman, a consultant specializing in this industry, says in *BusinessWeek*: 'Next-generation lithium-ion batteries will add at least $8,000 to the price of a plug-in when all the electronics are included. For drivers to save money on the Volt (a Chevrolet, GM plug-in), production will have to reach 1 million cars a year, and gas will have to pass $5 a gallon.' In other words, at least one euro per litre. In Europe, people are used to similar (or higher) fuel prices, however in the US, fossil fuels are still relatively cheap. Apart from investing in sustainable technology, the American government must also consider increasing the price of petrol and diesel.

Finally, let's also not forget that we need lots of electricity for this change-over. The situation differs by country. The French with all their nuclear stations would most probably be able to handle the change-over but the Dutch electric network company Enexis stated recently that 'If 5% of Dutch people were driving electrically, it would be risky but if 20% converted, all our fuses would blow.'

Trend 6. Moving towards sci-fi, with or without wheels

The flying car, which we all saw in Walt Disney cartoons like *The Jetsons*, seems to be on its way. In 2009, the American company Terrafugia introduced the Transition to the market – a futuristic two-seater car with foldable wings. The Transition is not intended for short flights, but for longer distances of between 150 and 800 km. To be able to fly the Transition, you do need to have a flying licence. You would also need to have a fairly sizeable bank account, as the Transition costs $194,000. However, you can't just take off if you are stuck in a traffic jam. Just as with a normal light aircraft, the Transition does need a relatively long airstrip.

The Dutch entrepreneur and inventor John Bakker has been able to interest a number of investors in a hybrid car which can both fly and drive along roads. This vehicle goes by the name 'Personal Air and Land Vehicle' (PALV). Bakker, who worked for the National Air and Space Laboratory, has brought together a group of experts to develop plans and attract more investors. Ultimately, the plans will lead to a real flying car. The goal is to have the PALV reach speeds of 200km/h on land as well as in the air. This vehicle should be environmentally friendly with a fuel consumption of 1:30. The PALV needs no new infrastructure and can be used on the current road network. It uses the existing roads, airports, heliports and fuel pumps. If the motorway is blocked, you fly; if the weather is poor or it's after dark, you drive,' according to Bakker.

The flying car seems like a great idea, but it does pose problems. Problems which need to be solved quickly. These cars fly above motorways, so have to be able to withstand strong winds. We can't have them crashing into bridges. They also pose new challenges for the traffic police; before you know it, there could be horrendous traffic accidents in the air and on the road, or both. More trivially, what if the paparazzi took a snapshot of an actress sunbathing naked on her roof terrace from a flying car and put the photo on the Internet? Also, it would be easy to break into a house with a flying car. You could fly up to any block of flats, stop in front of a window on the fourteenth floor, jimmy the window, drop off a mate who burgles the apartment, gets back into the car/plane and off you go.

Eco-friendly cars can be found across all segments and brands. Even Hummer, which has the most energy unfriendly image, has produced the ecological-minded Hummer O$_2$, where the carriage work is made from a type of algae which converts CO_2 into oxygen. It seems too good to be true: a Hummer that consumes CO_2 rather than belching it out! No wonder GM wants to dump the company.

Trend 7. Moving towards an increase in hybridization of vehicles

Public transport just isn't sexy. Many people are scared of it, it can be slow and involve many changes, and doesn't provide a door-to-door service. In contrast the car offers a cocoon of safety and convenience. In the coming years, there will be other alternative transport solutions. For example, there will be hybrid forms of bicycles and mopeds such as the new bicycles from Batavus with an electric motor and cool looking design – very comfortable for travelling short distances. There are also electric motor scooters. A retro-looking scooter called EVT was launched recently, it has no exhaust pipe, makes no CO_2 emissions, and runs on lead acid batteries. You plug it into a socket, and hey presto, about four hours later the batteries are charged and you can scoot around for approximately fifty kilometres. The retail price for a standard model is 2,300 euros. In the past, 'green' was the colour associated with the back-to-nature freaks. These days, green is linked to stylish trendsetters. Such trendsetters will make sure that environmentally friendly means of transport are also seen as trendy by the rest of us, even if the majority of sales are in the big cities.

In the not too distant future we'll see hybrid cars, hybrid bicycles and hybrid buses emerging. There will be all sorts of new means of transport such as the Segway and more frequent use of rollways and escalators. In light of obesity scares and a desire for general fitness people might even be inspired to use their own legs. Wouldn't it be great to improve our health and preserve the environment in the process?

Trend 8. Moving towards the electrification of city transport with Streetrollers

Traffic congestion in cities is soaring. In the future city centres will become less accessible by car. Taxes on driving cars in city centres will be raised, as has been the case in London and Singapore. Yet many people won't use the bus, tram or subway to enjoy city centres and all their attractions. We'll see new hybrid modes of transport emerging in cities in the near future. The Segway was the first to emerge on city streets. Bicycles, either regular or electric, will enter the market in even greater variety than already is the case today. In China, for example, 100 million electric bikes are already being used in cities alone. Electric scooters are already here. The newest invention for congested cities is the Streetroller, which will be seen in cities all over the world from 2010 onwards.

The Streetroller looks like a flat platform, with four small wheels. Available in several colours, it has an electrical motor and is designed to be ridden by one person. It's currently priced at 3,950 euros and can be ridden for 20 km before the battery needs to be recharged, which takes five hours. It weighs 34 kg and can travel at up to 12 km per hour. The new series, due out in 2010, is expected to be able to travel 40 km, recharge in two and a half hours and weigh 24 kg.

Silent and environmentally friendly, the Streetroller produces no CO_2-emissions, uses electricity only and, because of the four wheels, feels more stable than the Segway. Patrick van der Velden, a former Shell-engineer, is the father of the Streetroller. For more than twenty-five years he worked as a supply-chain professional for the oil company in various countries and locations. During his trips round the world he saw all kinds of vehicles. Patrick also noticed the trend for vehicles to become ever larger, carrying more and more empty seats over relatively short distances. Strangely enough there were hardly any solutions on the other side of the spectrum, for example for the transportation of just one person with his luggage. If only he could create a solution in this area there would be a huge untapped market potential.

After twenty-five years Patrick decided it was time to change his life altogether and start afresh. Together with his new wife he founded the company CMI Europe and decided to focus on mobility concepts. He wanted to develop a very small, green vehicle, which could be used in all urban areas. Although the idea started to grow in his mind, he had yet to work out what form it would take. Over the months he saw various interesting products, some of which he bought to study, reasoning that they could be useful one day.

On a sunny afternoon in September 2006 Patrick sat down with the young designer Steven van der Veen to discuss his ideas. He went into his tool shed and grabbed an assortment of items. A foldable push cart, four separate wheels and a foldable scooter without wheels. Within five minutes these elements became the ingredients for his new idea. Over the following months Patrick and Steven worked on ideas for the product that would come to be known as Streetroller.

A year later they had worked out all the details for a multi-functional platform and built a conceptual model. This would be a good starting point for future developments and new technology. From this point on they started to work on an appealing design. The Streetroller needed to be simple, safe and very user friendly: in short, easy to use for everyone.

CMI has introduced the Streetroller in various industries for business usage. This covers industrial compounds, large logistics warehouses, hospitals and recreational parks. After due trialling of the platform and technology they will make the Streetroller available for consumer usage.

In a real cradle to cradle (C2C) fashion they designed the Streetroller to be fully recyclable. The concept is future proof, with new technology such as iPhone interface, solar panels, fuel cells, new lightweight materials and merchandise articles in the pipeline. For logistical handling the Streetroller has been designed to carry various sizes of standard ISO transport boxes, carton boxes, crates of beer, small fire extinguishers etc.

CMI believes the current economic crisis is exactly the right moment to introduce this innovative and green mobility concept. It is more than a gadget, providing a very useful low cost alternative form of transport for city centres, shopping malls and the factory floor. The Streetroller can be user configured and is an ideal platform for promotional teams.

Patrick was inspired by the standard Model T Ford platform of 1909 from which a complete new industry emerged. He also studied the Apple philosophy for products and processes. With CMI and their Streetroller he hopes to change, move and inspire everyone. In early 2010 the EU is expected to approve the Streetroller for use in city streets. Asian governments are likely to approve it earlier. And then: rolling, rolling, rolling!

In conclusion

Over the next couple of decades, the car, 'the favourite pet' of many an individual, will become the subject of regulations to reduce CO_2 emissions and the dependency on fossil fuels. The first outlines for the future of the car look positive: by 2020, half of the considerably rejuvenated global fleet of cars will run on environmentally sustainable biofuels. Hybrid engines are already here. With regard to sustainable car technology in the future, it seems that the electric car has the best chance. However, how the energy for these cars will be generated isn't yet clear. The most obvious options are fuels cells that convert hydrogen to electricity and batteries that store electricity from the grid. With all that sorted it is only a question of managing the busy roads.

In the future, we will see toll roads and driver charging introduced in many countries. Since many of the normal roads, at least in urban areas, have become log-jammed, more and more people will be prepared to pay to drive in lighter traffic: the private sector will meet this demand if governments don't. Tolls and parking fees could be levied in a flexible manner using currently available technology such as Vialis, so that energy friendly cars can drive and park more cheaply than those cars that emit more CO_2.

And if, despite all these measures you still find yourself stuck in a traffic jam, you can always choose to fly in your hybrid car/plane!

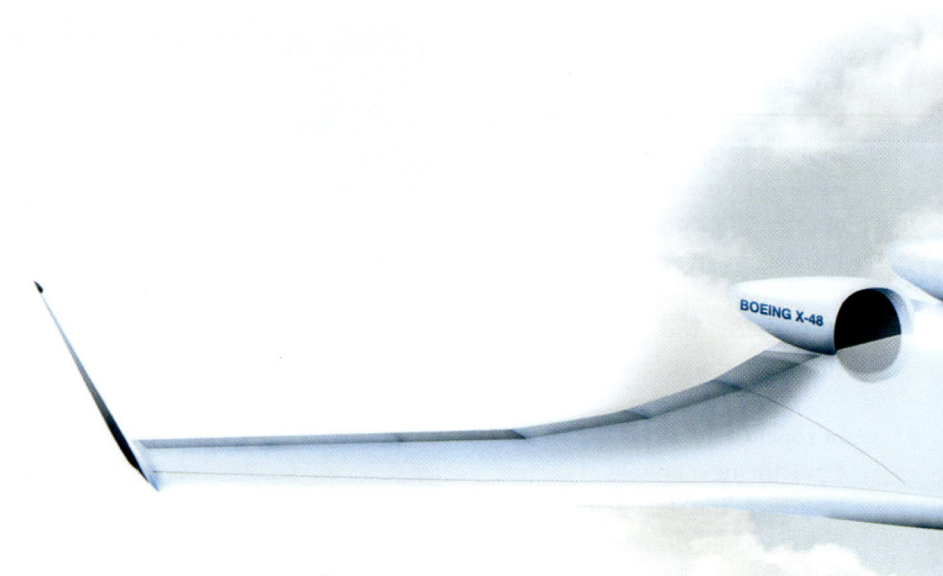

Megatrend V

Towards increasing pressure on the aviation sector

Currently, global flights account for around 2% to 3% of total CO_2 emissions. Planes emit a range of other gases as well, some of which contribute to global warming while others have a cooling effect. Greenhouse gases released at high altitude are more harmful to the environment than those released closer to the earth. According to IPCC, the climate institute of the United Nations, the negative environmental effect of flying is 2.7 times greater than the actual CO_2 emissions. In his book *Heat*, George Monbiot claims that the continually expanding aviation industry overshadows the energy savings in all other fields. 'Flying must be reduced by some 90% in the future, however painful it may be for those involved. That means that flying must in fact be rationed: there must be limits on the number of flights per airport and people must only be allowed to take a limited number of flights. It is only then that the world can achieve its objective of CO_2 reduction.' Monbiot is as serious as others in the industry are light-hearted about the future of aviation. As is often the case in life, the truth is probably somewhere in between.

During the last couple of years, the aviation industry has developed an image problem as a result of its high CO_2 emissions. Interestingly, the IT industry is a more significant contributor to global CO_2 emissions – but you seldom hear anything about that. Research into the environmental cost of the IT industry has been carried out by environmental physicists at Harvard University. They found that a simple Google search causes the emission of 7 grams (0.25 oz) of carbon dioxide. This emission is due to the specific electricity costs of the user at home as well as those at the Google data centre, yet this sector doesn't have an environmental image as poor as that of the aviation industry.

The aviation industry will face problems in the future. Apart from the expected government measures intended to reduce CO_2 emissions, peak oil, and therefore more expensive fuel, is a particular concern. As there are fewer alternatives to flying than to road traffic, it may be expected that the price of an air ticket will rise considerably when a barrel of oil again reaches $150 or more.

Are there no alternative energy sources available for planes? Can kerosene not be replaced by ethanol, electric batteries or hydrogen, as is the case with cars? At the moment, no. Researchers at the University of Florida recently announced that they had developed a technique that has made it possible to fly using hydrogen. However, to do so, you would need such enormous quantities that there would be no room left on board for passengers or cargo. Bio-fuels are suitable when mixed with kerosene, but not as a fuel in itself. Several years ago, there was only a very small percentage of mixed bio-fuels. At the start of 2009, Air New Zealand carried out a test flight with a 50/50 mix of kerosene and jatropha oil. The flight was successful. Test flights have also been conducted in America and Japan. It is hoped that the test results will lay the basis for an aviation industry that will use jatropha oil as a fuel within three to five years. No hybrid planes have as yet been developed.

Growth market

After the current recession, the world economy will start growing again, bringing with it more business travel; world-wide, the middle classes will grow substantially, resulting in a strong growth of foreign holidays. In 2006, the aviation sector posted a turnover of 470 billion euros. For many years, the sector ran at a loss, but it made a profit of 5 billion euros in 2006, despite an oil price of $70 per barrel. That year, 752 million passengers were transported around the globe, which is 6.7% more than during the previous year. This sector grew in productivity by 56% over the last five years. In 2002 the aviation industry was only able to make a profit if oil cost $22 per barrel or less, presently they can turn a profit with an oil price of $70 per barrel.

So, we are flying more than ever, particularly as tourists. Research carried out by the Central Statistics Office showed that 37% of foreign holidays were taken by air in 2006. In 2002, this figure was only 30%. In the same period, the number of short flights rose from 10% to 14%. The number of holidays by air rose globally by 10% per year. That means a 100% increase in seven to eight years if the current trend continues.

We expect that when the economy starts to recover the aviation industry will begin to grow annually by about 5% per year; however that figure could be higher if China and India really do become financial super powers with corresponding lifestyles for their citizens. Price busters such as easyJet and BudgetAir have been able to make relatively short flights as cheap as or even cheaper than similar journeys taken by car or train, so the only reason not to fly nowadays is a fear of flying. Flying at bargain basement prices will surely stop eventually. The question is how to push those costs up. Increasing the taxes on flying is a non-starter. The airline companies would simply cut their costs, and then charge the taxes to their passengers, who have no option but to pay.

As noted above, rising oil costs will have an impact and may lead some to consider more carefully how they use their travels. In the future, people will no longer automatically fly internationally to business meetings. Virtual meetings, with systems such as those developed by HP and Cisco will increase considerably in the coming years. It will also eventually be possible to project holographic 3D images into the air rather than onto screens. The *VirtualMe* will arrive. The idea is that you will be able to sit at a table in your office (in Paris, Amsterdam, London – wherever) while opposite you the moving image of your Shanghai based colleague is projected into the air floating above the table. You will look at each other as if you are sitting at the same table. However, even if this comes to pass, experience has shown that virtual meetings best work with people you already know. So with international work increasing, we will still find that people continue to travel for business in order to *bond*, to strengthen the contact and to maintain camaraderie.

At the same time, many people just like travelling. Meeting other people, experiencing other cultures, 'being let out', away from home, possibly even having a business affair. The eternal reasons for travel will still be applicable in the future. For holidays, people will still catch a plane. There will be more expensive flights in dedicated business travel aircraft. The most expensive will be the supersonic business plane which Cessna and Aerion are currently working on. This is the successor to Concorde. Due to the price, flying in this aircraft will only be possible for the world elite. But this group is growing in size. Millionaire Fairs will soon be held not only in cities such as Amsterdam, Ghent, Marseille, Moscow, Dubai and Shanghai, but in countless other cities. The number of billionaires grows globally at a spectacular rate, in 2006, by about 8% to 9.5 million. However, the recession did have a dramatic effect on these growth numbers.

Shorter distances will no longer be flown as frequently as new types of trains and buses will replace short flights. This market has boomed in the last couple of years. In his book *Heat*, George Monbiot calculated what the CO_2 emission per passenger would be for the various modes of transport for a trip from London to Manchester. With an occupancy of 70%, a flight generates 63.9 kg per passenger; a car journey with 1.5 passengers generates 36.6 kg per passenger; a train filled to 70% capacity generates 5.2 kg per passenger; and finally a bus with 40 passengers generated the lowest emissions with only 4.3 kg per passenger.

For mid-range flights, aircraft carrying 150–200 passengers are now being produced which fly more efficiently than the current models. For intercontinental flights, there will be larger aircraft, which will be able to carry up to 1,000 passengers per flight, which will be radically different in design from current planes. Boeing is already testing an initial design. People will continue to look for a way to fly more quickly. Currently, Boeing and NASA are testing the jointly designed scramjet, a cross between a jet engine and a rocket. As with a jet engine, the scramjet draws oxygen from the air to burn the fuel. As with a rocket, a scramjet can reach extremely high speeds. You could fly from London to Sydney in two hours, instead of twenty. Yet, CO_2 emissions remain a bone of contention. One potential solution is Boundary Layer Suction (BLS); a thin layer of air is pumped out from around the wings, resulting in reduced resistance for the aircraft. This means that less fuel is required. Flying needn't be rationed, as some have advocated, because CO_2 reduction measures outside of this industry will have positive consequences. There will be a certain degree of flight limitation, and this could well take various forms.

In the run-up to 2050, there are nine different trends to be observed in the aviation industry.

Trend 1. Unorthodox aircraft design from within the industry and beyond

The industry organization, the IATA, wants the sector to fly in CO_2 free aircraft by 2050. Across the world, there are developers huddled over revolutionary aircraft designs that will bring this objective ever closer. President of the IATA, Giovanni Bisagnani says: 'Within fifty years after the first flight made by the Wright brothers in 1903, we had a plane with jet engines. This means that an aircraft without emissions should be achievable too within fifty years.'

The IATA chief is perfectly correct. People are capable of great things, especially when they are put under pressure. Over the past couple of decades, the aviation industry grew astronomically but as a result, became lazy. Cars have changed enormously since the 50s, but planes haven't. Today's airplanes still look just like the Boeing 707 that took to the air back on December 20, 1957: a cylinder with engines under the wings.

As a result of factors such as CO_2 emissions and lifestyle changes, current airplane design has had its day. In the years to come, the airline industry will have to modernize and remodel itself. To start with, there will be much larger planes. The first, the recently launched A380 from Airbus, is able to carry 800 passengers per flight. Together, Boeing and NASA are working on a new type of plane, the X48, which can also carry around a thousand people. This concept plane, BWB – Blended Wing Body – forces a fusion of fuselage and wings. From above, a BWB aircraft looks like a flying wing. It has no tail functioning as a stabilizer. For the most part BWB passenger aircraft will be computer controlled as computers are more competent than humans when it comes to making the many steering corrections that are necessary to keep the plane stable. This aircraft would fly 30% more energy efficiently than current aircraft. The military version could be ready in ten to fifteen years, the passenger version five to ten years after that. However, aviation companies will have to cooperate. Whether these concepts are realistic or whether they are just marketing ploys, remains to be seen. *The Economist* reports that many passengers will feel uneasy during a BWB flight due to the short but broad design; the interior is more like a cinema than a conventional plane.

The enormous pressure on the industry to either come up with innovations, or have limits imposed by government, makes new coalitions and initiatives more probable in the future. There will have to be more action. In the past, a manufacturer designed an aircraft and then a prototype was shown to the aviation companies, who ordered the planes and that was it. New aspirations within the industry are stirring up a lot of energy, bringing changes in the role divisions between the various parties, as well as attracting new parties, who are trying to develop more efficient aircraft in new forms of co-creation.

Trend 2. Moving towards new generation fuels, more efficient aircraft, faster fleet renewal, return of the airship and new style air miles

Oil companies are currently working on new generation fuels with much lower CO_2 emissions. The IATA expects that this will be available by 2012–2014 and that the industry will then convert to its use. Fuels will also be developed by companies who aren't necessarily part of the fuel or aviation industry. One example of this is the young Californian biotech company Amyris Biotechnologies. Director John Melo says: 'We cultivate micro-organisms which produce fuels. That's what it boils down to. Small creatures, that's what they are, which are only bred for the fuel that they produce in the same way that cows are bred for their milk and meat, and mink for their furs. This will be a new type of bio-industry. We have already successfully developed microbes which produce the important malaria medicine artemisinin. Partly stimulated by Virgin Airlines, which has set up its own energy department recently, Amyris has decided to apply the same procedure to flying. We want to have microbes producing low CO_2, cheap fuel for airplanes.

'Amyris's own microbes are now able to produce a kerosene-like fuel, which complies with the Jet-A quality standard of the aviation industry. The production method is also more environmentally friendly than traditional fuel production methods. In any case, this trend will lead to a split amongst environmental activists: animal lovers, who are already unhappy about the bio-industry, will not be pleased with the considerable growth of this industry. The question that arises is how "animal-like" are these microbes? And how well are they treated? There will be great debate between the animal and environmental activists, as the environmentalists are intent on finding any means of reducing CO_2 emissions. And microbes are just not as cute as seals...'

Aircraft manufacturers are already designing planes that are more efficient than the old planes that are in dire need of replacement anyway. Just as with cars, the old ones are always the worst polluters. The Boeing 777 and 787 are already a great deal more efficient than earlier generations; Airbus planes are more efficient yet.

However in the long term this will not be sufficient. There will have to be restrictions on airport expansions. There will be less business and commercial travel by air and more overland travel, for example by high-speed train. Travel distances of around 2,000 kilometres will probably no longer be permitted by plane. Over such distances, the CO_2 emissions per person travelling by plane are twelve times that of rail travel.

In the future, trains will also be much quicker. But this will only make a positive contribution if their CO_2 emissions are addressed and they are run on electricity. Such electricity will come from nuclear power stations and alternative energy sources.

Ships will be using alternative energy sources in the future and sail more quickly. There is already a particularly striking prototype freighter called *Orcelle*, also called 'the Green Flagship'. It is the result of an initiative set up by Wilhelmesen Wallenius Logistics, a Scandinavian transport company specializing in logistics and car transportation. This futuristic cargo ship can transport 10,000 cars. It is also equipped with solar panels, sails and fins. At a length of 250m, it can sail at a maximum of twenty knots and is propelled using fuel cells, hydrogen and solar energy. The ship uses no oil and thus emits zero CO_2. It cost 1 billion euros to build. It will probably never be copied in exactly this form but it is an extremely inspiring model for the sea freight industry.

In the medium term, there will be restrictions on the number of flights to specific airports as well as individual air miles travelled, but there will be a difference: everyone will have a limited number of kilometres that they may fly annually. Of course, people would start trading with each other: auction websites such as eBay would be the ideal breeding ground for such dealings.

Trend 3. The Zeppelin's comeback

Apart from economy and speed, luxury is also part of the new face of flying. Sometimes, luxury is more important than speed. Time is money but when you have more than enough money, a slightly slower means of transport isn't objectionable as long as the journey is in the lap of luxury. Air-cruises by Zeppelin are consequently making a comeback. The Zeppelin? Yes, there is still a glimmer of hope for that nostalgic means of transport with its unprecedented luxury and almost zero CO_2 emissions. In a couple of years, we expect that air-cruises and Zeppelin trips will be on offer as the absolute pinnacle of luxury: visiting all sorts of exotic locations around the world in the most exquisite comfort. In spite of its slow speed (max. 150km/h) the airship has many advantages. It is quiet, and as it can fly very low, the views are absolutely stunning. Floating just above the tree-tops, you can admire wildlife through open windows. Because of this low altitude, Zeppelins are however rather weather sensitive. In countries such as England, Germany and Switzerland, Zeppelin sightseeing trips have always been on the agenda. Unfortunately, such Zeppelins are generally smaller models that only hold a maximum of thirteen people without any overnight accommodation.

Trend 4. Moving towards less travel per person on average

The tourist industry has grown considerably over the past couple of decades. Up until the 1970s, long haul tourism was solely for the rich. Since then, holiday travel has gone mass-market. The tourist industry now amounts to 500 billion euros per year, according to the World Travel & Tourism Council. As a result of this trend, CO_2 emissions have risen proportionately. Following the example of countries like Bhutan, it can be expected that some regions and countries will concentrate on returning to the policy of tourism in the 1970s: tourism that is only accessible to the rich.

In various developing countries, where tourism is a considerable source of income, it is seen by some as 'western green colonialism'. Alex Khajavi, director of the Costa Rican Nature Air Group, specializing in eco-tourism, says: 'environmental awareness is an issue for rich countries. These countries try to impose their ideas on the rest of the world. Developing countries actually have the right to overuse nature, as rich countries once did; but the world's ecosystem is no longer able to cope with it. The travel industry must come up with a global system of eco-tourism as a standard and not just as some eccentric, expensive label.'

part 2. The new energy economy: outlines and trends

According to Sonu Shivdasani, director of the hotel chain Six Senses, there isn't much time left. 'If the climate trend continues and we continue to use the current technology to transport people and to supply hotels with energy, the word tourism will soon be an empty concept and the tourist industry will collapse completely.' Stelios Haji-Ioannou, chairman of easyJet, rejects this. 'Environment? Fine, but it won't come to that. We have to make sure that travel isn't seen as some sort of sin. People shouldn't be made to feel guilty if they want to see the Acropolis.'

In any case, tourism will become more expensive over time: some regions will become the preserve of the rich while others will be more accessible. It will become less common for people to take regular city trips and numerous holidays throughout the year. However, as the world's population and the middle classes grow, the total tourist industry will not shrink in size. It will in fact continue to grow, but not at the same rate as over the past couple of decades. More environmental measures for the entire industry are unavoidable. Such measures will vary from taking fewer warm showers in your hotel, to washing hotel bed linen less frequently, and also installing alternative energy sources in hotels and across the entire entertainment industry. In the tourist industry, which works in conjunction with the aviation industry, new policies will have to be implemented and new parties created in order to curb climate change.

Trend 5. Moving towards diversification in the industry and the introduction of emissions trading

There will be diversification in the industry. Mergers between aviation and rail companies could possibly occur. But more unlikely alliances are also conceivable. For example, Virgin Airlines recently started its own fuel division. There is an enormous growth in the market for emissions trading, in other words the trade in CO_2 emissions rights. The principle here is that 'the polluter pays'. In some European sectors such as the steel and chemical industries, such licensing systems are already in use. Based on the free market process, there is a trade in emission rights. The government is not involved in this; companies feel more responsible with this system of emissions trading, as 'proprietors'. They behave more like managers and less like calculating citizens.

The aviation sector will have to deal with emissions trading from 2011. Regional and global emissions trading systems will be introduced. Long term institutional investors such as pension funds will also invest considerably in such systems. Once the economy has improved, this could be a mega-market in the long to medium term for pension funds. Pension funds could become interesting partners for the aviation industry.

Trend 6. Moving towards climate off-set programmes

Climate off-set programmes will increase in number. Passengers will be able to 'redeem' their travel by paying a supplement. With this money, trees will be planted or support given to the development of new energy forms. It is expected that such funds will also be used for the treatment of 'silent CO_2 disasters', such as those that have occurred in Malaysia and Indonesia. Large regions of mangrove swamp are falling victim to deforestation. The wood is highly desirable and, once removed, the empty swamps are turned into oil palm plantations. One of the consequences of this deforestation is that the water level in these regions has fallen dramatically and the greenhouse gas methane, that is naturally stored in the swamp, is escaping. This is occurring on an enormous scale. Indonesia is now globally the third largest emitter of greenhouse gases, whereas it would in fact only be twenty-first without this particular emission from the swamp areas. At least 8% of global greenhouse gas emissions are caused by exploitation of swamps and wet lands. The 'Mega-Rice' project started by the

Indonesian government in 1994, resulted in construction over large areas of the Kalimantan rice fields. The soil isn't suited to this. Unfortunately, the fragility of this eco-system was not considered at the time. Together, these regions produce as much greenhouse gas as Germany, The Netherlands and Belgium put together. The expectation is that emission off-set funds will be used for the management of such projects in the future. They could possibly also be used for the funding of measures to manage global overpopulation as this is and remains the real problem.

Companies and governments, which are large-scale aviation consumers, are buying into this idea. The Belgian government already wants to pay an eco-bonus for every flight made by its employees, thus allowing money to be invested in sustainable energy or reforestation. Various Dutch government organizations and companies have already made this so-called 'climate neutral' flying everyday practice. The term is of course misplaced: flying is and remains an activity that comparatively causes a lot of environmental damage. The suggestion that it could be made harmless by planting a couple of trees is obviously rubbish. At the same time, we know that people will not willingly give up their right to fly. The expected, discouraging effect of the eco-bonus or a climate certificate is limited. Few travellers will abandon flying. However their willingness to pay will be greater than if the tax went straight into the treasury. The good news is that the principle of emissions trading that was introduced for European companies in order to comply with the Kyoto Agreement, has now been expanded to include consumers.

Trend 7. Moving towards alternative flying technology and merging airspaces

Aircraft engine manufacturers such as Rolls Royce and General Electric are working on engines that run on alternative energy sources. Peter Elbers, former communications manager at KLM, expects that it will still take some time before they are brought onto the market. 'The ethics of flying is for us one of the most important subjects of the future. KLM's approach is threefold. We are completely committed to reducing CO_2 emissions at source; we want to control environmental effects; and we want to off-set emissions. You can already see that this is becoming widely accepted in the rest of the industry. Reduction of emissions can occur by renewing the fleet, by flying shorter routes, and with better air control. In 2006, KLM had to make 3,200 hours of flight detours due to noise regulations and air traffic control queues. That's a lot of CO_2! We are also going to reduce the weight on board, taxi on one engine and use as little fuel as possible at the airport itself.'

This also results in a dilemma within the environmental movement. The management of air traffic, partly due to the noise emission standards that have to be maintained for local residents, results in more CO_2 emissions. Thus, noise and CO_2 concerns contradict each other. Over the coming years, this contradiction will become more evident; however, due to the significance of CO_2 reduction as part of the social debate, noise emissions standards will have to be amended. This development will lead to a reduction in the number of people living in the vicinity of airports.

Airspaces around the world will in future be clustered together into a limited number of larger airspaces. Peter Elbers of KLM explains: 'In Europe, we now have twenty-eight airspaces, which results in a lot of inefficiency. The amalgamation into one European airspace would result in a reduction of 6% in CO_2 emissions. If this were also carried out across the globe, the CO_2 emissions from this industry could fall a lot more.'

Trend 8. Moving towards a growth in *cynicism* amongst governments and environmental activists

The aviation industry will, in the future, be affected more frequently by measures introduced by governments under pressure from environmental activists (who often clock up quite a few air miles themselves!). These are officially meant to force the sector into emitting less CO_2. In reality, such measures are used to wipe out general budget deficits, as is the case with car transport. There will be an initial angry response from the car and aviation industries. However, it will quickly be acknowledged that

part 2. The new energy economy: outlines and trends

a focused lobbying and communications strategy will be necessary to deal with the issue. Peter Elbers again: 'there is not one single guarantee that governments which collect money will invest it in the environment, rather than in a larger welfare state. The price rise for the consumer does not automatically ensure that they'll fly less, as there are no alternatives to long haul. So, it doesn't really help the environment.'

Such political opportunism will lead to more cynicism within the industry and an uncertainty in combating CO_2 emissions. For every two steps forward, there will be one step backwards.

Trend 9. Moving towards fewer empty seats and more imaginative financing from the industry

The more unoccupied seats on a plane, the higher the actual CO_2 emission per passenger. In other words, the plane itself emits a certain amount of CO_2 during a flight; if there are two hundred passengers on board each of them is responsible for a portion of those emissions. If only thirty passengers are on board, each of them is responsible for a much higher portion of the emissions. It is expected that the industry will begin to offer empty seats at much more favourable fares than is now the case. This will keep the CO_2 emissions per passenger as low as possible. This of course doesn't reduce the total emission, but it does make the flight more efficient.

In the future, more and more aviation entrepreneurs like Richard Branson of Virgin Airlines will make money available to the Dr Emmett Browns of this world to devise original solutions for the CO_2 issue. Branson promised $25 million for the most original idea to reduce annual CO_2 emissions by a billion tonnes. This initiative led to the development of some very interesting ideas being submitted to Virgin from all around the world.

In conclusion
Together these nine trends will dramatically alter the aviation industry over the coming decades. There will be new alliances and associations. Why shouldn't the IT company HP, which develops Halo virtual meeting systems, work closely with an aviation company which specializes in business travel? In this way, one brand could offer the product – business trips (both live as well as virtual) – to the client. Moreover, better prices could be offered due to scaled economies.

The industry has always been perceived as sexy, which is partly due to its madcap inventors. The creativity of many a Dr Emmett Brown will be stimulated to discover a solution to the industry's CO_2 issue. Such solutions will be financed through existing and new parties in and around the sector. The biggest problem that will have to be managed in the near future is the opportunism of governments, which use the CO_2 issue as an excuse to cream off extra income to alleviate general budget deficits. With the help of action groups, creative environmental saviours, bloggers and other parties, the industry will have to agree on a 'coalition against opportunism'. It's worthwhile considering what could happen in the medium-to-long term if all these trends failed: up to 80%–90% fewer flights than now, with a growing world population…

Taking the plane out of the emissions equation

Green flying. A realistic possibility or an unreachable dream? In the last few years, aviation has become a high-profile target for climate change campaigners precisely because our industry has failed to convince enough people that previous technological advances will be repeated in the future.

In the last forty years, the aviation industry has succeeded in making planes 70% cleaner and 75% quieter than the jets that were flying in the 1960s. Similar giant leaps forward are being planned right now for the coming decades. Yet the aviation industry, which contains some of Europe's best-known companies, has been uncharacteristically silent when it comes to speaking out about technologies that will increasingly take the aircraft out of the climate change debate.

It is for this reason that easyJet has become the first airline to outline the environmental requirements that must be met by the next generation of short-haul super-clean aircraft, and has unveiled its design of what such an aircraft, which could be ready for operation by 2018, could look like.

We're calling it the 'ecoJet'. It would be 25% quieter and emit 50% less CO_2 and 75% less NOx than today's newest aircraft (the 737 and A320 families of aircraft).

These are big numbers, but they are achievable within the very ambitious timeframe we have set. For the 'ecoJet' is not Star Trek – it is based upon technology that is being developed right now by some of the biggest names in the aerospace industry.

With an average aircraft age of only three years, our fleet of 175 aircraft is already the youngest of any major airline in Europe. But as we are committed to the most environmentally efficient future, if the 'ecoJet' were to be made available today we would order a large number of them for fleet replacement and to achieve the 'green growth' that our industry must achieve.

If a reduction in aircraft CO_2 of 50% is achievable by 2015–2020, just think what we could do by the middle of this century. While the 'ecoJet' is based upon impending technological advances in airframe components and engine technology there is a revolution still to come in fuel technologies. As soon as the next generation of aircraft after the 'ecoJet' is available we'll be at the front of the queue to order them.

Possibly then emissions-free flying could be a reality.

Cor Vrieswijk is COO of easyJet.

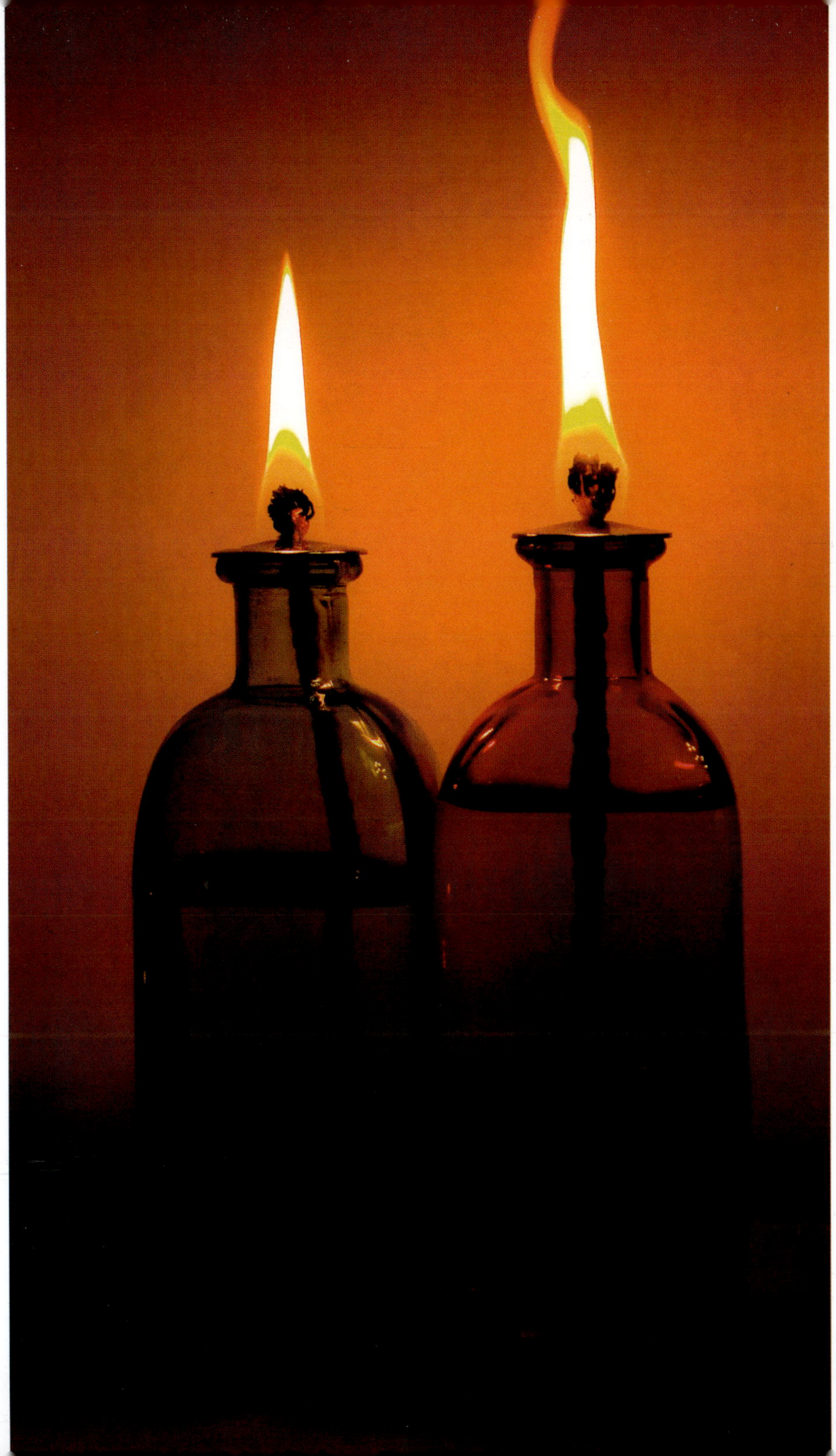

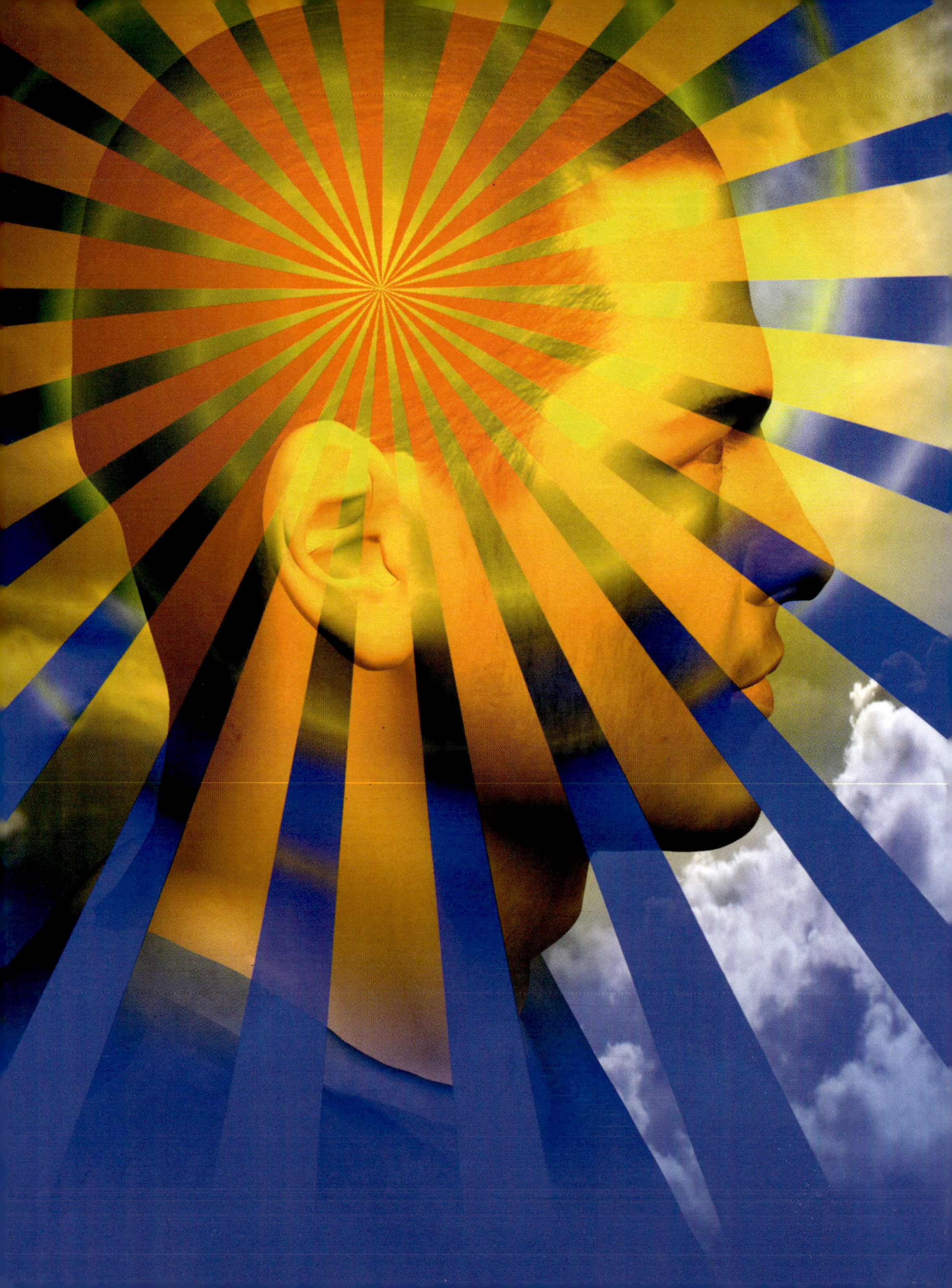

Megatrend VI

Towards innovations in energy supply

Energy companies have played an important role in the energy market since they were privatized. One of the results of this is that we are seeing more and more mergers, at both the national and international level. There are still a lot of smaller fry appearing on the market as well, in particular, those specializing in green energy.

Renewable energy companies are currently experiencing difficulties, as their projects are capital intensive with many projects only paying returns at a much later date. Due to the crisis, many banks have discontinued their investment in sustainable energy, which is already affecting the green energy companies. These companies are no longer receiving funds for expensive projects such as the construction of offshore wind farms or the development of new energy systems. This is however where our future lies. Typical of this trend is the Danish Vestas Group, which is the largest producer of wind turbines in the world. They had to reduce their production drastically in November 2008. This sector has also had similar difficulties in the US. The wind energy developer, Renewable Energy Systems Americas, has halved its production relative to its 2008 output. American solar energy companies, such as OptiSolar, Ausra, Heliovolt and SunPower, once investors' favourites, had to dismiss staff in 2009.

The entire sustainable energy research and development sector has had to adjust its once sunny future expectations downward in the current barren economic climate. Apart from the lack of funds, the sector has also suffered under a diminishing demand. With the current economic situation, fewer people are installing solar panels on their roofs for example. In the short-term things look rather bleak for the renewable energy sector. Traditional energy companies are suffering less from this crisis, as they're able to rely on the steady cash flow from consumer energy supplies.

The reticence of banks to lend to the new energy sector is putting agreed climate objectives in danger. Credit guarantees from the state could offer a solution. This has already been reported to a certain degree in some countries, such as Denmark, Germany and France.

The megatrend for modernization amongst energy suppliers is composed of six sub-trends.

Trend 1. Moving towards a significant growth in underground storage of CO_2 and a new growth in coal fired power stations

In the future, we need to think not only about developing technology that produces lower emissions, but also technology that cleans up existing concentrations of greenhouse gases. One of the most interesting techniques is the capture and underground storage of greenhouse gases. This is also called *sequestering*. This technique is still very much in its developmental phase, mainly in Norway and Germany, and at the moment can only be done on a small scale and under test conditions.

This method allows the capture of CO_2 to take place, temporarily chemically binding the greenhouse gas to another material before it escapes. The price of such capture equipment is quite considerable, in total about three-quarters of the total cost of capture, transport and storage. However, this is good value for money in the industrial and energy sectors, in particular amongst heavy CO_2 polluters such as coal fired power stations and the cement industry.

In the past, oil companies used carbon dioxide as a sequestering agent on a limited scale. They pumped CO_2 into nearly empty oil or gas fields to increase the pressure in those fields, thus forcing the 'liquid gold' to the surface. In the Canadian state Saskatchewan, sequestering was carried out on two oil fields. These sites are now being monitored to see what happens to the underground CO_2. We certainly wouldn't want all that carbon dioxide to leak to the surface. Moreover, there is a high risk to the people and animals living in the vicinity of such fields if concentration levels are too high. Using seismographic technology, the underground CO_2 in Saskatchewan has been monitored over the past couple of years, while experiments are carried out on the effects of underground explosions etc. Don White, research scientist with the Geological Survey of Canada, reports in the *Technological Review*: 'We have demonstrated fairly convincingly that you can monitor the CO_2 under the surface by using seismic technologies.' Even so, many of the questions on the dangers of underground CO_2 have not yet been answered. We don't know what happens to the gas over the long term or what its impact on sub-surface water might be.

Much research will have to be done into sequestering as a solution to the CO_2 issue. Unless the cost of wind and solar energy fall considerably in the near future, the combination of coal fired power stations with sequestering is simply the cheapest solution. Coal would once again be the dominant source of electricity.

Globally, there are still enormous quantities of lignite and coal available. Consequently, many countries are starting to build coal fired power stations, on the assumption that sequestering technology will be feasible in the near future. In the US, there are already about 600 coal fired power stations. In the European Union, there are 50 new coal fired power stations planned between 2009 and 2014. China sees a new coal fired power station open every two weeks.

At the start of the twenty-first century, coal, which is still available in abundance around the world and is still relatively cheap, seems to be once again socially acceptable as a source of energy. Over the coming years, more and more coal fired energy plants will be built, in spite of the damage to the landscape resulting from coal mining as well as the enormous CO_2 emissions released during coal production. The IEA predicts that at least 44% of our electricity will come from cheap but dirty coal by 2030. The revival in coal fired power stations is a result of the potential for sequestering. But that isn't operational anywhere yet.

Environmental organizations are watching these developments closely. The Alliance for Climate Protection and several other prominent environmental organizations launched a campaign in the USA 'to debrand the myth of clean coal,' pointing out that there's no conclusive evidence to confirm that the process will work as is hoped and as the marketing claims. The campaign was designed to combat the well-funded coal industry, which formed a trade association in April 2008 to promote the idea of clean coal. Joe Lucas, vice president for the American Coalition for Clean Coal Electricity, says in *Newsweek* that the technology does exist, although it's still in early development stages: 'With the current research being done, we think we can get the technology up and running within ten to fifteen years.' When a pro-coal man admits that it will be another ten to fifteen years before this technology works, we suggest: no more coal fired power stations for the moment. Let's concentrate on alternative and nuclear energy.

We have to accept that the West will not be able to prevent countries such as China from building new coal fired power stations; a sensible route here would be to invite China to cooperate in the development of sequestering technology. Chinese inventiveness is legendary!

Trend 2. Moving towards offshore wind farms

Wind energy is one of the most sustainable forms of energy for the future, even if more work needs to be done on the cost/yield ratio. We can only presume that wind energy will generate electricity that grows ever cheaper. In the early eighties, it cost three times as much as now. Thus, the development curve is promising.

Globally, the percentage of electricity that is created by wind energy is low – only 1%. Nevertheless, in a number of European countries, this percentage is considerably higher: 20% in Denmark, 10% in Spain and about 7% in Germany. Wind energy is also increasingly utilized in the United States, where the capacity increased by 45% in 2007 to nearly 17 gigawatts. In China, the development of wind energy is even more advanced. Since the end of 2004, the capacity has doubled annually. According to the Danish market research agency BTM Consult, the capacity will increase globally from 94 gigawatts at the end of 2007 to 290 gigawatts by 2012. Wind energy will then be responsible for 2.6% of all electricity generated. By 2012, this percentage will be 6% according to BTM Consult. The IEA predicts that by 2030 14% of the electricity generated in the European Union will be created by wind energy. Due to the economic recession, such predictions will have to be adjusted downwards, since investments in sustainable forms of energy have also fallen. On the other hand, many countries are committed to their green objectives: the European Union wants to create 20% of its energy from sustainable sources in ten years' time; and the Department of Energy in the US wants 20% of its energy to come from wind farms by 2030. With such ambitions, there are incentives such as tax credits and feed-in tariffs that we hope will be implemented in the US by the new Obama government. The goals in Asia seem even greater, even if there are as yet no official objectives. It is expected that within five years Asia will be the largest market for new wind turbines.

Apart from the cost aspects, there are still a number of obstacles that prevent a greater application of wind energy. Countries such as Denmark and Germany have been dotted with modern wind turbines for the past twenty years. When there were only a couple, everyone thought that they were spectacular. However, complaints about 'horizon pollution' due to the presence of these windmills are increasingly common. The construction of offshore wind farms that are out of sight from the coast could be a solution to this.

Also, the current power grid is unsuitable for the supply of wind (and solar) energy and needs to be adapted. Transmitting wind power from rural areas with strong winds to populated areas with high demand will require expensive new transmission lines. At the moment, China's biggest utility, State Grid Corp., is pouring money into the multibillion dollar field of electric power transmission. The company says it began operating a 1 million volt commercial power line in January 2009, which is much more powerful than the 765,000 volt systems used in the United States, Europe and other places. State Grid Corp. said 'ultrahigh voltage' transmission systems will be able to link Chinese cities to distant hydroelectric dams in Brazil or Africa. So maybe the solution for the transmission of wind energy and solar power will come from China.

One of the biggest problems with wind energy is the fluctuation in the creation of energy, and therefore the matching of supply and demand. When there is no wind, there is no power. Then when there is a strong wind there is surge of energy. The Dutch inventor Rudolf Das has come up with a technically feasible solution: an offshore wind farm with a subsurface-lake power station. Energy atolls – islands of 10 × 16 kilometres – are built alongside the offshore wind farms. These atolls are in fact circular dikes surrounding a large inland lake of 30 to 40 metres in depth. When there is a strong wind and thus a surge of energy the lake is pumped dry. When there is a lack of wind, the lake is allowed to slowly refill. This delivers 1500 watts of power over twelve hours. Dutch energy companies are financing research into this solution. As well as offering a solution to the problem of fluctuation in the energy supply, this proposal also allows energy to be generated more efficiently and in response to demand. When demand is high, energy from both wind and from the process of refilling the lake can be used, so providing double the power. When demand is low, but wind speeds are high the power station doesn't have to be shut down as there is a system for discharging excess energy.

Trend 3. Moving towards more intelligent and cheaper solar energy
At first glance, the sun is the ideal source of energy. No other source gives as much, as often and for as long as the sun. However, we haven't yet discovered a way to harness this energy on a large scale.

In the summer of 2007, a solar power plant was put into operation in the Mojave Desert just to the south of Las Vegas. This power station has a capacity of 64 megawatts: enough power to provide energy to forty thousand American homes. The station, which is called Nevada Solar One, covers an area of 1.5 km^2. The plant doesn't use solar collectors, but mirrors. These mirrors concentrate the solar energy which is then used to heat synthetic oil to a temperature of 400 °C. This oil, in turn, is used to convert water into steam to power a steam turbine. Such stations are called Concentrating Solar Power plants, or CSP plants for short.

In Southern Spain, a similar, so-called solar thermal energy or solar mirror plant was put into service, with a slightly smaller capacity of 50 megawatts. Such solar mirror plants are also springing up in Australia, Algeria, Morocco, Egypt, Jordan and Portugal.

For the time being, solar energy is only really viable in sun-drenched regions. A few years ago, scientists began to calculate just how much energy our deserts might produce. Take the biggest desert in the world, the Sahara, as an example. In theory, a 90,600km^2 (35,000 miles^2) chunk of the Sahara – smaller than Portugal and a little over 1% of its total area – could yield the same amount of electricity as all the world's power plants combined. A smaller square of 15,500km^2 (6,000 miles^2) could provide electricity for Europe's 500 million people. But of course, installing such an enormous solar power plant plus the infrastructure to get the power to Europe would be very expensive. Gerry Wolff, an engineer who heads Desertec, an international consortium of solar-power scientists, estimates it will cost about $59 billion to begin transmitting Sahara power by 2020. To supply Europe with 20% of its electricity needs, more than 19,300km (12,000 miles) of high-voltage direct-current (HVDC) cables would need to be laid under the Mediterranean. Furthermore, Europe will need to build completely new electrical grids if it wants to use renewable sources of power like solar energy. The ageing alternating-current lines, built largely for the coal fired plants that supply 80% of Europe's power, are inadequate for carrying a larger load. Germany's government-run Aerospace Center, which researches energy, estimates that replacing those lines could raise the cost of building solar plants in the Sahara and sending significant amounts of power to Europe to about $465 billion over the next forty years. Generous government subsidies will be needed – a potentially unpopular idea while Europe is in recession.

In the meantime, there are all sorts of technological developments with regard to solar energy. The Californian company Cool Earth Solar recently came up with a notable invention to increase the amount of light that falls on a solar cell. Solar cells are expensive so it only makes sense to use them efficiently. Normally, large mirrors controlled by motors are used to concentrate light onto the cell. Unfortunately, these are prohibitively expensive. Cool Earth works with balloons that have a diameter of around 2.5m. These balloons are coated with a mirrored layer on one side. The inside of the mirrored part of the balloon works like a concave mirror, which intensifies the sunlight 400 times. Such balloons are cheap in comparison to the traditional motorized mirrors. In 2009, Cool Earth opened a 1 megawatt test plant using this technology in sun-baked California.

There are other promising inventions in the field of solar energy. The Dutch energy company Nuon will soon launch solar cell foil. This resembles wallpaper with solar cells built into it. There is a layer of silicon on the foil. The layer of silicon is the most costly component of a solar panel, but on the cell foil, it is much less expensive. This not only lowers the material costs, but also the amount of energy that is required to make these solar cells. Since the foil is flexible and light, the transportation and installation costs are considerably lower. The foil is rolled out across the roof, plugged in and before you know it, you've got power. In 2009, a test factory was built for this foil. It is expected that the cost price of energy generated by the foil will eventually come close to that of conventional energy. A similar technology, which will also perhaps be used in the future, is spray paint that incorporates solar cells. The Technical University of Delft is currently developing this.

There are, of course, many other ideas that could be utilized in the future. Daniel Nocera, a chemistry professor at MIT, is currently working on the application of photosynthesis as a way to conserve solar energy. Photosynthesis is the process by which green plants use the sun's energy to convert carbon dioxide and water into carbohydrates and cellulose, in other words sugars and chlorophyll. In fact, photosynthesis converts solar energy into chemical energy, which can then be stored. Nocera is ultimately striving for a society that can meet its energy needs using only water and sunlight.

All sides are working hard on the development of new technology, but for the time being, individuals will have to be satisfied with solar cells in the form of panels and collectors. Globally, the current capacity of solar cells is 3 gigawatts. By 2010, this is expected to have risen to 10 gigawatts. The greatest challenge is the production of cheaper and thus more widely available solar cells. Currently, they are manufactured with expensive, rare materials such as platinum or silicon. The market for solar cells has, from the start, been determined by the supply from the silicon providers rather than by the demand. There is enough demand, if only the price was more reasonable. Due to the economic situation, the price has recently fallen considerably. In 2009, there was apparently an oversupply of modules and components from the more than 250 suppliers worldwide. This provided a potential boon for local governments, utilities and others trying to roll out new solar-power projects. A report by Lux Research Inc., a New York based energy research firm, says global *spending* on solar power is expected to decrease by nearly 20% to $29 billion in 2009, from $36 billion in 2008. But the amount installed will decline only slightly, reflecting more favourable pricing for buyers. Juiced by government spending, such as the Obama economic stimulus package, the solar-power market is expected to grow to $70 billion in annual investing by 2013.

Trend 4. Moving towards the resurrection of nuclear energy

For a long time, nuclear power stations were taboo in many countries. A large portion of public opinion was against it. The association of nuclear energy with nuclear weapons didn't help, nor did the danger posed by nuclear waste. These issues were discussed time and time again by its opponents. For many decades, the majority of politicians didn't dare allow an increase in the number of nuclear power stations. But a combination of tight climate-change targets, energy-security worries and a wobbly economy has caused a rethink in a lot of countries. At the moment, nuclear power is at least being considered once again, and thus a great battle has already been won.

Nuclear energy is still relatively expensive. According to a new collective study carried out by the Keystone Centre consisting of twenty-seven American experts, the (nuclear) power industry and environmental groups, the price of electricity from a new nuclear power station is 6 to 8.2 euro cents per kilowatt hour. At this price, nuclear energy is more expensive than electricity generated from coal, gas and land wind turbines. It is comparable to the current cost of electricity from offshore wind energy. However, when the 'hidden costs' of CO_2 reduction and storage are taken into consideration the picture is completely different.

The idea that nuclear power is the potential saviour of humanity due to its low CO_2 emissions was deemed a 'myth' in July 2007 by the Oxford Research Group. This group of scientists reported that nuclear energy can never supply the required energy needs. Globally, there are 429 nuclear power stations responsible for 16% of global electricity production. Twenty-five new power stations are currently under construction, and in total seventy-six are planned. However, this won't make a difference, as electricity requirements are set to increase by 50% over the coming twenty-five years. In order to fulfil the increasing need, 3000 nuclear power stations would have to be built. This comes down to one new nuclear power station per week. Currently they are constructed at a rate of only 3.4 stations per year. Moreover, the Oxford Research Group report reiterated the notorious safety risks surrounding nuclear energy.

Nevertheless, France has shown that nuclear power can be a serious energy source. After the United States, France is the largest producer of electricity generated from nuclear energy. In 2006, there were fifty-nine nuclear reactors active in twenty nuclear power stations spread across the country. The oldest nuclear power stations date from the early 70s. These will have to be replaced around 2020. In a country of baguettes and TGV trains, nearly 80% of power is generated in nuclear power stations. What's more, the CO_2 emissions are negligible. The fact that France still has power stations which run on fossil fuels is due to nuclear power stations not being able to supply the demand for energy consumption during peak hours. Nuclear energy production is not as flexible as gas and coal are: there is more to it than just adding some coal to the fire when more electricity is needed.

Apart from France, Lithuania, Sweden and Finland respectively generate 72%, 47% and 26% of their electricity from nuclear energy. The majority of nuclear power stations which are due to be built are in Finland and Eastern European countries. Fortum, a Finnish energy group, has lodged an application to build a new nuclear plant. This would be the country's sixth. Four are in operation and a fifth, the world's largest, is under construction. Poland plans two nuclear power stations to reduce its dependence on coal. For the same reason, Slovakia is planning two nuclear power plants. Russia has three under construction and eight more planned for the coming years.

And to complete the list, here are some figures from the International Atomic Energy Agency: in the United States, there are 103 nuclear power stations; one is currently being built; and two new ones are being planned. The majority of activity is to be found in Asia. Countries which have little in the way of raw materials, such as China, Korea and Japan, are very focused on nuclear power. China has ten nuclear power stations, is building five and has at least thirteen planned. In Japan, the figures are respectively fifty-five, two and eleven; South Korea, twenty, one and seven. Globally, there are now 485 nuclear reactors, 29 being built and 64 being planned.

Nuclear energy's comeback is unavoidable, and gradually more people will realize this. Nuclear energy is demonized a lot less than ten years ago, with increasing numbers of people accepting new nuclear power stations. Banks are no longer refusing to finance these plants as had been the case in many countries over the past twenty years. New backers, with input from venture capitalism, will happily finance such plants without thinking twice. Principles won't solve the environmental problem and more parties will realize that. Opposition towards nuclear energy is steadily becoming more of a rearguard action. However, living in an emo-cracy as we do, the emotional appeal against the supposed dangers of nuclear waste must be taken seriously, and must be approached using careful emo-communication.

Trend 5. Moving towards a greater focus on the development of nuclear fusion

As a source of energy, nuclear fusion has enormous potential. Nuclear fusion takes place naturally in stars. Under conditions of extreme heat and pressure, hydrogen nuclei combine to form helium atoms, releasing enormous amounts of energy. This process of fusion provides a constant supply of light and warmth to the earth thanks to the sun. Nuclear fusion converts matter to energy, so a 1000-megawatt fusion reactor would require an amazingly small amount of fuel. It would burn the equivalent weight of around ten cubes of sugar per hour. A kilogram of hydrogen could generate as much electricity as 11,000 metric tons of coal.

But a process that is natural in the sun is not easily reproduced in a lab. For half a century physicists around the world have struggled with the problem of bringing nuclear fusion under control. Fusion – as opposed to fission, which drives all commercial nuclear power plants – could solve a number of problems related to energy generation. The general public has lost all hope in fusion – the first experiments with it began in 1979 in Great Britain, the so-called Joint European Torus – but scientists working in the field of plasma physics appear to be making significant progress now, some thirty years later.

However, if commercial-scale fusion works, the dream of having (almost) clean energy in abundance will come true. Can the human race run the risk of not perfecting a technology that could one day replace all nuclear-fission and coal fired power plants?

Nuclear fusion has also created renewed interested in space travel. While in the 1960s the United States and Russia travelled into space for political gain, there are now a multitude of participants: the US, Russia, China, India, Japan and Europe (ESA). They have all announced plans for new trips to the moon; this time it is no longer about territory but also about mineral mining. There is a lot of helium-3 on the moon, the perfect fuel for nuclear fusion. Nuclear fusion using helium-3 is ideal as almost no radioactivity is released. On top of that, the fusion process is manageable. This mineral is almost non-existent on earth. Millions of tonnes of helium-3 can be found on the moon's surface, swept there by solar winds. It could be transported to earth under pressure in the form of a liquid gas. A cargo of twenty-five tonnes of helium-3 would last for ten weeks, supplying earth's total energy requirements. Cosmo-chemist Ouyang Ziyuan from the Chinese Academy of Sciences, who is now in charge of the Chinese Lunar Exploration Program, has already stated on many occasions that one of the main goals of the program is the mining of helium-3. 'Each year three space shuttle missions could bring enough fuel for all human beings across the world.' In January 2006, the Russian space company RKK Energiya announced that it considers lunar helium-3 a potential economic resource to be mined by 2020. The investment in space travel could really take off, even if there are still people who consider the whole nuclear fusion adventure unrealistic or wishful thinking.

Trend 6. Moving towards a maximum decentralization of energy resources and consumers who also become energy suppliers

These days we all know how dependent the world economy is on energy resources. Businesses, government and consumers all need to use energy in their daily lives. There is a widespread awareness that we can't go on wasting our energy resources and damaging the environment the way we have done so far. At the same time demand is rising due to a growing population especially in the emerging markets. This causes one of the biggest dilemmas of our time: how can businesses and economies grow and get greener at the same time?

A big obstacle for a sustainable solution is the lack of understanding and cooperation between businessmen and environmentalists. In the past the first group did not believe that a solid enterprise could be built with solid profits, based on social and environmental principles and the second group thought that any profitable enterprise could only be a polluting one. Fortunately today we know better.

A good example is the Dutch company MLB Energy. This company proves that future enterprise will be based on a new economy with foundations in social and environmental principles on one side, and solid business principles with sound profits and a sound return on investments on the other. MLB Energy has developed a business concept based on these principles. The business concept will have an enormous leverage on the political stage as well. MLB's approach guarantees a maximum decentralization of energy resources and therefore diminishes the dependence on energy resources from other countries in political instable regions. The MLB business concept is based on three pillars:

- The energy producing systems MLB Energy uses must have a production price per kilowatt of no more than €0.049. The average production price per kilowatt of the systems MLB uses is less than €0.02. MLB Energy's unique selling point is the range of systems, which makes it possible to put the best possible systems for any given location together, dependent on the local needs. By combining these different systems the result in every location where MLB Energy will produce renewable energy is much bigger than just the sum total of the systems
- The energy saving systems MLB Energy has to offer vary from car engines (up to 80 miles to the gallon), to air-conditioning systems (cost reduction up to 95%), desalination systems that produce over 1.5 million litres of drinking water per day with just a 150kWh generator fuelled either by wind power, solar energy or both, and construction systems.
- The MLB Energy Foundation will have a local foundation for every community where MLB Energy produces energy. The foundation will receive 4% of the local turnover per annum to be used in socially responsible developments such as hospitals, schools, housing and sanitation.

Therefore not only does MLB Energy produce renewable energy with considerable profits while paying employees fair and better than average wages, it also develops the community or the region. MLB Energy is developing projects in several countries such as the Netherlands, Germany, Pakistan, India, Ukraine, USA and Turkey. The people who work for MLB Energy and who live in these communities and regions will become economically viable. The consumer driven economy will henceforth grow and it will grow without pollution. Large parts of the world are extremely poor and therefore have no part in the world economy, nor are they interesting for the consumer driven economy – at this time. MLB Energy wants to change this and multiply the world market by creating jobs based on sustainable energy.

This expansion of the consumer market can't be based on anything other than sustainable energy and better than average wages. The oil based economy is coming to its end, whether we like it or not. Prices of oil and (liquid) gas will increase. Ten years from now China will need 80 million barrels of crude oil per day. The worldwide need for crude oil is currently 95 million barrels per day.

Jobs are the basis for economic growth so jobs should be created in the renewable energy sector. Renewable energy can guarantee work and income for as long as we live. Many people who currently have a very poor outlook will become economically viable. Decentralization of energy resources will not only make us independent of politically unstable countries, but will also create an immense consumer market. Decentralization will also take care of a better division of wealth in the world.

In the future oil companies will utilize more wind energy, traditional energy companies will merge and new financiers and unlikely associations will arise in the energy sector. Over time the identity of the supplier will become ever more vague.

The energy landscape will consequently change radically over time. Even the classic differentiation between energy supplier and consumer will become unclear. Currently, much is being invested in the development of a completely new generation of central heating boilers. Boilers that run on natural gas like a sort of mini-electricity power station already exist. When there is a surplus of energy generated, the boiler returns the surplus to the energy company. The electricity meters don't just go forward, they can also move in reverse! Everyone becomes his or her own boss when it comes to energy supply. If people (or groups of people) can create their own energy and each individual house becomes a mini energy power plant, the role of traditional energy companies in society will change. In 'the century of the individual', the autonomy of the individual will become an important subject for energy companies.

In the political arena it seems clear that decentralization of energy resources is the top priority. MLB Energy is commited to turning every energy using building (from houses to offices to factories) into an energy producing unit, supplying power at a price that is lower than with traditional energy producers. Energy dependent countries are the ones to profit most from this. A development of a new knowledge-based industry with a focus on renewable energy will have a considerable effect on the present power that energy-resource-rich countries naturally have. No longer will they be able to dictate prices on the world market.

Energy companies naturally have difficulty letting go of the existing way of doing business. The share holder principle is an obstacle they can't overcome. The gigantic costs of their production sites and the need to satisfy the stock exchanges make it next to impossible for them to invest in renewable energy. Although political pressure is increasing, these companies can't invest serious amounts of money in new and insecure developments. This means that innovation in renewable energy has to come and will come from outside.

With innovations as with all new products the way the market is approached and entered is of the utmost importance. MLB Energy has decided to develop an ever growing range of renewable energy systems. This makes the company less vulnerable than companies that have based their business only on wind parks and/or solar parks. MLB Energy has as an extra positive selling point: the possibility of combining different systems to optimize the production with repect to local needs and possibilities. Their systems can therefore be used all over the world.

The selection of the energy production sites is based on feed-in tariffs and focused on regions with a currently poor projected future. This combination guarantees MLB Energy a very fast time to market at low cost (no red tape) with a secured income for a long period of time. Because MLB Energy establishes a local foundation wherever it produces energy, it is asked by communities and regions to develop activities as soon as possible.

Current producers of alternative energy systems focus on licences and subsidies. Hardly any systems are sold or offered to non-energy companies and private consumers – except for small-scale wind turbines. Due to the high pricing and the non-existence of a return on investment (even with subsidies) there is hardly any interest in the current alternative energy systems. Furthermore it is hard to cut through the red tape to get any subsidies.

MLB Energy will force a breakthrough by offering several small alternative energy systems free to private consumers. The private consumer will become a client and will have a discount on his energy bill. The surplus of alternative energy produced by all these households will be sold by MLB Energy at regular prices. MLB Energy uses only systems with an attractive return on investment. The return on investment is without subsidies or emission rights. These are to be seen as extras.

By combining these different systems and technologies it is possible to build a business that is technically, commercially and financially very solid. Everything produced by MLB Energy systems can be sold and therefore makes a contribution to the company's profit.

Here's an example of how one system works. The waste management system gasifies all kinds of waste and turns waste into high quality heat, power and fertilizer. The high quality heat and power will be sold; the fertilizer will be used for the algae production. The algae production leads to bio-diesel and algae-cake. The algae-cake can be sold to the pharmaceutical, cosmetics and agricultural industries and will also be used for the production of power. The roofs of the algae production units (10 hectares each) will be used for solar-energy production.

In conclusion
Together, six trends form the megatrend of renewal of the energy companies. Governments will still have a strong role to play in driving the future strategies of energy companies; energy nationalism will grow stronger; and old and new forms of generating energy will emerge. Wind energy will come in many forms, as will solar energy. Nuclear energy is experiencing a glorious renaissance. The future is now.

Solar energy as a wildcard

Futurologists vehemently oppose the decisiveness with which trends are described. Frequently, trends create a false sense of security that suppresses the urgency to find solutions to important questions. To offset this, wildcards will be formulated more often in future investigations. Wildcards are events that are not very probable but if they do occur will have enormous consequences. An example of a wildcard is the September 11 attack on the World Trade Center in New York: impossible to predict, with enormous consequences.

It is advisable to regard the almost inevitable breakthrough in solar energy as a wildcard, when considering the most common philosophies on energy issues. After all, anyone who now postulates that the oil price will be low in 2025 because by that time the majority of energy used will come from the sun would be seen as a dangerous outcast.

In the meantime, solar collectors have become a trend on the market. Solar cell manufacturers can barely deal with the demand. The share prices of such equipment are extremely high on the venture capital market. There is now speculation on the third generation of solar cells, long before the second generation has even been developed. The cost price of solar cells is falling steadily. Amongst the developers of solar cells, there is a sense of a self-fulfilling prophecy. It is the same as in IT. Moore's Law, which predicts that the performance of a chip doubles every eighteen months at the same price, has been accepted by the industry for more than thirty years. The new generation of chips is being designed without their applications even being completely clear. It is the same with solar cells.

Recently, tension in the energy debate has been running high. The fossil fuel community is waging war against the converts to solar energy. Both parties are fighting over the profits of CO_2 trading, energy subsidies and regulation from which the other party may not benefit.

Maybe the futurologists are themselves the most frustrated. They know that it requires little effort to describe the technological road map that will lead to a lower oil price in 2025. They also know that this technology, based on already existing techniques, will not be implemented in the battle between the two camps. Thus, anything that is unjustly regarded as a wildcard will appear to be the genuine article. As a result of this human shortcoming, the arrival of a new era has been delayed, a time when Al Gore will no longer need to make a film in the hope of protecting the planet from decline.

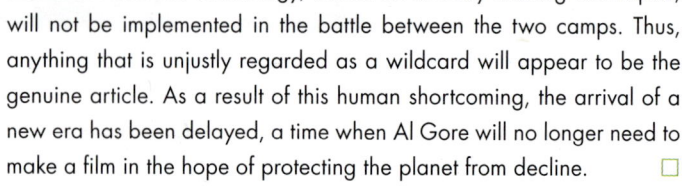

By Professor Wim de Ridder
Professor Wim de Ridder is professional member of the International Futurology Association.

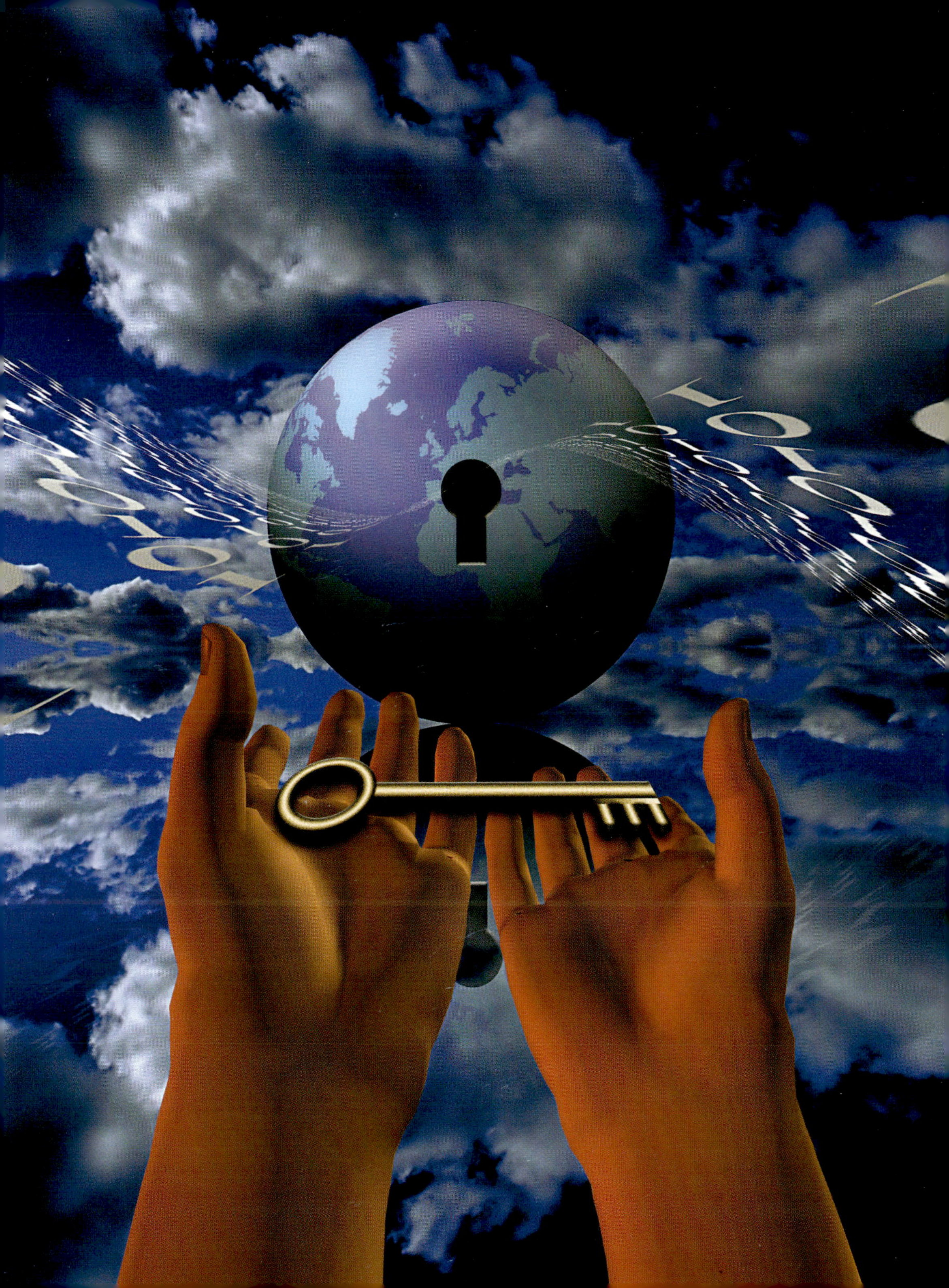

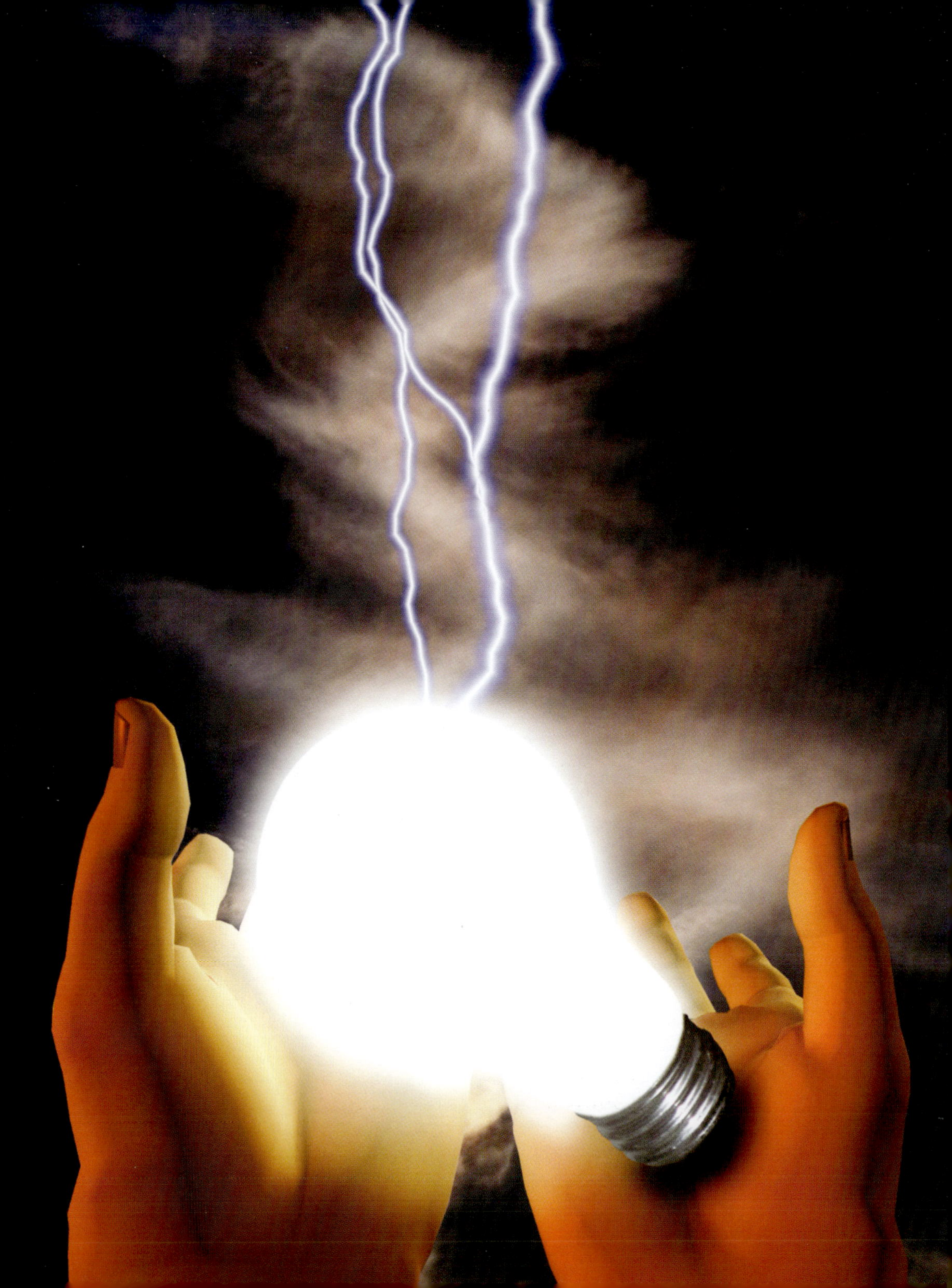

Megatrend VII

Towards new concepts of life and work

The way in which we have organized our work over the past century has led to more mobility as well as more energy consumption. Unfortunately, this process has not made the majority of people any happier. Humans are passionate but also rather lazy. They like to work a little, potter a little, and relax a little. However, the way in which we have arranged our work, with its rules and regulations, protocols and decision trees, has made work a lot less pleasurable than it was at many points in the past. The necessity of reducing our energy consumption and the need for individuals to have more autonomy, self-management and a different balance between work and recreation, makes a new division between living and working necessary. Reduced mobility leads to lower energy consumption, lower CO_2 emissions and less damage to the environment. This megatrend is very interesting in relation to the topic 'life without oil'.

Trend 1. Moving towards a blurring between living and working

For the majority of people, living and working have been very separate. However, these two concepts are becoming more intertwined. You can work at home and deal with your private business at work. This is possible because employers and managers are more focused on their employees' productivity and results than on their physical presence. More and more companies are classifying larger numbers of their employees as flexi-workers. A company such as Hewlett-Packard now classifies 8% of its employees as flexi-time workers. Freelancers and IWPs (independents without personnel) make less of a distinction between living and working. Working at the kitchen table, even if it isn't in line with HSE regulations, is the norm rather than the exception amongst most independent entrepreneurs. It used to be the case that working at home was considered 'typically female', as women could combine it with looking after children and managing the home. Current technology has made working at home very attractive to men as well. Why would you want to sit in traffic for an hour if you could just log on to the business network at home and run through your emails before driving to work after rush hour? The percentage of home-based workers will increase considerably in the near future. The greatest hurdle here is not a lack of potential tele-workers, but management. Bosses often think that tele-workers are lazy. They want to keep an eye on their employees all day long but they forget that this doesn't improve productivity. Research shows that home-based employees are, in fact, more productive. A win–win situation, surely. If you respect your employees and trust them to do their jobs, they will respect you in return and get the job done. At the same time, employees will also assume more responsibility. People are just like small children: if they are watched all day long, they are more inclined to lower the standard. Managers must jettison their prejudice towards home-based workers and learn to work alongside these virtual employees. As a manager of a team that works partly from home, you must be goal-orientated. Otherwise you'll just end up doing a head-count and reading time cards every morning.

Working from home can lead to isolation. To combat this, we have to arrange to meet each other. Meeting up is also good for team spirit. However, if the work place is primarily a meeting point, are little offices with desks the most suitable arrangement or would it be better to have a coffee shop set-up similar to that in the Dutch offices of Interpolis in Tilburg, where they first introduced flexi-working ten years ago? Can an employee based at home be trusted with confidential information belonging to the company or clients? What do you do if this confidential information is left lying about? In spite of concerns, such issues will become the norm both in freelance practices and in large companies. The new Rabobank Netherlands head-office in Utrecht has been designed with the flexi-work space in mind. One of the characteristics of this concept is liberating employees from a fixed time and fixed workplace. When you have to be 'at work' you just find a suitable, available spot on your arrival.

There are companies like IKEA which have introduced green measures into their work contracts. The furniture giant offers its employees cheap loans if they want to trade in their old, polluting car for a clean one. It even reimburses the cost of new particle filters for its employees' diesel cars. The courier company TNT is considering non-contractual incentives for staff that choose to go green. It has realized that it's a bit strange for the company to aim for carbon neutrality if staff are still driving to work in Hummers every day. A third example is Canon, the camera and printer manufacturers. Canon keeps an account of how environmentally (un)friendly employees' driving conduct is. Every month, employees receive an email with an evaluation of their driving habits. There's a score for everything: wear and tear on brakes and tyres; fuel consumption; and of course fines and damage. If employees' driving skills aren't up to scratch, they get lessons in how to drive more CO_2 efficiently including how to brake and change gears differently.

The concept of an e-government, or a digital government, is also emerging. Already we are seeing DigiD (digital identity) being used more and more. This allows individuals and companies to enter electronic governmental services with a log-in code. In future, such identification methods will be expanded and improved. Why should you need to go to the registry office for every little certificate if you can identify yourself from your home computer with DigiD, and then just request the necessary documents? Do registry offices and other administrative services even need to remain in the home

part 2. The new energy economy: outlines and trends

country? Certainly, the Dutch tax office has seen some of its administrative activities being relocated to India.

However it may progress further. The future is in flexible work and the blurring between living and working. With the mobile telephone, employees are available anywhere, even on holiday. Work and recreation time interlink with each other.

One of the consequences of this is that we no longer need to hit the road every day, which leads to less work-related travel. Less travel means lower CO_2 emissions. If fewer people are going into an office, there are fewer work places required, which in turns means that less office space is required. This of course makes a big difference when it comes to energy consumption.

Trend 2. Moving towards new transport projects and new types of roads

Over the past ten years, we have seen much of Western Europe's industrial production out-sourced to low-wage countries, particularly to countries in Eastern Europe and the Far East. This has meant a rise in the number of transportation kilometres. As transport becomes more expensive due to increases in fuels costs, there is a possibility that some of this production will return to Europe, where automation will have to keep labour costs down. However, we can't expect a major return of industrial production to Europe, as the costs of container shipping are so low that there is effectively no real competition. The shipping industry is also working hard to make its ships more environmentally friendly. The Japanese shipping company, NYK Line, is currently experimenting with ships equipped with metal sails. In addition, solar collectors are fitted to the sails making use of both the wind and solar energy.

Long before the CO_2 issue reared its head, the Dutch Das brothers dreamt of making sea transport more profitable than goods transport by road. They realized that this could be achieved if the cruising speed of shipping could surpass that of road transport. This would partially alleviate Europe's motorway traffic problem. They envisage European ports being linked by 'short sea truck transporters'. 'Eventually, a trailer will drive onto a short sea truck transporter in the evening in Stockholm, just before the driver needs to take his allocated rest-time. This he can do onboard along with a hundred or so colleagues. They can eat and drink in the large spherically-shaped canteens. Despite any pitching or rolling, these canteens remain as still as if they were still docked in the harbour thanks to the stabilizing effects of gyroscopes. Drivers sleep in their cabins or they can pay extra for a berth with shower facilities. Two hydraulic propellers on the underwing provide the basic power for the ship. Three gas turbines contribute to the maximum cruising speed of ninety kilometres per hour on the open water. The hundred metre long ferry for lorries sails from Stockholm to Rotterdam in sixteen hours. Simultaneous loading and off-loading of lorries over the entire length of the decks allows a very short turnaround-time. The following morning, the driver can drive off the boat refreshed and head for his final destination. The specifications of future lorry ferries are impressive. Three decks provide space for about one hundred lorries. Heavy loading is done through onboard rails. Computers determine the deck placement of marshalling areas, so that loading and unloading can be done as quickly as possible. This is a fast boat with rounded edges and strong colouring.'

On the subject of ships and lorries, the Das brothers let their imaginations go wild: 'The past couple of years have stood out as quite remarkable in the development and sales of consumer goods. A number of well-organized companies, which started in their homeland as nothing more than grocers, managed to bring one supermarket after another to prosperity and have grown into mega-companies with branches all over the world. Sooner or later, we can expect that one of these supermarket giants will discover that they are no longer bound to the mainland due to global standardization in distribution.' According to the futurologists, the big-time grocer will build extremely large model mother ships, which are anchored outside territorial waters and act as warehouses. And what is the advantage of these sailing distribution centres? In politically unstable countries, such a branch carries little risk. Loading and unloading of products is not hindered by border blockades. The mother ships are linked to each other over the water and can follow changing consumer trends. The brothers do not expect that these new shipping markets will spring up out of nowhere from one day to the next. Compare them with the offshore industry. First, there was a demand for mineral mining at sea. Then, came the specialized platforms and boats.

It is expected that over time investors other than the government will build toll roads for commuter traffic; possibly even 'double-decker' toll roads above the normal roads. Then, it won't be necessary to buy any land. Pension funds, banks or venture capitalist companies would be able to build and utilize these types of roads. Car drivers would be able to choose between normal roads and toll roads. This would of course vary from region to region. In many European regions, the population is shrinking. The EU estimates a population reduction of between 20% and 40% during this century. We can expect some areas to be very quiet, with traffic-free pleasure trips along pretty roads. They will be like large, open-air theme parks bringing in the tourists. However, in other more urban European regions, pressure on the roads will only increase. There will be 'a permanent rush-hour' and these 'areas of concentrated activity' will require extra roads. Such roads will be built, with the government surrendering their monopoly on road building and exploitation in these areas. There will be new coalitions and parties that will be exempted by governments. It wouldn't be unimaginable to think that in the future a company like ING Bank, which has 30% of all Dutch transport and distribution companies in its client base, might build toll roads for lorries. Lorries belonging to their clients would receive a discount. Older transport projects will also be overhauled. Why can't lorries with silent engines make deliveries and collections in the cities at night? Why can't the drivers enter clients' warehouses with a chip card, collect or deliver packages and then lock up shop again? Everything could be run more efficiently than is currently the case. Even the roads could be used more efficiently. Currently, work is being carried out on a floating road for use when The Netherlands is flooded.

Trend 3. Moving towards an increased virtual mobility
Much future mobility has a virtual character to it. A visit to the doctor won't be as frequent. The e-doctor has now taken over from the *flying doctor* in the Australian outback. Surgeons in American can now carry out operations in London hospitals by remote. In these new times, distances are being blurred. This makes a difference to mobility and thus to CO_2 emissions.

We are seeing a *virtualization* of our mobility in other areas. There is currently a digital environment being created which combines the Internet virtual world 'Second Life' with the 'actual world' of Google Earth. You could call it 'Second Earth'. Designed in 2003, Second Life is a virtual 3D environment where users can lead a 'second life'. Users live their second life via a so-called *avatar*, a digital representation of the user whose appearance they design themselves. They can also design homes and other buildings if they wish. Second Life looks like a gaming environment but is no game. Combining it with the maps and views of Google Earth takes it up another level. For example, imagine that you want to buy new wallpaper and furniture for your living room: rather than heading out to your local furniture store you could go digital shopping. Then, instead of trying to envisage how your choices will look in your home, you could try it out in the digital 3D version of your home before you buy. The salesperson's avatar would wave his or her magic wand to make the wallpaper change. We anticipate that in five years' time, with the continued growth of the bandwidth of our Internet connections, we will be able to experience a photo-realistic experience via our computers. It will be very much like living in a 3D movie world.

Online shopping is very popular amongst the older generation, who apparently don't like going around all those shops on their mobility carts. Many older people feel that purchasing groceries via the computer is much safer, as they don't have to leave their homes and go outside where they could encounter all sorts of sinister characters. In research carried out for Microsoft into Internet use in England, it showed that 76% of over fifty-fives 'regularly shop online' in comparison with 74% of young people.

We also expect a growth in the digital assistant. Currently, it is either you or your secretary who arranges meetings. Soon, your computer will do this independently. Patients at some dental practices can already arrange appointments digitally. On a website, the patient can see when there are free appointment slots, and can then register for treatment at a given time. Gone are the secretaries of yore. This new age is creating all sorts of new and exciting possibilities. Such developments will make a difference to mobility and thus to energy consumption. However, there is a downside to all this digitalization. It was recently calculated that the extremely popular buying and selling done through websites such as eBay, leads to many additional kilometres being driven. It used to be that second-hand gear was put away in the attic to be put out with the rubbish one day (or simply forgotten!). Now, there are people who will drive hundreds of miles to pick up some second-hand item, with all the resulting extra CO_2 emissions. And we used to think that recycling was environmentally conscious.

Trend 4. Moving towards intelligent building and CO_2 neutral homes

In Darmstadt, Germany, the first so-called 'passive house' was built in 1991. This is a type of home that uses only 10% of the energy required by a normal home for its heating and hot water. Using ultra-thick insulation and complex doors and windows, the passive house is encased in an airtight shell, so that barely any heat escapes and barely any cold penetrates. That means a passive house can be warmed not only by the sun, but also by the heat from appliances and even from occupants' bodies. Decades ago, attempts at creating sealed solar-heated homes failed because of stagnant air and mildew. But new passive houses use an ingenious central ventilation system. The warm air going out passes the clean, cold air coming in, exchanging heat with 90 per cent efficiency. A home that is sealed hermetically may sound suffocating, but in fact passive houses have plenty of windows and all can be opened.

There are now an estimated 15,000 passive houses around the world, the vast majority built in the past few years in Germany, Austria, Switzerland and Scandinavia. Moreover, their popularity is spreading. The European Commission is promoting passive-house building, and the European Parliament has proposed that all new buildings meet passive-house standards by 2011.

At the moment the first passive house is being built in the United States. In Germany the added construction costs of passive houses are modest (about 5% to 7% more than a conventional building) and, because of their growing popularity and an ever larger array of attractive off-the-shelf components, the costs are decreasing. But the sophisticated windows and heat-exchange ventilation systems needed to make passive houses work properly are not readily available in the United States. So their construction, at least initially, is likely to entail a higher price differential.

The Passivhaus Institut, which was founded a decade ago, continues to conduct research, teaches architects, and tests homes to make sure they meet standards. It now has affiliates in Britain and the United States.

Apart from new types of homes such as the passive house, existing homes and normal new developments must from now on comply with stricter environmental requirements. Warm and cold groundwater layers will be used more often for the heating and cooling of a house. In the summer, the water circuit of the house is cooled by water pumped up from a cold groundwater layer. The groundwater that has been heated up in this way is then pumped back into the warm groundwater layer where it is stored. In the winter, the process is reversed. The water originating from this warm groundwater layer now warms the house's water circuit. The cooled groundwater is pumped back into the cold groundwater layer. In some areas the installation of this type of geothermal water pump has not been left to private individuals but has become the responsibility of the government. One such instance is the city council of The Hague that delivered a new housing development of four thousand homes with geothermal heating. Water heated to 75°C was pumped up two kilometres from inside the earth. In France and Germany, there is large-scale building of homes that are made cosy and warm with geothermal heating systems.

In conclusion

Living and work will blur and run into each other more and more in the coming years. You won't need to be out and about for every meeting or shopping trip. With the emergence of virtual meetings, you will no longer need to take a plane for every overseas meeting.

Moving towards green sea-going cargo?

Globalization entails more cargo transport over land, over water and by air. With the introduction of container transport on cargo ships, sea-going cargo transport has grown considerably across the globe in the past couple of decades. For some products, parts can come from twenty different countries. End products can be bought all over the world. American Buick cars contain parts which come from far and wide. The cars are then made in the US to be transported all over the world and sold. The ever-growing demand for 'outsourcing' and assembly has meant that the past couple of decades have been a real treat for the shipping industry.

The world now has all the means available to make the twenty-first century a Golden Age for humanity, as long as we manage all the different sources of conflict. In times of great economic growth, there is now another topic for the sea-going transportation sector: energy consumption and responsible environmental policy.

As one of the largest shipping companies in the world with a fleet of eight hundred ships, NYK wants to set a good example for the industry on these issues in the future. We aim to reduce our ships' fuel requirements; we want energy consumption without sulphur. We want all ships to be connected to 'shore current' when they dock in harbour, using more environmentally friendly energy from the mains grid. We also want to use fuel cells for our small ships, as well as for all the trucks that drive between our ships. Unfortunately, ships longer than 300 metres will not be able to sail from The Netherlands to Japan using fuel cells. We are, however, supporters of a wider use of nuclear energy both in our company and across the industry as a whole. We support the development of project ships where new intentions and technologies are created and tested, even if they aren't always successful.

We are already making advances with these objectives. 'Money makes the world go round' was featured in our integration course. Consequently, we give bonuses to our NYK captains who achieve the annually highlighted environmental objectives. Every year, the oil consumption of our fleet has to decrease by 3%. Experience has shown that the environmental bonuses help to achieve this objective. We want to develop this environmental bonus system further by including measures to reduce CO_2 and other pollution. At all levels within NYK Line, environmental concern has become part of standard procedures. For quite some time, we have supported various environmental organizations, which help to keep us on track. That helps, as sometimes it takes a fresh pair of eyes to put things into the proper perspective. ☐

By Hans de Vink

Hans de Vink is Chief of Environmental Management of the shipping company Nippon Yusen Kaisha (NYK) in Europe.

part 2. The new energy economy: outlines and trends

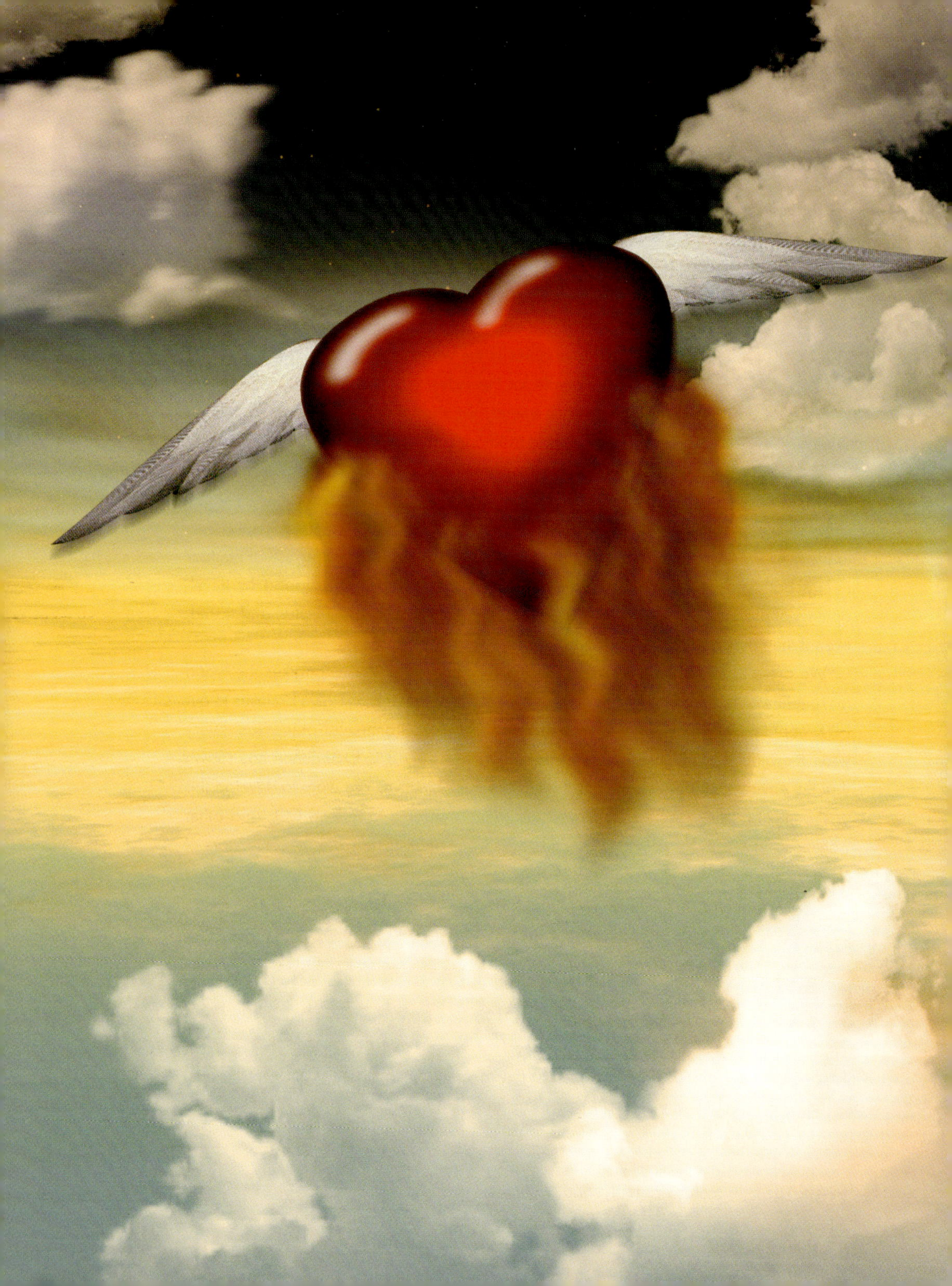

part 3

Energy agenda for the future

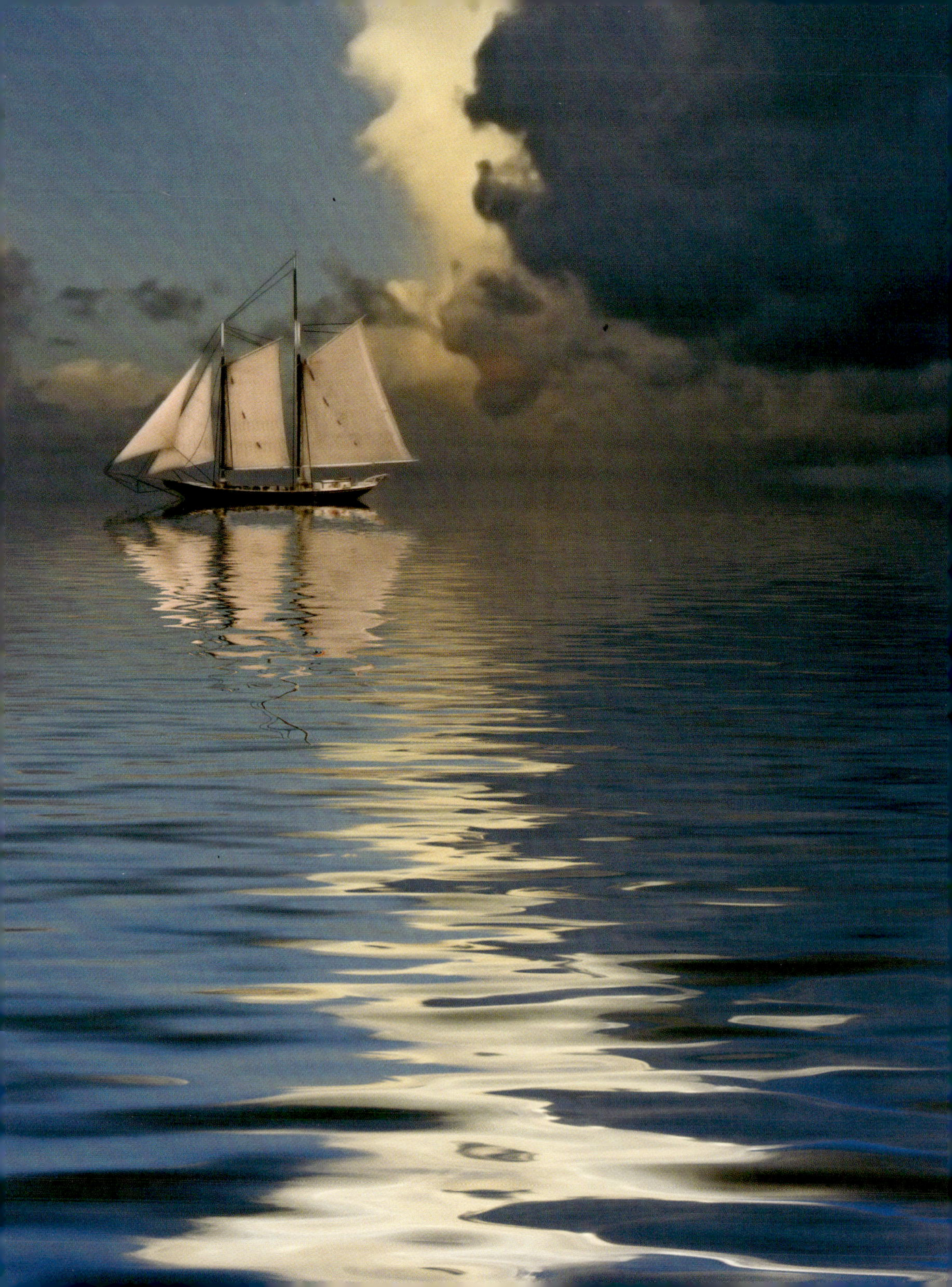

You've nearly finished the book.

In part one, you learnt that there was a time when we lived without oil. You also now know that although oil has brought us much, there are alternative energy sources available. Even at the dawn of the oil age, the Model T Ford, the world's first mass-produced car, originally ran on bio-fuel. There were also electrical cars during this period. The return to these more sustainable forms of energy will have to be implemented by the car industry over the coming years. This turn-around, which not only affects the car industry, will help create many new jobs, making us as individuals, companies and nations independent of oil and gas producing nations. Having read this book, you will now know that there is still £3,000 trillion in oil sitting beneath the earth's surface with many vested interests trying to prevent us from switching over to other sources of energy. There are huge conflicts of interests. You will also now understand that there is a global subsidy industry that supports the continuation of this slavery to oil. This can only be eliminated with direct action. Governments will have to play a role in this. We should also realize that the sense of urgency about the need to switch to the new energy economy has temporarily subsided as a result of the economic situation.

Part two explained that there are seven megatrends in the new energy economy. These trends are extremely promising. Soon, we will be able to drive electric cars or cars partially powered by bio-fuels. We will be able to make every household self-efficient with regards to energy. We can be more efficient with energy due to new inventions such as LED lights. We can be mobile in our work, and contribute to a cleaner world with green IT. We can collect energy from many different types of waste, making chicken manure into biomass. We will be able to not only run our cars on biomass, we will even be able to build cars using biomass (which is also called white biotechnology), making them biodegradable as well. We will be able to fly planes on bio-diesels made from the jatropha plant with no detrimental effect on our food supply. We can also maintain the tropical rainforests by paying the owners to manage their land. President Jagdew of Guyana came up with this idea to reduce the temptation to chop down the jungles. We can do a lot to mitigate the serious consequences of global warming, and learn to live with it. Building green is possible. Alas, climate change will continue partly due to the 'bathtub effect' we described in this book and we will have to make the best of it.

How can we turn all this into concrete and practical action for ourselves even though it may all seem so far from our own doorstep? This is where we offer some practical ideas.

Are you an individual and an energy consumer?
- Buy a smaller, more efficient car, if possible a hybrid.
- Try not to live too far from your work, and if possible try to work from home every so often.
- In general, try not to constantly be on the move.
- Replace old, energy-squandering electrical equipment with energy-efficient goods. Even though such equipment is initially more expensive, it will earn its keep as it uses less energy.
- When you buy, pay attention to the product's carbon footprint. Buying local products saves transport kilometres.
- Improve the insulation of your home.
- Replace your energy wasting central heating boiler with its circulation pump with a high efficiency boiler – circulation pumps for central heating account for between 5% and 10% of a private home's electricity bill.
- Move over to green energy.
- Where possible, buy smart products that are networked and can be energy managed.
- For anyone with a garden: remove the paving stones or lawn, and create a green garden, grow your own fruit and vegetables if you have the space.
- Form action groups (use the Internet for this) to exert pressure on local and national politicians. They need to tackle the conversion to the new energy economy more quickly and forcefully.

Are you a politician or a manager?
- Invest in public transport (particularly in the USA).
- Stop the dispersed construction (building?) of suburbs, particularly in the US.

- Reduce taxes on smaller, more efficient cars.
- In the USA, a guaranteed minimum price for oil would be a decisive factor in making R&D into alternative energy sources cost-effective. In other countries, such a guaranteed minimum price is less of a factor. Take Brazil as an example. With all that sugar cane, mass use of biofuels is possible.
- Apart from emissions trading for various polluting sectors and industries, emission budgets for private individuals could also be used to reduce CO_2 emissions. The former British environment minister, David Miliband, has already suggested such plans. A personal carbon budget makes the individual more conscious of the environmental effect of his or her own actions. Under this system, if you wanted to exceed your annual allowance you would have to purchase more emission rights.
- Consider that the move to a new energy economy will lead to political instability and unrest in oil-producing countries. For example, Russia is completely dependent on oil and gas exports. Countries such as Russia need help in building an alternative economy. Russia used to be a very important agricultural country. With the growth in the world's population, there is a greater market for food. It is important to help Russia to make that economic shift using agricultural knowledge and technology.
- Bear in mind that in some oil dictatorships, such as Iran and Venezuela, the rulers are criticized when the price of oil is low, and the countries will suffer when oil exploitation comes to an end. In retaliation they might be tempted to make military incursions into neighbouring countries or start a (nuclear) war. Within two years, Iran will have that potential. We must prepare ourselves for nuclear blackmail as well as political and religious fanaticism.
- Prepare for the end of all subsidy links with regard to old energy.
- Show vision and nerve.

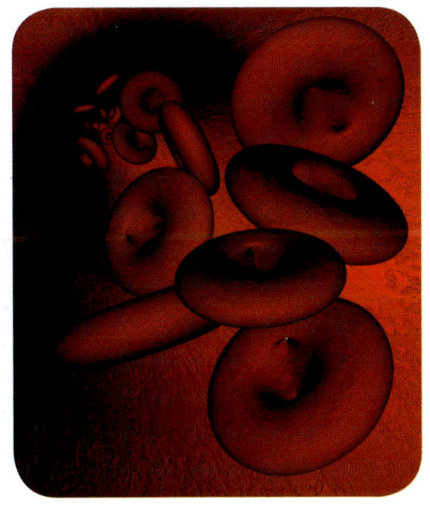

part 3. Energy agenda for the future

- At local and national level, you can do a lot to prepare your supporters for the switch to the new energy economy.
- Keep up to date with new developments. Land based wind farms deliver too little energy and are ugly; offshore and out of sight, they are acceptable and cost-effective.
- Link development aid from rich to poor countries to a stringent family planning policy and education program about the dangers of over-population.

Are you an entrepreneur?
- You know that the economy changes like the seasons and that we are currently in an economic winter. After this winter, the economic spring will arrive. The winter has the advantage that you can get rid of dead wood; new leaves will replace old leaves. In an economic winter, the real entrepreneurs will emerge. The most intelligent entrepreneurs will grab their chance now. During a recession, there is trouble and affliction every day. Think back to the recession in the 1980s. Mass unemployment, economic shrinkage and social unrest were all characteristic of this period. Something that depressed everyone. However, it was then that we saw the birth of the mobile phone, the PC and the Internet. These three things were the keys to the blossoming of the economy and its growth. Entrepreneurs who, during the last recession, had an eye for such things, started great companies or updated existing companies so that they successfully rose out of the ashes of the 80s. If you are an entrepreneur now, it's up to you to recognize the new energy economy. And use it to your company's advantage. It all starts with awareness.
- Don't just try to keep all your own products and production processes as climate neutral as possible, make the whole process more energy efficient. Transport kilometres (delivery, distribution) increase the carbon footprint of many products. Use the recession to bear this all in mind. People are now more susceptible to change than when everything was going well.
- Ensure that your employees are aware of their use of heating and lighting as well as paper consumption. Make them think about how

they use their computers and the miles they travel. You can encourage this by introducing incentives.
- Look into potential energy subsidies in your country. The majority of governments have arrangements that subsidize investments in making companies more sustainable.
- Introduce flexi-working.
- Allow your employees to work from home more often (less commuter traffic).
- Use tele-conferencing tools, so that there is less need to drive or fly to meetings.

Are you an oil company?
- Use all that money that you have earned over the last couple of years for R&D into alternative fuels, and not to buy back shares. Invest in bio-fuels, better batteries for electrical cars, hydrogen technology, wind and solar energy.
- Re-invent yourself as a new energy producer. Then, you'll deliver real shareholder value, even in the medium term.

A new day has begun…
With these hints and tips we complete this book about the future of energy. If we manage our energy consumption and respect the earth and nature we will return to our roots as humans.

The utilization of new technology will make this shift possible. However, it will only be successful if we stop global population growth. We are too many on this planet, and as a result we are over-exploiting it. We have to reduce our numbers to 2 billion people, the population as it stood at the start of the twentieth century. We must prepare ourselves for the energy strains that this transitional period will bring with it. We must take the losers by the hand and guide them. Countries that are still dependent on oil exports must be helped to build new economies. We must curb those dictators who are watching their lucrative oil incomes disappear and who use (religious) fanaticism to start wars. Iran is the 'toughest cookie' in the international politics of tomorrow. Political and personal courage are needed, however difficult the future seems.

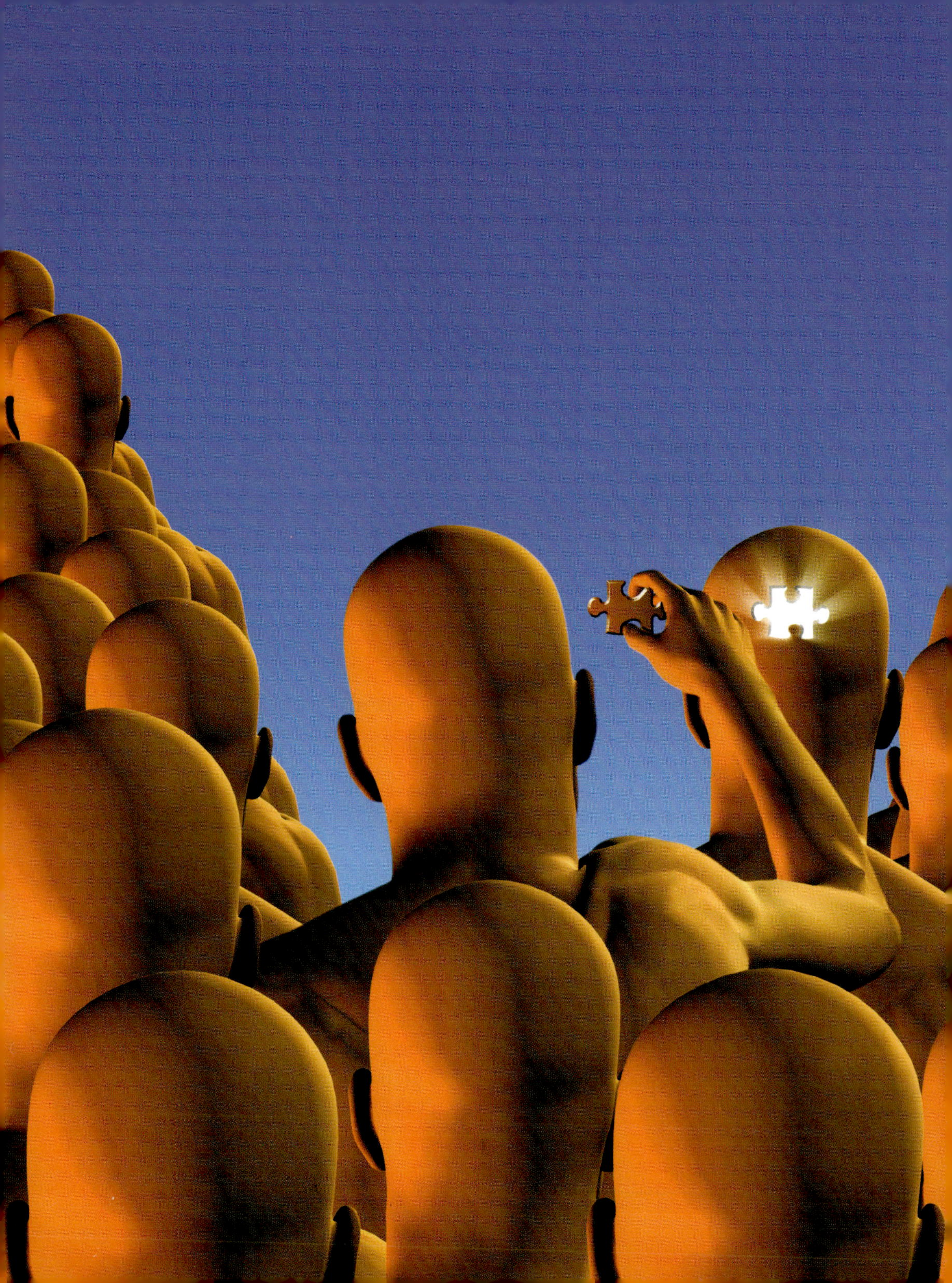

sources

Books

Archer, D. *The Long Thaw.* Oxford, 2009
Bakas, A. *Megatrends Nederland.* Schiedam, 2005
Bakas, A. and M. Buwalda. *De Toekomst van God.* Schiedam, 2006
Broecker, W. and Kunzig, R. *Fixing Climate.* New York, 2008
Brown, L. *Plan B 2.0.* New York, 2007
Carson, I. *Zoom.* New York, 2007
Crichton, M. *State of Fear.* New York, 2005
Croy, G. *The Energy Trail.* Singapore, 2008
Diamond, J. *Collapse.* London, 2005
Faris, S. *Forecast.* New York, 2009
Flannery, T. *The Weather Makers.* London, 2005
Friedman, T. *Hot, Flat and Crowded.* New York, 2008
Garvey, J. *The Ethics of Climate Change.* London, 2008
Gore, A. *An Inconvenient Truth.* Los Angeles, 2006
Greer, J. *The Long Descent.* Canada, 2008
Hasegawa, Y. *Clean Car Wars.* Singapore, 2008
Heinberg, R. *The Party's Over.* Sussex, 2003
Heinberg, R. *Power Down.* Gabriola Island, 2004
Hensen, R. *The Rough Guide to Climate Change.* London, 2006
Hensen, R. *Climate Change.* London, 2008
Juniper, T. *How Many Light Bulbs Does it Take to Change a Planet?* London, 2007
Knoke, W. *Bold New World.* New York, 1996
Kolbert, E. *Field Notes from a Catastrophe.* London 2007
Kroonenberg, S. *De Menselijke Maat.* Amsterdam, 2007
Kunstler, J. *The Long Emergency.* New York, 2005
Leeb, S. *The Coming Economic Collapse.* New York, 2006
Lovelock, J. *The Revenge of Gaia.* London, 2006
Lynas, M. *Six Degrees.* London, 2007
Middelkoop, W. and Koppelaar, R. *De Permanente Oliecrisis.* Amsterdam, 2008
Meadows, D., J. Randers et al. *Limits to Growth.* London, 2005
Monbiot, G. *Heat: How to Stop Planet Burning.* London, 2007

Murphy, P. *Plan C*. Canada, 2008
Pearce, F. *When the Rivers Run Dry*. London, 2007
Pfeiffer, D. *Eating Fossil Fuels*. Canada, 2006
Prahalad, C.K. *The Fortune at the Bottom of the Pyramid*. New York, 2005
Rees, M. *Our Final Century*. London, 2003
Reijnders, L. *Energie*. Amsterdam, 2006
Rifkin, J. *The Hydrogen Economy*. New York, 2003
Romm, J. *The Hype about Hydrogen*. Washington, 2004
Romm, J. *Hell and High Water*. New York, 2007
Sperling, D. and Gordon, D. *Two Billion Cars*. Oxford, 2009
Stern, N. *The Stern Review on the Economics of Climate Change*. New York, 2007
Strahan, D. *The Last Oil Shock*. London, 2007
Weisman, A. *The World Without Us*. London, 2007
Wilson, O. *The Future of Life*. London, 2002
Yergin, D. *The Prize, The Epic Quest for Oil, Money & Power*. New York, 1991

Articles

'As More Eat Meat, a Bid to Cut Emissions,' *The New York Times*, December 4, 2008.
'Environmental Issues Slide in Poll of Public's Concerns,' *The New York Times*, January 23, 2009.
'New Science Could Help Solve Climate Crisis,' *Reuters*, January 28, 2009.
'The Return of High Oil,' *BusinessWeek*, November 11, 2008.
'Climate Scientists: It's Time for Plan B,' *The Independent*, January 5, 2009.
'Dark Days for Green Energy,' *The New York Times*, February 4, 2009.
'Uitstoot kooldioxide daalt door kredietcrisis,' *NRC Handelsblad*, January 10, 2009.
'The Greening of the Corporation,' *BusinessWeek*, December 11, 2008.
'The Decline of the Petro-Czar,' *Newsweek*, February 15, 2009.
'The Energy Challenge,' *The New York Times*, December 27, 2008.
'Capitalizing on Climate Change,' *Der Spiegel*, November 14, 2008.

'Nuclear Fusion,' *Der Spiegel*, January 2, 2009.
'Nuclear Power in the Nordic Countries,' *The Economist*, February 14, 2009.
'Solar Power Equipment Prices Drop,' *Wall Street Journal*, February 19, 2009.
'Solar Energy,' *The Economist*, December 31, 2008.
'Out of Africa: Sahara Solar Energy,' *Time*, January 19, 2009.
'Exposing the Myth of Clean Coal Power,' *Time*, January 12, 2009.
'Wind of Change,' *The Economist*, December 12, 2008.
'Carbon Cost of Google Revealed,' *BBC*, January 12, 2009.
'Carbon: Europe's Lessons for the U.S.,' *BusinessWeek*, February 20, 2009.
'The Cost of Cutting Carbon,' *Technology Review*, December 31, 2008.
'Is Clean Coal Technology Fact or Fiction?,' *Newsweek*, December 9, 2008.
'Electric Cars are Cheaper and Faster,' *Newsweek*, January 31, 2009.
'Now We're Cooking With... Batteries,' *Newsweek*, November 23, 2008.
'The Electric Car Battery War,' *BusinessWeek*, February 13, 2009.
'Politically Incorrect,' *Businessworld*, January 23, 2009.
'US Auto Sales Hit 27-Year Low,' *BusinessWeek*, February 4, 2009.
'Here Comes Global Warming Legislation,' *BusinessWeek*, January 24, 2009.
'Climate Scientists: It's Time for "Plan B",' *The Independent*, January 5, 2009.
'Royal Philips Sheds Olds Businesses for New Directions,' *The New York Times*, December 24, 2008.

Websites

www.volkskrant.nl
www.parool.nl
www.ap.org
www.greenpeace.nl
www.wnf.nl
www.snm.nl
www.shell.com/scenarios
www.dw-world.de

www.yaleglobal.yale
www.fembusiness.nl
www.businessweek.com
www.nrc.nl
www.spiegel.de
www.nytimes.com
www.time.com
www.chrismartenson.com/crashcourse
www.technologyreview.com
www.telegraaf.nl
www.economist.com
www.bbc.com
www.elsevier.nl
www.reuters.com
www.anp.nl
www.peakoil.nl
www.wsje.com

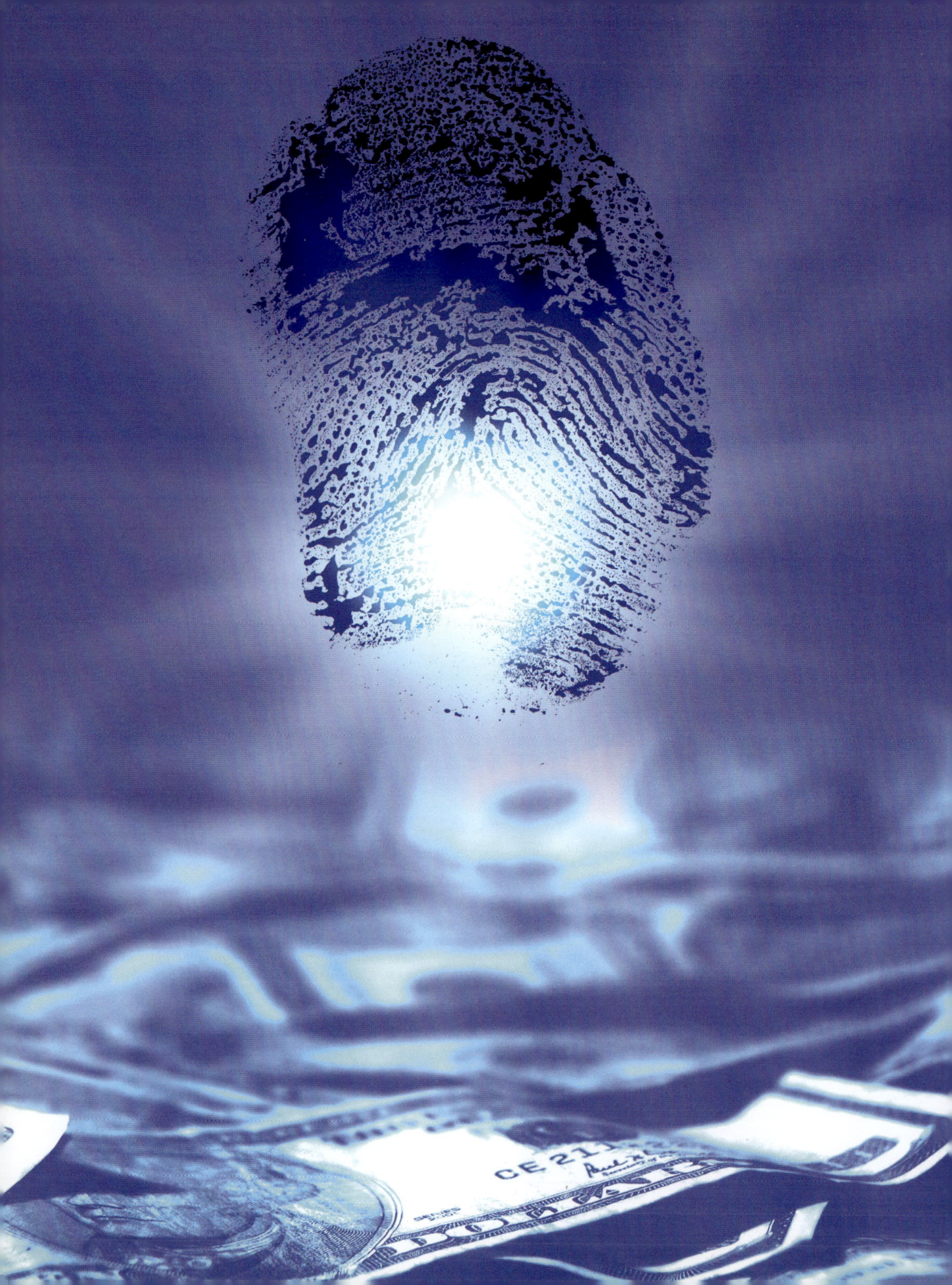

index

advertising agencies, 126–127
Aerion, 166
Agassi, Shai, 155
agriculture, 33–34, 59, 72–73, 114, 219
Ahmedinedjad, Mahmoud, 53
Ahmend Yamani, Sheik, 25
Airbus, 167, 169
air-cars, 145
air-conditioning, 58
air curtains, smart, 102–103
Air New Zealand, 164
airships, 170–171
airspaces, 175
air transport, *see* aviation
Alaska, 48
Algeria, 187
Alliance for Climate Protection, 183–184
Al Qaeda, 27
Amyris Biotechnologies, 168–169
Anderman, Menahem, 155–156
Arctic Ocean, 93–94
Argentina, 73
Audi, 139
Ausra, 181
Australia, 58, 90, 187
avatars, 209–210
aviation, 35–36, 57, 92, 105, 162–178

Bahrain, 58
Bakker, John, 156–157
Bali treaty, 65
Bangladesh, 116
BASF, 86
Batavus, 158
batteries, lithium, 153–156

Belgium, 86, 174
Ben & Jerry's, 98
Besam, 102–103
Better Place, 155
Bhutan, 171
bicycles, 157–158
bio-based materials, 113–114
bio-diesel, 149, 150
biodiversity, 34
bio-ethanol, 111, 149–150
bio-fuels, 33, 35, 36, 67, 99, 111, 149–152, 164, 217
biogas, 113
biomass, 217
biotechnology, 102–114, 168–169
Bisagnani, Giovanni, 167
Blair, Tony, 128
Blended Wing Body (BWB) aircraft, 167–168
BlueTec technology, 145, 151
BMW, 139, 140, 144, 145, 147
Boeing, 166, 167, 169
boilers, central heating, 196, 218
Boundary Layer Suction (BLS), 166–167
Bovenberg, Lans, 38–39
BP, 54, 148
Brandstätter, 47
Branson, Richard, 176
Brazil, 27, 34, 51, 65, 67, 72, 73, 101, 150, 219
BTM Consult, 185
BudgetAir, 165
Bush, George W., 74, 124, 140, 148

Canada, 27, 50–51, 58, 142, 182–183
Canon, 205
carbon dioxide (CO$_2$), 55–59, 104–105, 182–184
   see also greenhouse gas emissions
Carbon Disclosure Project (CDP), 104
carbon footprint, 101, 218
carbon off-set programmes, 104, 105, 173–174
Carbon Trust Fund, 89
cars, 33, 34, 37, 46, 57, 90, 92, 102, 114, 121, 125, 137–157, 161, 217, 218, 219
Castles, Stephen, 74–75
castor oil, 113–114
Centrica, 85
Ceres, 97
Cessna, 166
charities, 127–128
Chávez, Hugo, 53, 54
chemical industry, 109–114
China, 28, 33, 34, 38, 40, 51, 57, 58, 61, 66, 67, 72, 83–84, 89, 101, 137, 155, 158, 165, 183, 184–186, 192, 194, 196
chlorofluorocarbons (CFCs), 55, 56
   see also greenhouse gas emissions
Christian Aid, 74
Chrysler, 140, 141, 142, 152
citizenship, analytical democratic, 120–121
Citroën, 139, 142
clean energy investment, 21
climate change, 21–22, 29, 30–32, 39, 40, 42, 54–59, 63–64, 66, 67, 68–72, 74–76, 81–95, 97, 98–99, 112–113, 218
   see also greenhouse gas emissions
Climate Change College, 98
climate offset programmes, 104, 105, 173–174
Clinton, Bill, 69, 82
Clinton Climate Initiative (CCI), 82–83
clothes dryers, 122
Club of Rome, 29
CMI Europe, 159–161
coal, 35, 51, 66, 84, 88, 95, 182, 183–184
coalitions in energy market, 89–90
community spirit, 39
commuting, 37, 58
compressed air cars, 145
Concentrating Solar Panel (CSP) plants, 186
consumers, greening of, 119–135
Cool Earth Solar, 188
Cornelissen, Marc, 98–99
Costa Rican Nature Air Group, 171
cow farts, 72–73
credit cards, 'green', 104
crowd sourcing, 33
cups, plastic versus earthenware, 124–125

Daimler, 145, 146, 147, 148
Das, Robbert and Rudolf, 186, 206–208
deforestation, 65, 173
Denmark, 81–82, 155, 184, 185
Desertec, 188
developing countries, 34, 171

Diaz, Cameron, 143
DiCaprio, Leonardo, 143
DigiD, 205
digital assistants, 210
Drake, Edwin, 46
DSM, 109, 110–116
Dubai, 85

Easter Island scenario, 39–40, 41, 64
easyJet, 165, 177–178
Eck, Wouter van, 73
economic crisis, *see* financial crisis
EcoPaXX™ 113–114
eco-sleeping, 132–135
EDF, 88
e-government, 205–206
Egypt, 187
Ekman, Bo, 22
Elbers, Peter, 174–175, 176
electric cars, 33, 152–156, 217
electrification of city transport, 158–161
emissions trading, 105–107, 173, 174, 219
Empire State Building, 92
Endesa, 86
Enel, 86, 88
energy supply innovations, 181–199
Enexis, 156
entrepreneurs, 99–100, 220–221
environmental awareness, 123–124
E-ON, 85, 86, 88
environmental refugees, 74–75
European Union, 66–67, 83, 84, 86–87, 88, 89, 105, 138, 183, 185, 208, 211

family planning policies, 38, 220
farts, cow, 72–73
Fedele, Joe, 107
Fiat, 139
financial crisis, 21–22, 24, 27–28, 51–52, 75–76, 220
financial services, CO_2-neutral, 103–105
Finland, 88, 191–192
Flags scenario, 63
flexi-workers, 203–205
floating roads, 208
flying cars, 156–157
Food Council, 33
food production, 33–34, 150, 151
Ford Motors, 140, 142, 146
Formula Zero, 114
Fortum, 191
France, 81, 86, 142, 156, 191, 212
freelancers, 203–204
FreshDirect, 107–108
Friends of the Earth, 73
fuel cells, 35–36, 99–100, 148–149
future, energy agenda for the, 217–221
future scenarios, 38–41

G8 countries, 65, 82
gas, natural, 45, 51, 52, 62, 85–86, 88, 95, 147
Gas Exporting Countries Forum (GECF), 52
Gasuni, 86, 88
Gaz de France, 86
Gazprom, 85–86, 88
General Electric, 174
General Motors (GM), 140–141, 142, 145, 146, 157

geo-engineering, 30–31
Georgia, 52
geothermal heating, 212
Germany, 67, 81, 85, 86, 90, 138–139, 142, 184, 185, 188, 211, 212
global government initiatives, 82–83
globalization, 35, 36, 39, 62, 89
global warming, *see* climate change
Google/Google Earth, 163, 209, 210
Gordon, Deborah, 140
Gore, Al, 68, 69, 70, 71, 74, 76, 126, 127, 128, 200
Great Alarm, 69–70
The Great Global Warming Swindle, 126
greenhouse effect, *see* climate change
greenhouse gas emissions, 21, 26, 31–32, 35, 54–59, 63–67, 72, 82–84, 162, 163
Greenland, 42
Greenpeace, 91
guaranteed minimum price for oil, 52, 219
Guyana, 217

Haji-Ioannou, Stelios, 172
Hayward, Steven, 69–70
heavy oil, 51
Heliovolt, 181
helium-3, 193–194
Hewlett-Packard, 203
hidden hunger, 114–116
home working, 203–205
Honda, 140, 143, 146
Hormuz, Strait of, 52
households, economical, 121–123
Hummer, 143, 157

hunger, hidden, 114–116
Hunter, Joel C., 124
hybrid vehicles, 138, 143–147, 151, 152–156, 157–158
hydrogen cars, 144, 147–149
hydropower, 129–130
Hyundai-Kia, 146

ice, polar, 93–95
IKEA, 205
An Inconvenient Truth, 68, 69, 70, 76
An Inconvenient Truth... or Convenient Fiction, 69–70
independents without personnel (IWPs), 203–204
India, 28, 34, 40, 51, 57, 66, 67, 72, 101, 116, 137, 139–140, 165
individualism, 39
individuals, energy agenda for the future, 218
Indonesia, 173–174
industry, greening of, 97–114
information, energy, 101, 124–125
ING Bank, 208
Institute of Mechanical Engineers, 66
insulation, 122, 123
intelligent building, 211–212
Intergovernmental Panel on Climate Change (IPCC), 29, 63–64, 71, 72, 76
International Air Transport Association (IATA), 35, 36
International Atomic Energy Agency (IAEA), 192
International Energy Agency (IEA), 42,

183, 185
inter-nationalization, 63
Interpolis, 204
Investor Network of Climate Risk, 97–98
Iran, 27, 28, 46, 50, 52, 53, 54, 219, 221
Iraq, 46, 49, 50
iron deficiency, 116
Islam, 27, 53
Israel, 23, 46, 47, 155
Italy, 86, 142
ITER, 89
IT industry, 163

Jagdew, President, 217
Japan, 67, 121, 192
jatropha, oil, 164
Joint European Torus, 193
Jordan, 187

Keeling, Charles, 56
Kenya, 116
kerogen, 45, 50, 51
kerosene, 45, 46
Keystone Centre, 190
Khajavi, Alex, 171
Khomeini, Ayatollah, 47
Ki-Moon, Ban, 24
KLM, 174–175
Kondratieff waves, 22–23
Korea, 192
Kroes, Neelie, 87
Kuwait, 46, 49, 50, 58
Kyoto Protocol, 64–66, 68, 83, 105, 106, 174

labelling schemes, 101
Lang, Tim, 33–34
Large Cities Climate Leadership Group (C40), 82–83
Lavital, 133–135
Lawson, Lord Nigel, 70–71
LED lighting, 91–92
Lewiner, Colette, 106
Lexus, 140, 146
liberalization, end of, 85–89
light bulbs, 90–92
Lithuania, 191
Live Earth, 127–128
London, 83, 92, 158
London Eye, 92
lorries, 207, 208
Lovelock, James, 29, 30
Low Trust Globalization scenario, 62
Lucas, Joe, 184
Luther, Martin, 40
Lutheran scenario, 40, 41, 42, 64
Lux Research Inc., 190
Lyme disease, 104

malaria, 104, 116
Malaysia, 173
managers, energy agenda for the future, 218–220
mangrove swamps, 173
Martin, James, 27, 33
mattresses, 133–135
Max Planck Institution, 132
Mayan culture, 23
MDI, 145
meat consumption, 72–73, 124

Medvjedev, Dmitri, 53
Melo, John, 168–169
Mercedes-Benz, 139, 140, 145, 146
Meridian International Research, 154–155
Merkel, Angela, 66–67
Metcalf, Gilbert, 84
meters, energy, 119
methane, 55, 56, 72, 173
   see also greenhouse gas emissions
Mexico, 27, 65
micronutrient deficiency, 114–116
migration, 74–75
Miliband, David, 219
mirrors in space, 30–31
MLB Energy, 194–196, 197–198
Monbiot, George, 162, 166
Morocco, 187
MTV, 127
Myers, Norman, 74

NASA, 166, 167
nationalism, 39, 86, 89
Nègre, Guy, 145
Nepal, 116
Netherlands, 47, 81–82, 86, 174, 205, 208
New Zealand, 58, 73
Nigeria, 28, 48, 50
Nilas ice, 93, 95
Nissan, 146
Nocera, Daniel, 189
North Pole, 93–94, 95
North Sea, 48, 129–131
North Stream (NEGP), 86

nuclear blackmail, 219
nuclear energy, 29, 51, 88, 190–194
nuclear fission, 89, 193
nuclear fusion, 89–90, 192–194
Nuon, 188
NYK Line, 206, 213

Obama, Barack, 84, 105, 120, 124, 141, 142, 153, 185, 190
occupancy tax, 123
oil, 24–29, 42, 45–54, 61–62, 84–85, 95, 151–152, 163–164
oil companies, 52, 221
one-child policy, 38, 61
OPEC, 27, 46, 47, 49, 52, 84
Opel, 141, 142
Open Doors scenario, 62–63
OptiSolar, 181
Orcelle, 170
Ostrich scenario, 40, 41, 64
Oxford Research Group, 191

Pachauri, Rajendra, 22
passive houses, 211–212
Passivhaus Institut, 211–212
peak oil, 28–29, 42, 49–51, 61–62, 163–164
pension funds, 173
Perez, Carlota, 23
Peru, 65
petroleum, 46, 47, 48, 50, 51
Peugeot, 139, 142
pharmaceutical companies, 103–104
Philips, 91–92
photosynthesis, 189

Pichocki, Richard, 104
Playmobil, 47
plug-in hybrids, 152–156
Poland, 192
politicans, energy agenda for the future, 218–220
politics and oil, 26–27, 29, 52–54
population levels, 26, 33, 34, 37–38, 51, 61, 63, 64, 114, 208, 220, 221
Porsche, 139, 144–145
Portugal, 47, 187
power, energy as a means of exercising, 52–54
pressure groups, environmental, 126
profit orientation and environmentalism, harmonizing, 99–100
protectionism, 39, 86
public–private partnerships (PPP), 89, 90
public transport, 149, 157
Putin, Vladimir, 52, 53

Qatar, 54, 58

Rabobank, 204
rainforests, 26, 217
Reagan, Ronald, 85
Red Cross, 74
Rees, Martin, 39
reforestation, 29
refugees, environmental, 74–75
regional government initiatives, 82–83
religion, 27, 53, 70–72, 82, 124, 152
Renault, 142
Renewable Energy Systems Americas, 181

rice, 116
rickshaws, 139–140
RKK Energiya, 194
roads, 208
Rolls Royce, 174
Roquette, 110
Russia, 27, 29, 34, 42, 50, 51, 52, 53–54, 65, 67, 85–86, 88, 101, 192, 194, 219
RWE, 88

Saab, 140
Sahara, 187–188
Saudi Arabia, 42, 46, 50, 52–53
Saudi Aramco, 88
scramjet, 166
sea-going cargo, 206–207, 212–213
sea level projections, 76
Second Life, 209–210
Segers, Frans, 133–135
Segway, 158, 159
self-employment, 99
sequestering, 31, 35, 182–184
Shell, 54, 62–63, 88, 100
shipping, 170, 206–208, 212–213
Shivdasani, Sonu, 172
shopping online, 210
Sight and Life, 115
Singapore, 158
Singer, Isaac Merrit, 132
single-person households, 122–123
Six Senses, 172
sleep, 132–135
Slovakia, 192
socially responsible business, 63

solar cell foil, 188–189
solar energy, 36, 99, 181, 185, 186–190, 200
South Korea, 192
space travel, 193–194
Spain, 86, 142, 184, 187
Sperling, Daniel, 140
Sterman, John, 31–32
Stern, Sir Nicholas, 68–69, 74
Storch, Hans von, 71
Streetrollers, 158–161
Streiff, Christian, 139
subsidies, energy, 89, 188, 198, 221
suburbia, 37, 58
succinic acid, 110–111
Suez, 86, 88
sulphur particles, 31
SunPower, 181
supermarkets, 101–103, 107, 108
sustainability officers, 98
SustainGroup, 102
Sweden, 191

tar sands, 27, 50–51
Tata Motors, 145
tax, 84, 90, 92, 107, 119, 121, 123, 155, 165
Technical University of Delft, 189
technological revolutions, 23–24
tele-working, 37, 204, 221
Terrafugia, 156
terrorism, 27, 28–29, 126
Tesla, 152, 153
Thatcher, Margaret, 85
tipping points, 29, 33

TNT, 205
tourism, 164, 165, 166, 171–172, 208
Toyota, 140, 143, 144, 145, 146, 152–153
trains, 169–170
transportation, 32–33, 57, 125, 137–138, 143–147, 152–156, 157–161, 206–208
 see also aviation; cars
Turkey, 101

Ukraine, 52
United Arab Emirates, 50, 58
United Kingdom, 34, 46, 57–58, 81, 83, 85, 86, 88, 92, 121–123, 142, 210, 212
United Nations Environmental Programme (UNEP), 74
United States of America, 21, 46, 47, 51, 57, 58, 65, 68, 73, 83, 84, 105, 111, 120, 122, 123–124, 140–142, 146, 148, 150, 151, 152, 153, 155, 156, 183, 184, 185, 186, 191, 192, 211, 212, 218, 219
uranium, 51
urbanization, 34
urgency, need for, 42

valvematic technology, 145
Vauxhall, 140
Veen, Steven van der, 160
vegetarian diet, 124
Velden, Patrick van der, 159–161
Venezuela, 28, 29, 48, 50, 51, 52, 53, 54, 219

index

Venter, Craig, 151–152
venture capitalists, 90, 192
Venus, 55
Vestas Group, 181
Virgin Airlines, 169, 172, 176
virtual meetings, 165
virtual mobility, 209–210
Visa ClimaCount, 125–126
Vogtländer, Peter, 86
Volkswagen, 137–138, 144–145, 146

Wahabites, 27, 53
Wal-Mart, 149
water power, 129–130
water scarcity, 33–34
White, Don, 183
white biotechnology, 109–114
Wiedeking, Wendelin, 144
wildcards, 200
Wilhelmesen Wallenius Logistics, 170
Willems, Rein, 62, 86, 148–149
wind energy, 99, 129–131, 181, 184–186, 220
Wintershall, 86
Wolff, Gerry, 188
work life, 203–206
World Food Programme (WFP), 115, 116
World Wildlife Fund, 98

Yergin, Daniel, 26
Yom Kippur War, 46, 47

Zeppelins, 170–171
Zeropollution Motors, 145
Ziyuan, Ouyang, 194